ACKNOWLEDGEMENTS

The editor and publishers wish to thank the following people and organisations for their help in compiling this book or in providing photographs:

Angling Times
Bass Anglers Sportfishing Society
British Record Rod-Caught Fish Committee
Endeavour Deep Sea Group, Aberystwyth
European Federation of Sea Anglers
Gwynedd Oysters Ltd, Brynsiencyn
H.M. Coastguards
Inspector S. R. Richards, H.M. Coastguards, Swansea
Institute of Coastal Oceanography and Tides, Birkenhead
Lancashire and Western Sea Fisheries Committee, Lancaster
Local authorities throughout Wales
Mr. George Micklewright, Sully
A. Miles & Son, Anglers Supplies, Cardiff
Ministry of Defence, Tolworth, Surbiton
National Anglers' Council
National Coastal Rescue Training Centre (Commander Charles Thomson)
Severn River Authority, Malvern
South Wales Sea Fisheries Committee, Swansea
Sports Council for Wales, Cardiff
Mr. Lionel Sweet, Usk
Mr. Dave Taylor, Aberystwyth
Tope Angling Club of Great Britain
Welsh Anglers Council members
Welsh Federation of Sea Anglers, its officers and affiliated clubs
Welsh Fly Fishing Association
Welsh Water Authority and its officers
Welsh Record Rod-Caught Fish Committee
Welsh Tope, Skate and Conger Club

Where to Stay in Wales
Hotels listed in this guide offer fishing on their own waters or can arrange an angling holiday on the waters of a local angling club. For a more complete list of holiday accommodation suitable for anglers, on the coast or near rivers, the Wales Tourist Board's **'Where to Stay'** *guide of about 300 pages can be obtained at bookshops, or by post from* **Wales Tourist Board, Dept. AG, PO Box 151, WDO, Cardiff CF5 1XS.**

Cover: *Clive Gammon returns a tope to the sea at Broughton Bay, Gower.*

Wales Angling Guide

CLIVE GAMMON EDITOR

Third Edition

[illegible]

GAME FISHING

COARSE FISHING

INDEX

Designed and published by Wales Tourist Board

Printed by A. McLay & Co. Ltd., Cardiff.
ISBN 0 900784 48 2

Wales for the holiday angler

For a small country, Wales has a great deal of water. And almost everywhere, once you are clear of industrial South Wales (and even there you can get some surprises – cod at Cardiff, for example, and sea-trout within the city limits of Swansea) you are fishing in clean, unpolluted waters. If you are a sea angler there is infinite variety for you. Atlantic storm beaches that yield bass; rock stations from which you can latch into a big tope, piers and jetties for fun-fishing for whiting and flatties. That's from the shore. At sea, you can hunt blue shark and porbeagle in South West Wales, go for pack tope and rays in Cardigan Bay and further north. If you're a specimen hunter, the Welsh Record Fish list is an obvious target. It is now well established but there's plenty of scope to improve on present records.

River fishing? We have some of the most available salmon fishing in the UK and unrivalled sea-trout fishing, a great deal of which is available to the visitor for a moderate fee. We wouldn't claim to be so well endowed with coarse fishing, but big fish hunters will be surprised at the big tench that come out of Bosherston Lake in South Pembrokeshire – and at the quality pike that Llangorse Lake, near Brecon, and Bala Lake can provide.

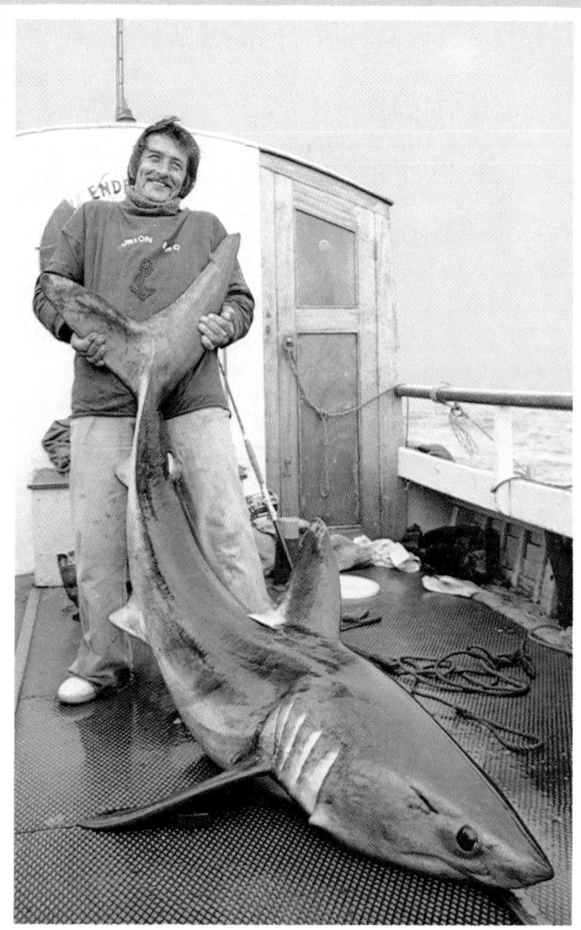

The Welsh record porbeagle shark caught by Peter Redfern of Measham, Leicester, fishing with the Endeavour Group boat out of Aberystwyth in the summer of 1978.

Exhibition of Fishing
Fishing gear through the ages, nets and flies as well as coracle fishing in a 200 ft × 50 ft pool and fly tying demonstrations, occasionally form part of the Welsh Folk Museum's 80 acre attraction, 5 miles west of Cardiff. Open daily.

Summer fishing begins early in Wales, on an early summer day for Clive Gammon's Gower beach tope, released to fight another day. Albert Harries' world record tope of 74 lbs 11 ozs was caught just a few miles away across Carmarthen Bay. Bass stay all winter in mild South West Wales waters. All around Wales they're big. George Micklewright's 16 lbs 3 ozs specimen beat a 12 lbs 2 ozs Colwyn Bay Bass Festival winner which had stood for only a month. There have been bigger ones: 20 lbs on a Menai Strait commercial line and nearly 19 lbs from Cardigan's Teifi estuary.

Salmon from the Wye represent 30 per cent of all fish of that species rod caught in England and Wales combined and according to the *Salmon and Trout* magazine of November 1972, sea trout, which run the faster, western flowing rivers of Wales – and the Conwy – are much bigger and in far greater numbers than anywhere else in Britain.

Though tope may be the staple fishing for the boat angler and bass for his beach counterpart, what of the specialist hunter? A good 130 lbs Aberystwyth porbeagle shark emphasises that bigger fish are about. Porbeagle represent a big challenge to visiting anglers, but like the blues, though there are plenty in Welsh waters, they have been pretty well ignored by locals. Brandon Jones' Barry-caught 44 lbs 8 ozs cod underlines a winter attraction around South Glamorgan shores.

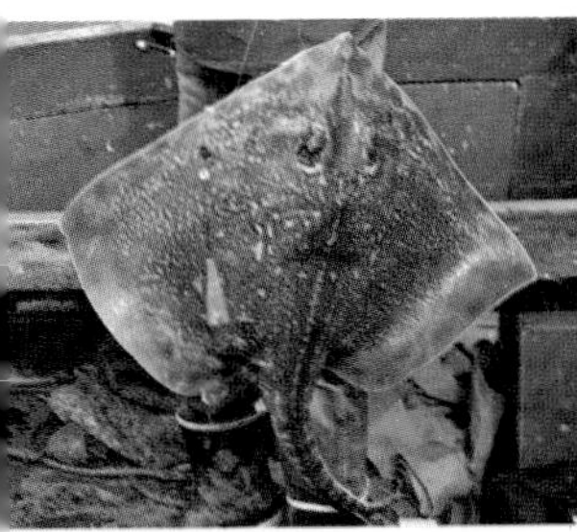

Sea fishing marks and facilities of Wales are illustrated in detailed maps on pages 68 to 73 inclusive.

Angling opportunities in the eighty-three most important game rivers and lakes of Wales will be found on pages 80 to 104

Bring your specialist gear if you're visiting one of the coarse fishing centres illustrated on pages 106 to 110.

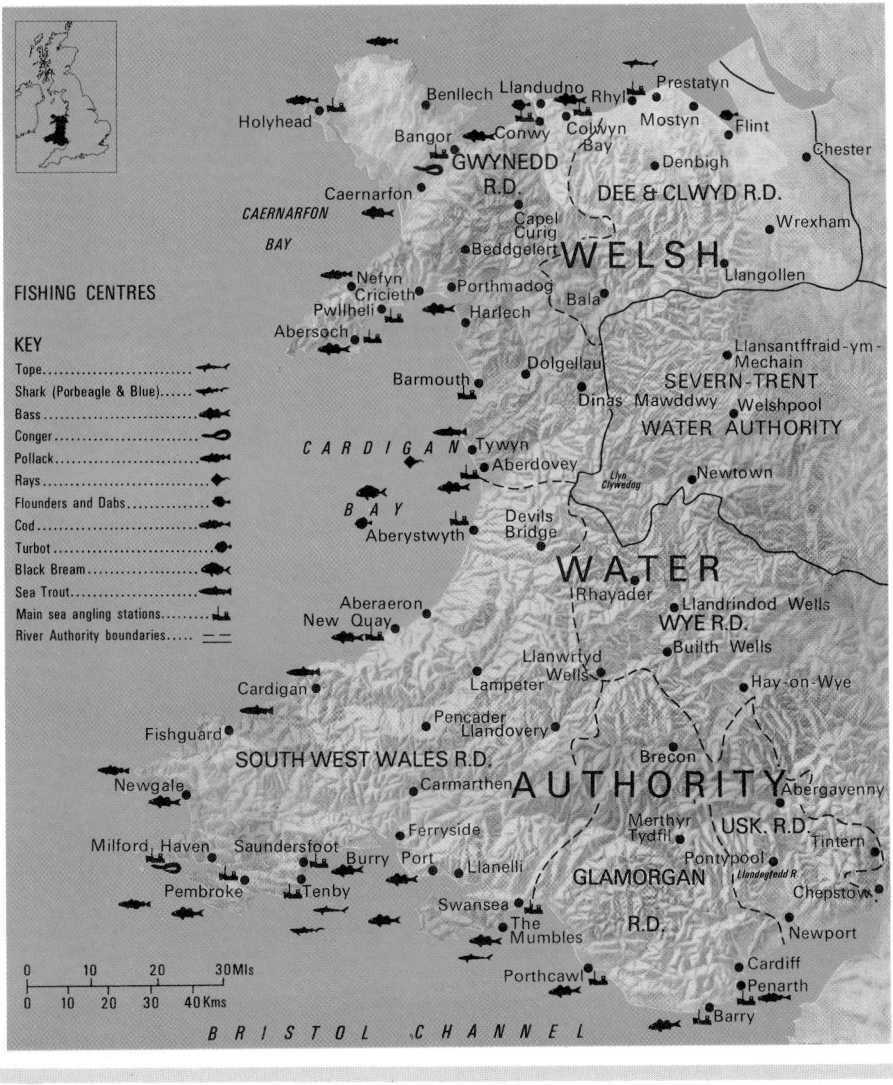

FISHING CENTRES

KEY

- Tope
- Shark (Porbeagle & Blue)
- Bass
- Conger
- Pollack
- Rays
- Flounders and Dabs
- Cod
- Turbot
- Black Bream
- Sea Trout
- Main sea angling stations
- River Authority boundaries

WELSH WATER AUTHORITY

GWYNEDD R.D.

DEE & CLWYD R.D.

SEVERN-TRENT WATER AUTHORITY

WYE R.D.

USK. R.D.

GLAMORGAN R.D.

SOUTH WEST WALES R.D.

CAERNARFON BAY

CARDIGAN BAY

BRISTOL CHANNEL

Holyhead, Benllech, Llandudno, Rhyl, Prestatyn, Mostyn, Flint, Chester, Bangor, Conwy, Colwyn Bay, Denbigh, Caernarfon, Capel Curig, Wrexham, Beddgelert, Llangollen, Nefyn, Cricieth, Porthmadog, Pwllheli, Bala, Harlech, Abersoch, Llansantffraid-ym-Mechain, Dolgellau, Barmouth, Dinas Mawddwy, Welshpool, Tywyn, Aberdovey, Llyn Clywedog, Newtown, Devils Bridge, Aberystwyth, Rhayader, Llandrindod Wells, Aberaeron, New Quay, Builth Wells, Llanwrtyd Wells, Lampeter, Cardigan, Hay-on-Wye, Pencader, Llandovery, Fishguard, Brecon, Newgale, Carmarthen, Abergavenny, Merthyr Tydfil, Ferryside, Tintern, Milford Haven, Saundersfoot, Burry Port, Llanelli, Pontypool, Llandegfedd R., Pembroke, Tenby, Chepstow, Swansea, The Mumbles, Newport, Cardiff, Porthcawl, Penarth, Barry

0 10 20 30 Mls

0 10 20 30 40 Kms

Beaches, estuaries and bays

Sixteen ounces of beach-casting rod, a multiplier or good fixed spool reel loaded with 300 yards or so of 15 lbs b.s. monofil, a box of hooks and leads, and you have the freedom of many miles of excellent shore-fishing for bass, tope and flatfish that you'd be hard-pushed to find the equal of anywhere else in the UK and you don't need a licence or permit of any kind (see note on private land). There's orthodox white-water surf fishing for bass almost everywhere from the Gower Peninsula to Anglesey (the sport actually started down in West Wales, around the beginning of the century). For this majestic form of fishing, choose a shallow storm-beach where big rollers send in tables of water into which the bass forage. Here's the top half dozen – the numbers refer to the map page in this book: Dinas Dinlle (35), Porth Neigwl (38), Borth (47), Newgale (54), Freshwater West and Frainslake (57), and Rhosili (66). There's much estuary fishing too, which features, broadly speaking, bass in summer and flounders in winter. The beaches east of Beaumaris (25), Holy Island's narrows (31), the Teifi estuary at Cardigan (50), Milford Haven's creeks (57), and the Towy/Gwendraeth area (63) all give of their best.
There's low water reef fishing for bigger bass at Gogarth (Llandudno) (23), Menai Strait (25), Marloes (57), and Caldy Island (61), but probably the most exciting beach fishing of all, which is almost unique to Wales, is casting half a herring or mackerel from the sand to contact hungry tope which may go up to 60 lbs in weight, and make sure you have at least 300 yards on that reel! You can do this in the Menai Strait (25) off South Pembrokeshire beaches (61) and Broughton Bay on Gower (66).

Evening in the surf at Manorbier, the best time for bass fishing on holiday beaches.

The bait problem

Bait! What a problem that can turn out to be sometimes. This guide devotes a special item in each coast section to the best baits to use, how to use them – and where to find them.
Live rag – sometimes lug – can be bought only in bigger towns: in Cardiff, Swansea and Llandudno, Colwyn Bay and Rhyl. Preserved baits have found their way into almost every tackle shop but they have yet to gain the confidence of serious sea anglers. Where there is a fishing industry, a few shops will sell frozen herring, squid and mackerel – at Tenby, for example, which even has frozen razor fish.
Don't worry overmuch about bait going off before you use it (except ragworm); lug, squid, razorfish and clam can fish better for its being a bit high. You will need a light garden fork and, for crabbing, a pair of old leather gloves – as well as a plastic carton of salt for razor fish.

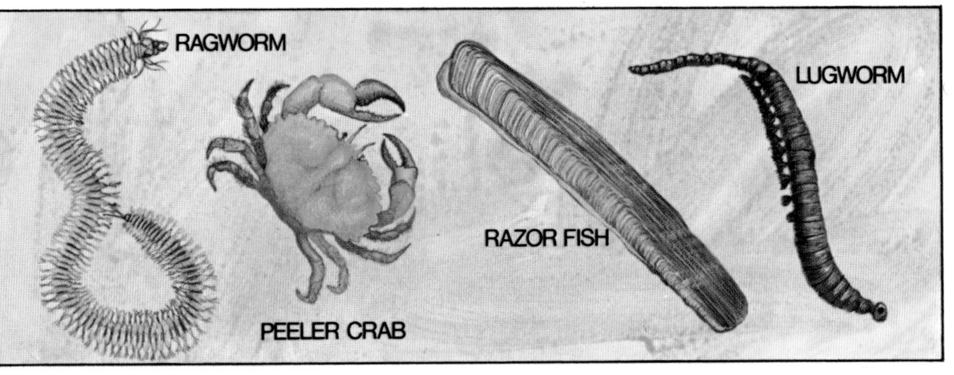

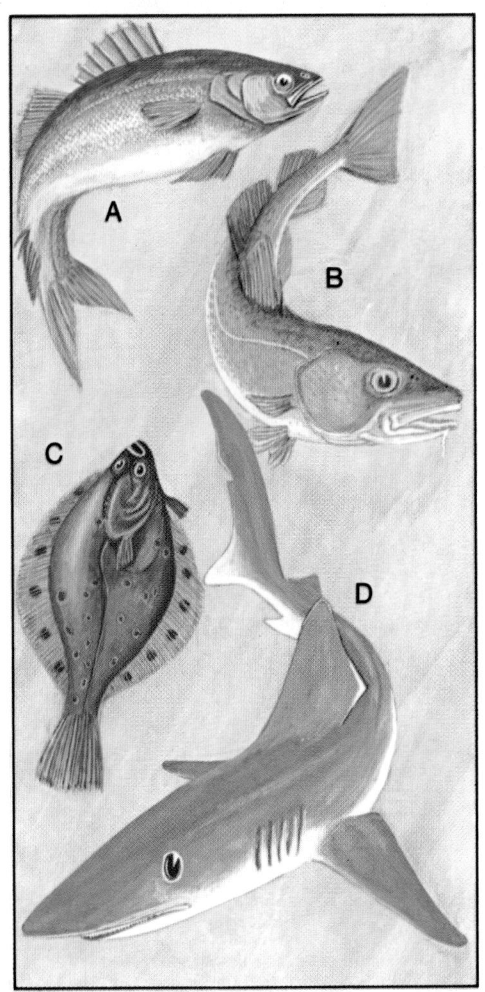

A. BASS

Silver, strong, with eight or nine sharp spines on their back, most shoaling school bass weigh 1–2 lbs. The minimum size is 10 inches nose to tip, but under 3 lbs should be released. They shoal to 5 lbs to 7 lbs over reefs, weedy ground and in island races. 8–18 pounders are loners.

B. COD

A winter visitor to the South Glamorgan and North Wales coasts, from early November to early spring. In hard winters they stay to April, even May, but in mild or frostless winters they are gone by early January. Codling, lovers of big lug/squid cocktails, run from 2½ lbs to about 4 lbs, with many fish 5 lbs to 8 lbs, some 15 pounders, the few 20 lbs plus and the Welsh record of 44 lbs 8 ozs.

C. PLAICE

Locally common over shallow clean sandy ground or where mussels live, this tasty flatfish is often confused with the red spotted flounder, an estuary-loving relative. It likes rag worm on a fine wire long-shanked 2/0 hook, sometimes on a wobbling white spool.

D. TOPE

Common offshore between Swansea and Rhyl, May to September, and inshore from May in Carmarthen Bay, and June in Menai Strait, tope are fished chiefly from Rhyl, Aberystwyth and Saundersfoot. 5–7 feet long, slaty-blue black and white belly, they take frozen herring and mackerel on 8/0 wire traced hooks to 300–400 yards of 18 lbs or heavier line.

Piers and jetties

You'll find a convenient pier or jetty at almost every Welsh coastal resort – as well as a bunch of hopeful anglers fishing from the end of it! It's a social occasion for most of them – a few flatties, a dogfish or two and they are perfectly happy with the companionship and the day out.

Surprisingly, though, Welsh piers can offer some good fishing if you are willing to break away from convention – to lower a small live bait or a peeler crab close to the ironwork for a marauding bass or to rise at crack of dawn to floatfish for mullet that haven't yet been scared away by the crowds. There's usually a small charge to take your tackle on the pier – and remember to bring a dropnet along with you to land your fish, since it isn't likely there'll be one provided.

Top: *Barry breakwater and lighthouse: the lighthouse end is out-of-bounds but there are plenty of good positions outside the railings for winter cod and whiting.*
Bottom: *Llandudno Pier and Great Orme headland.*

TIDES AND TIDE TABLES

Why worry about tides and heights; if there's water there, why not fish it? Why not indeed – you can break a record and a rule at the same time. Yet ignoring the tides and their effect probably accounts for the old belief that only 10% of the fisherman bag 90% of the fish caught.

Low water, high water

6 hours 10 minutes approximately separates dead low water from high water. So high water tonight is about 40 minutes later than high water last night. As a rough guide, a flat, bait-filled mark fishes better for tope, bass and flatfish soon after it has been covered by the tide. Deeper water marks that attract rays, conger, small turbot, cod, whiting and dogfish, usually fish better later in the tide when a good drop of water has covered the mark.

Shoaling mackerel, garfish, pollack, coalfish and bass, enjoy high tides, calm, warm evenings or morning high tides.

Springs and Neaps

The height of the tide, published in tide tables in metres or feet, measured over a convenient dock entrance sill, or from a chart datum (it doesn't matter for our purposes) tells the angler if the high tide will bring water to the top of the beach (spring tides) or only a little way up the beach (neaps), or to some point between. Conversely, springs mean that tides go out further and more bait beds and better fishing positions are revealed. Spring tides (the highest measurements in the tidetables), with plenty of water moving about (but the time it takes from low water to high water and back stays the same), mean livelier conditions, faster races, more dangerous overfalls, and weights being swept into snags. It can also mean more fish, but only if you can stay on the bottom. Up to 2 knots is normal. Around 3 knot tides are manageable by upping the weight and drifting. One has to use fine, water-scything wire lines from 4 knots, and in 5–7 knot tides it's best not to be about at all. The flow is fastest in the 3rd and 4th hour after low water and after high water, and around headlands, over reefs and between islands.

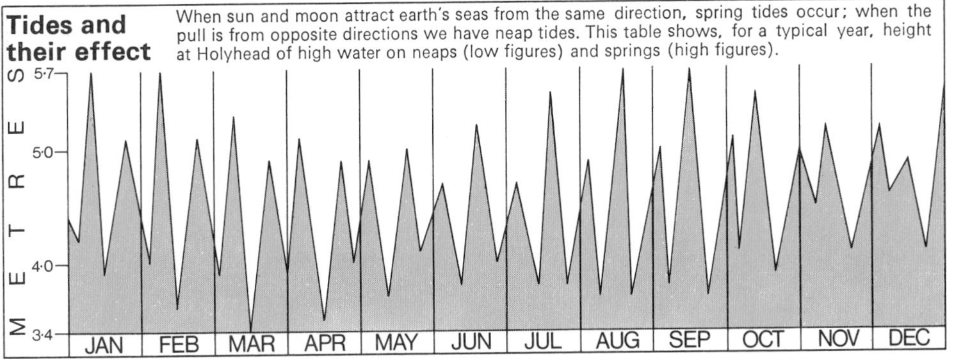

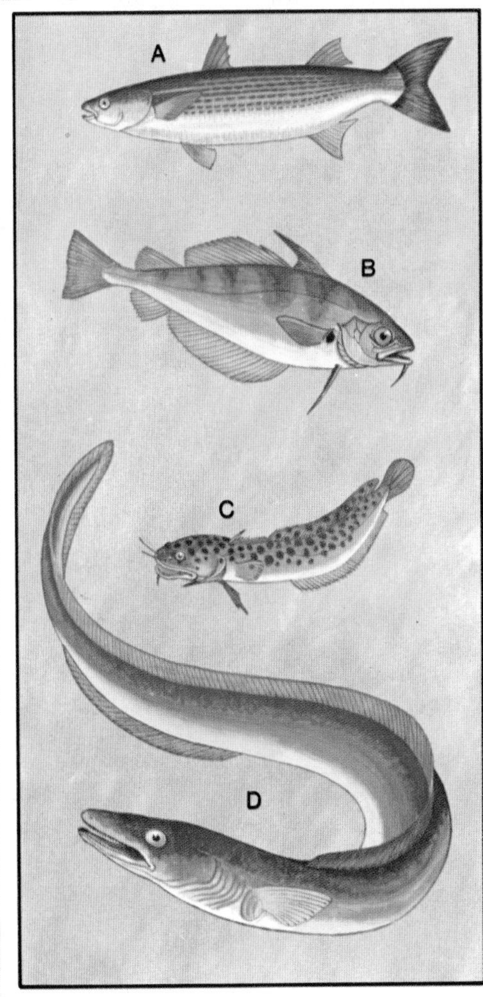

A. GREY MULLET

Scraping and sucking their way around the estuaries and harbour walls of Wales, grey mullet taste dreadful. Fine line, small hooks, Numbers 8–10, light floats, a bait they're used to – harbour rag, cheese, bacon, cockles! – and those beautiful silver-sided fighters with the four-spined dorsal fin give a good account of themselves.

B. POUTING

Ubiquitous pout whiting, golden with black bars and a tiny chin barbel, shoal inshore bait stealing with a sharp, stabbing knock from pier anglers seeking cod and whiting. Over rough ground in deeper water they run to $1\frac{1}{2}$–2 lbs.

C. ROCKLING

With the pouting, rockling, the 3-, 4- and 5- bearded, are members of the cod family. Barbels protruding from the lips and chin, immediately identify these little fish, frequently caught about piles and rocks.

D. CONGER

Feared and respected, conger vary from the 4 pounders of South Glamorgan's coast to 75 pounders-plus known to haunt the conger holes in 10 fathoms, 50 yards from the shore near the hulk of HMS *Warrior*, Pembroke Dock. Hobbs Point jetty, nearby, and Mumbles pier, Swansea, are two favourite conger hot spots. Big ones hide away in daylight, stalking around after dark to take fresh mackerel chunks. Strong gear – swivelling hooks on 50-lb wire traces – to braided lines and strong reels, help move their backsides from rocks and crannies.

Rocks and records

Rock marks at Giltar Point face Caldy Sound, a noted bass area.

Rock fishing is an exhilarating, extrovert sport that you can practise on most of the coastline around Dyfed, Lleyn Peninsula and North Anglesey, though you'll need to be fit and cautious. Wear commando-type boots for a grip on the rocks and take care not to fish when there's a big swell or in circumstances where you could be cut off by the tide. And never go rock-fishing alone!

Having said those cautionary words, it's time for the fishing. And what fishing it can be! Casting from a South Pembrokeshire rock platform for tope. Watching an orange-topped float bob in the white foam of a rock gulley where colourful wrasse and broad shouldered pollack hit and run. The delicate art of lobbing a soft crab on to a patch of sand between weedy stones for a big bass. And the wild excitement when a mackerel shoal homes in near the rock where you are standing with a spinner at the ready!

ROTTEN BOTTOMS AND FLOAT LEVELS

Choose paternoster (A) or ledger (B) tackle but maintain one, preferably two, weaker snoods (the rotten bottom) to the smallest possible streamlined lead; you renew the shorter chaffed snapped snood instead of losing the lead, and are able to snap out of a snag without losing your fish. (C) demands hand holding and extreme alertness to compensate quickly for the lack of hook snood length. (D) Float fish for bass, mackerel, pollack, pouting and wrasse.

Minimum casting strengths				
Line lbs.	8	12	18	25
Weight ozs.	2	3	4	5

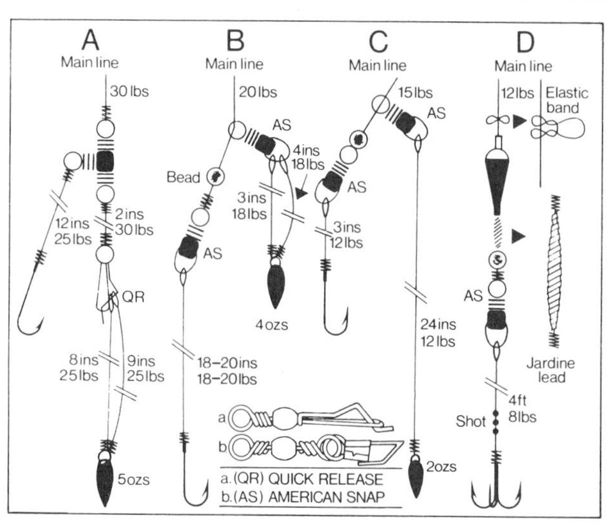

Going metric

Increasingly your fishing line strength will come expressed in Kilos not lbs; here is a brief conversion table:

Pounds – Kilogrammes

lb	*Kg*	*lb*	*Kg*
1	0.454	8	3.629
2	0.907	9	4.082
3	1.361	10	4.536
4	1.814	20	9.072
5	2.268	25	11.340
6	2.722	50	22.680
7	3.175	100	45.359

Record Fish Claim Form

Holiday anglers should make themselves familiar with the Record Fish Claim Form on page 113, in case they should catch a record specimen. It should be remembered that two independent witnesses (not relatives) are required before a claim can be made, and a certificate of identification of the species must also be produced.

1 *A fine bass of 16 lbs 3 ozs, the Welsh rod-caught record, caught on the Rhosili storm beach by George Micklewright of Sully, South Glamorgan*

2 *A plump John Dory, an unusual Welsh record fish of 5 lbs 7 ozs with its captor, young Michael Barlow pictured with Vic Haigh, skipper of Aberystwyth's Endeavour I.*

RECORD FISH

Now well established the Welsh Record Committee for rod-caught sea and freshwater fish has scrupulously examined all existing claims and has thrown out a number which could not stand its rigorous examination, replacing them with comparatively high but realistic qualifying weights. When you have caught a fish which you believe to be a record, you should contact the Record Fish Claim Recorder as soon as possible by telephone, letter or telegram. His address is: *Mr. R. G. B. Elliott, General Secretary, Welsh Record (rod caught) Fish Committee, 'Grande Vue', 16 Cambria Road, Old Colwyn, Colwyn Bay, Clwyd LL29 9AG. Tel. Colwyn Bay* (0492) 55666 (*after* 6 *p.m.*). He will advise you on which procedure to then follow in completing the Report Form – a sample is given on page 113 – preserving the specimen for identification.

British Record (rod caught) Fish Committee
If the fish is really big roughly the same procedure applies to gain British Record rod-caught fish committee acceptance. *Its secretary is: Mr. P. H. Tombleson.*
Tel. (0733) 54084, but first apply through the Welsh Record Committee. A complete list of British Records – including boat and shore records for sea fish of one pound and over – can be obtained from the offices of the National Anglers' Council, 5 Cowgate, Peterborough PE1 1LR.

Angling Times Report Stations

Catch a big fish and you will want it properly reported and authenticated. These tackle shops, etc, will help you get it officially recognised.

Aberaeron: J. Evans & Son, 1 Alban Square. Tel. (054 553) 356.
Aberystwyth: J. E. Rosser, 3 Queen Street. Tel. (0970) 7451.
Bangor: Ron Edwards, 6 Dean Street. Tel. 2811.
Barmouth: 'All Sports & Hobbies', Beach Road. Tel. (0341) 280240.
Bridgend: Brian Rowe, Fishing Tackle & Bait, 20 Queen Street. Tel. Aberkenfig (0656) (721) 459.
Caernarfon: Howard's Fishing Tackle, 72 Pool Street. Tel. (0286) 2671.
Cardiff: A. Miles & Son, Anglers Supplies, 172 Penarth Road. Tel. (022) 20723.
Cardigan: M. & A. Williams, 10a Pendre. Tel. (0239) 2038.
Carmarthen: Doug Sports, 11 Lammas Street. Tel. (0267) 7334.
Colwyn Bay: T. S. Ronald, 52 Sea View Road. Tel. (0492) 30651.
Connahs Quay: Mrs. I. M. Williams, Fishing Tackle, 316 High Street. Tel. (0244) 813373.
Conwy: Dennis Haywood, 'The Bridge'. Tel. (049263) 3494.
Dale Sailing Co., (Mr. F. C. Reynolds), Dale. Tel. (06465) 349.
Dolgellau: 'Celfi Diddan', Eldon Square. Tel. (0341) 388.
Fishguard: Cwm Boat Stores, The Quay, Lower Fishguard. Tel. (0348) 3250.
Haverfordwest: County Sports, Old Bridge. Tel. (0437) 3740.
Llandudno Junction: The Anglers Corner, The Bridge. Tel. Deganwy (0492) 81073.
Llanelli: R. Thomas, 76 Stepney Street. Tel. (05542) 3659.
Menai Bridge: Ken Johnson, Devon House, Water Street, Menai Bridge, Isle of Anglesey.
Milford Haven: Dudley Marine & Sports, Upper Charles Street. Tel. (06462) 2787.
Newport (Gwent): Dave Richards Angling Supplies, 8 Caerleon Road. Tel. (90) 54910.
Newport (Dyfed): W. Beynon Williams, Fishing Tackle, West Street. Tel. (023976) 265.
Pembroke Dock: W. T. V. Humber, 46–48 Dimond Street. Tel. (06463) 2511.
Porthcawl: G. S. Jackson, 14 Well Street. Tel. (065671) 2511.
Porthmadog: J. & R. T. Davies, 49 High Street. Tel. (0766) 2464.
Port Talbot: Selwyn Jenkins, 45 Station Street. Tel. (06396) 2787.
Rhoose: Berkeley Stores, Rhoose, Barry. Tel. (91) 247.
Rhyl: W. M. Roberts (Rhyl) Ltd, 131 High Street. Tel. (0745) 53031.
St. David's: Chapman Sea Food & Tackle Shop, 25 Nun Street. Tel. (043788) 333.
Saundersfoot: Saundersfoot Marine The Harbour. Tel. (0834) 812149.
Swansea: Capstan House, Beach Road. Tel. (0792) 54756.
Tenby: Morris Bros. (Tenby) Ltd, Troy House, St. Julian Street. Tel. (0834) 2306.
Tywyn: F. R. Porter, Sports Shop, 8 College Green.

RECORD SEA FISH LIST *Main Fish*	WELSH SHORE			WELSH BOAT			BRITISH BOAT			BRITISH SHORE		
	lbs	*ozs*	*drms*	*lbs*	*ozs*	*drms*	*lbs*	*ozs*	*drms*	*lbs*	*ozs*	*drms*
Angler Fish	62	2	0	37	0	8	82	12	0	68	2	0
Bass	16	8	5	12	10	0	18	6	0	18	2	0
Bream, Black		VACANT		4	5	0	6	14	4	4	14	4
Bream, Red..		VACANT			VACANT		9	8	12	3	0	0
Brill		VACANT		4	9	0	16	0	0	5	12	4
Bull Huss	15	2	12	17	4	0	21	3	0	17	15	0
Coalfish	3	0	0	6	3	0	30	12	0	16	8	8
Cod	44	8	0	25	0	0	53	0	0	44	8	0
Cod, Poor	0	4	0	0	4	0	0	10	5	0	10	5
Dab	2	9	8	1	12	0	2	12	4	2	9	8
Dogfish, Lesser Spotted ..	3	9	4	3	7	8	4	1	13	4	8	0
Dogfish, Spur	11	10	1	14	6	8	21	3	7	16	12	8
Dragonet	0	4	7	0	4	7	0	4	12	0	4	12
Eel, Conger..	23	12	4	56	4	0	109	6	0	67	1	0
Flounder	2	12	0	2	9	12	5	11	8	2	7	0
Garfish	2	0	0	2	6	9	2	13	14	2	1	2
Gurnard, Grey	0	6	8	1	2	4	2	7	0	1	8	0
Gurnard, Red	1	0	0	4	9	7	5	0	0	2	10	11
Gurnard, Tub	12	3	0	9	1	0	11	7	4	12	3	0
Haddock		VACANT			VACANT		12	10	1	6	12	0
Hake		VACANT			VACANT		25	5	8	5	0	0
Halibut	10	0	0	10	0	0	212	4	0	14	0	0
Herring		250 grams			250 grams		1	1	0	1	0	0
John Dory	2	0	0	5	7	0	11	14	0	4	0	0
Ling		VACANT		16	10	0	57	2	8	15	5	11
Lumpsucker	7	14	0	2	0	0	6	3	4	14	3	0
Mackerel	2	9	0	2	8	0	5	6	8	4	0	8
Megrim		VACANT		1	1	4	66	0	0	50	0	0
Monkfish	50	0	0	57	0	0	1	0	8	2	10	0
Mullet, Golden Grey ..	2	10	0	1	0	0	10	1	0	9	6	8
Mullet, Grey Thick Lipped	9	6	8	5	6	7	3	8	0	3	10	0
Mullet, Red..	0	12	8	1	1	0	10	3	8	8	1	4
Plaice	5	0	4	4	2	4	25	0	0	14	12	0
Pollack	9	3	8	17	13	8	5	8	0	3	0	0
Pouting	1	5	13	3	9	0	37	12	0	25	4	0
Ray, Blonde	10	0	0	28	0	0	5	11	0	4	8	0
Ray, Cuckoo	4	4	0	5	10	0	4	0	0	4	0	0
Ray, Sandy	2	0	0	2	0	0	16	4	0	13	8	15
Ray, Small Eyed	13	0	0	11	8	4	59	0	0	51	4	0
Ray, Spotted	4	9	10	5	9	8	6	3	4	7	12	0
Ray, Sting	10	0	0	49	0	0	38	0	0	19	0	0
Ray, Thornback	15	9	0	26	8	0	19	6	13	10	10	4
Ray, Undulate	3	0	0	3	0	0	1	0	0	1	1	4
Rockling, Shore	0	7	2	0	7	2	0	9	4	0	9	4
Rockling, Five Bearded ..	0	9	0	0	9	0	3	2	0	2	14	8
Rockling, Three Bearded ..	2	9	12	2	8	0	0	7	12	0	7	12
Sand Eel, Greater	0	8	0	1	1	0	3	4	8	2	5	13
Scad, Horse Mackerel ..	1	0	0	2	5	0	0	6	4	0	6	4
Sea Scorpion, Long Spined	0	5	0	0	5	0	2	3	0	2	2	8
Sea Scorpion, Short Spined	0	11	6	0	11	6	3	0	0	4	12	7
Shad, Allis	1	8	0	1	8	0	3	2	0	3	2	0
Shad, Twaite	1	14	0	1	2	8	218	0	0	75	0	0
Shark, Blue	40	0	0	114	6	8	500	0	0	75	0	0
Shark, Mako	40	0	0	50	0	0	465	0	0	75	0	0
Shark, Porbeagle	40	0	0	138	8	0	280	0	0	75	0	0
Shark, Thresher	40	0	0	40	0	0	226	8	0	150	0	0
Skate, Common	25	0	0	50	0	0						
Smooth, Hound (m-mustleus)	14	14	12	9	4	0	28	0	0	14	14	12
Smooth, Hound (m-asterias)	7	8	6	17	0	0	20	0	0	23	2	0
Sole	1	14	4	2	9	8	4	0	0	4	3	8
Sun Fish	10	0	0	108	0	0	108	0	0	49	4	0
Tope	48	0	0	74	11	0	74	11	0	54	4	0
Trigger Fish, File Fish ..	3	6	8	2	7	9	4	9	5	4	6	0
Turbot		VACANT		19	8	6	32	3	0	28	8	0
Weever, Greater		VACANT		2	4	0	2	4	0	2	0	0
Whiting	2	12	5	4	6	2	6	4	0	3	2	0
Witch	1	2	13		VACANT		1	0	0	1	2	13
Wrasse, Ballan	6	8	9	3	0	0	7	8	5	8	6	6
Wrasse, Corkwing ..	0	10	0	0	10	0	0	11	4	0	11	4
Wrasse, Cuckoo	1	4	0	1	0	0	2	0	8	1	4	8

With acknowledgements to: The British Board (Rod-caught) Committee, National Anglers Council and to Cyngor Pysgotwyr Cymr (Welsh Anglers Council). Welsh Record (Rod-caught) Fish Committee.

Boat fishing

Boat-fishing in Wales has only recently established itself, but already the results show that there is a wealth of fishing to be exploited. Established centres include Aberystwyth, Caernarfon, Conwy, Rhyl, Milford Haven, Tenby and Swansea and it is likely that others will develop within a very short time.

There is a great variety of fishing. The South West offers drifting for blue shark and reef pollack fishing, as well as spinning for shoaling bass. The shallow, unexploited and easily-fished waters of Cardigan Bay have big shoals of tope and plenty of skate. There are more tope and bass off Abersoch and exciting fishing still to be discovered where Anglesey juts into the Irish Sea.

Anglers recognise three types of boat fishing. Firstly, deep sea angling from fast, strong well-skippered craft, venturing up to 15 or 20 miles, often in pairs, when winds are steady up to Force 5. Fitted with radio navigation equipment and echo sounders, they pinpoint and farm wrecks, underwater pinnacle rock and prolific banks and gullies, in a degree of comfort. Then there's the lobster and tripping boat turned angling special. They catch as much as they do because fish are plentiful and their skippers' knowledge so vast. Safe, but slow, often open and uncomfortable, they plod about within the three-mile limit to get to their own time-honoured marks.

The third category are amateurs – often strangers to the coast – who put to sea in assorted craft, from pram dinghies to luxury cabin cruisers without any clear idea of where the fish are.

The detailed information and accompanying maps are intended to give chauffeured anglers an idea of where they are being taken, and, for the owner-driver, to aid him find fish and avoid danger to himself and others.

The end of a good day's fishing, Endeavour I and II head for Aberystwyth from a tope and ray mark 18 miles out in Cardigan Bay.

BEAUFORT WIND SCALE AND DESCRIPTION

This is the scale of wind strengths referred to in weather forecasts.

Beaufort number	*Wind*	*Statute mph*	*Beaufort number*	*Wind*	*Statute mph*
0	Calm	—1	6	Strong Wind	25–31
1	Light Air	1–3	7	High Wind	32–38
2	Slight Breeze	4–7	8	Gale	39–46
3	Gentle Breeze	8–12	9	Strong Gale	47–54
4	Moderate Breeze	13–18	10	Whole Gale	55–63
5	Fresh Breeze	19–24	11	Storm	64–75

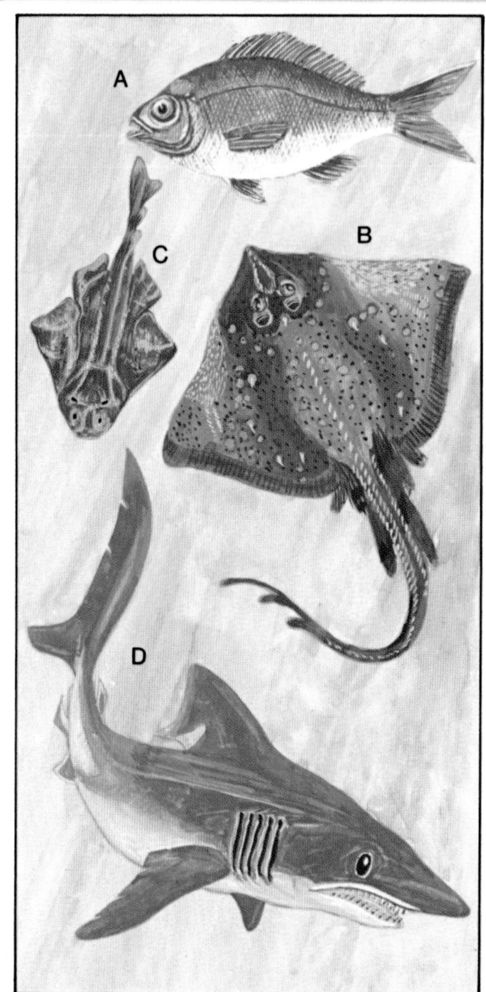

A. BLACK BREAM

Though its cousin, the common or red sea bream is frequently seen, black bream – a smoky blue running usually to about 3½ lbs – are less commonly caught. They are established along Sarn Wallog and Sarn Cynfelyn, a narrow rocky finger of reef extending under Cardigan Bay from the coast 3 miles N or Aberystwyth.

B. THORNBACK RAY

Common in deep water over sandy ground off the coast from Rhyl to Porthcawl – particularly in Cardigan Bay and Carmarthen Bay and even 14 miles inside Milford Haven at Garron Pill (55), probably breeding. On average bigger than in the rest of the UK. Grey brown, it has four rows of thorn-like hooks along the back.

C. MONKFISH

Fishing's bighead, the monk fish, in appearance half dogfish, half ray, is common off Lleyn, South Pembrokeshire and sometimes in the Swansea area, in late summer, getting up to 5 feet long and 60 lbs in weight. Sometimes called the angel fish – not to be confused with the angler fish.

D. PORBEAGLE SHARK

A frequent summer visitor to the south west corner of Wales and Cardigan Bay in 10–15 fathoms over sand. Though reputed to swallow dogfish whole, they feed mainly on mackerel shoals. A mighty torso, with a sharp snout and keel-like ridges each side of the tail, and weighing between 100 lbs and 250 lbs in Welsh waters, they call for specialist equipment and tactics.

Weather Forecasts

Times of BBC Forecasts – British Summer Time.

Shipping Radio 4 1500 m (200 kHz)
Daily 0015 0625 1355 1750

Land Forecasts
Radio 4 1500m (200kHz), VHF 92–95mHz.
Radio Wales 341m (882kHz)
Monday–Friday
0658 0758 1255 1755 2159 2400
Saturday
0655 0758 1257 1755 2158 2315
Sunday
0755 0855 1257 1755 2157 2315

Gale Warnings Radio 4 1500m (200kHz).
When received and then on next hour.

Weather forecasting services are also provided by:

Meteorological Office, R.A.F. Station, Valley, Anglesey. Tel. (0407) 2288.

Aberporth Royal Aircraft Establishment, Meteorological Office, Tel. (0239) 810117.

Gloucester Meteorological Office. Tel. Churchdown (0452) 855566.

Meteorological Office, Glamorgan Rhoose Airport. Tel. (0446) 710343.

Post Office, Tel. Swansea (0792) 8011 *during summer for Swansea Bay, Carmarthen Bay and Gower Coast.*

An indication of the weather at the time and in the immediate vicinity can often be obtained from Coastguard Stations around the coast. Telephone numbers are shown under 'useful telephone numbers' in each section.

Full details of weather forecast arrangements are included in a useful leaflet 'Meteorological Office Services – Weather Bulletins and Gale Warnings for shipping including Fishing Vessels', Met. O., Leaflet No. 3, 1976, *published on behalf of and available from The Director General, Meteorological Office (Met. O. 7a), Eastern Road, Bracknell, Berks. RG12 2UR. (Tel.* (0344) 20242).

This Coastguard service is tailor-made for the boat owner. It offers safety coverage to those who regularly use local waters and to those who make longer passages. Its aim is to give the Coastguard a record of the movements of craft and in times of distress provide immediate information vital to the saving of lives.

The old CG66 scheme has been reorganised with two main aims (a) to provide the information necessary for the coastguard to mount a successful Search and Rescue operation, and (b) to promote closer links between the Coastguard Service and all small craft owners and users. All you need to do is fill in a simple, post-paid card, obtainable from Coastguard Stations, marinas, yacht clubs and harbour masters' offices – wherever you see the circular Safety Scheme 'Issuing Authority' disc. Describe your craft, its equipment and your normal sailing area, and then send the card back to the Coastguard station. The card, and perhaps a photograph of your craft if this is available, will be retained at the Coastguard Rescue Headquarters for your area so that if you or your craft are reported overdue or in distress then the necessary information to make Search and Rescue action more effective will be at hand.

Each card includes a tear-off section which you can leave ashore with a reliable friend or relative – so they will know the Coastguard Station to contact should they be concerned for your safety.

Cards should be renewed annually or whenever significant changes occur to your craft.

The service is entirely free and is simply designed to assist small craft safety and to improve Search and Rescue effort.

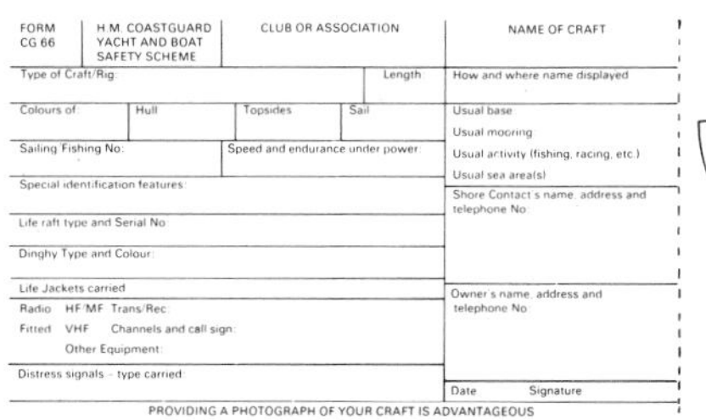
FORM CG 66 | H.M. COASTGUARD YACHT AND BOAT SAFETY SCHEME | CLUB OR ASSOCIATION | NAME OF CRAFT

Type of Craft/Rig: | Length: | How and where name displayed

Colours of: | Hull | Topsides | Sail | Usual base: | Usual mooring: | Usual activity (fishing, racing, etc.) | Usual sea area(s)

Sailing/Fishing No: | Speed and endurance under power:

Special identification features:

Shore Contact's name, address and telephone No:

Life raft type and Serial No:

Dinghy Type and Colour:

Life Jackets carried

Radio Fitted: HF/MF Trans/Rec: | VHF Channels and call sign: | Other Equipment:

Owner's name, address and telephone No:

Distress signals – type carried:

Date | Signature

PROVIDING A PHOTOGRAPH OF YOUR CRAFT IS ADVANTAGEOUS

THIS PORTION SHOULD BE RETAINED AND PREFERABLY LEFT ASHORE WITH SOME RESPONSIBLE PERSON CONCERNED WITH YOUR SAFETY.

Porthdinllaen, home of a RNLI lifeboat on Lleyn Peninsula.

Emergency Services

HM Coastguard is the authority responsible for initiating and co-ordinating Marine Search and Rescue measures for vessels and persons in need of assistance.

For search and rescue assistance it is only necessary to dial 999 and ask for 'Coastguard'; the Coastguard Rescue Headquarters will then deploy lifeboats, helicopters, Coastguard teams and search parties, Police, etc.

For advice, local knowledge and reports of weather conditions local Coastguard Stations may be telephoned direct; the following stations are constantly manned:

(a) Coastguard Rescue Headquarters Holyhead – Tel. Holyhead (0407) 2051.

(b) Coastguard Rescue Headquarters St. Anns – Tel. Dale (06465) 218.

(c) Coastguard Rescue Headquarters Mumbles – Tel. Mumbles (0792) 66534.

(d) Coastguard Fishguard – Tel. Fishguard (0348) 3449.

(e) Coastguard Barry Island – Tel. Barry (91) 5016.

Constant Watch is maintained on Channel 16 VHF, and the MF Distress Watch on 2182 kHz supplements the coverage of the Coast Radio Stations.

Intermediate, Regular and Auxiliary Stations maintain special watches at various times (specifically when 'casualty risk' exists) or carry out mobile patrols using Land-Rovers.

A feature of the last few years has been the number of anglers who have lost their lives through being swept from exposed ledges and rocks or have been lost from overloaded small craft without even the simple precaution of wearing a life jacket. It might also be mentioned that an isolated angler could well be the only person in a position to assist a fellow sportsman who gets into difficulty; consider the possibility, how could you help him? Where is the nearest telephone? Have you something which could help him to float or assist him to land? If you are going afloat do leave details with someone reliable ashore, including a full description of the craft, number of occupants etc, and keep them informed should you change your plans and when you return.

Useful publications obtainable from the Department of Trade. Apply to:
Information Division
Department of Trade and Industry
Room 306
Gaywood House
Great Peter Street
London SW1 3LW
Tel. (01) 212 8698

1. Search and Rescue: HM Coastguard (Free).
2. Seaway Code – A guide to small boat users. (Free).
3. Safety on small craft (HMSO, 75p).

Sea tackle

The sea angler's basic tackle – the rod, reel, line, weight and hooks or lure – is designed to carry out only a limited number of tasks perfectly. Equipment designed for one class of fishing can be used in the circumstances of another, but only with some loss of ability to present the bait at the right place, way and time, or else with a loss of enjoyment (of feel) and, perhaps, a reduction in the chances of landing the fish. If you can only afford one rod, choose it from the classes of rod illustrated – the brand-name is a matter of personal choice – rather than one advertised to be a jack-of-all-trades. At least it will have the merit of being entirely suited to the class of fishing you do most. If you can afford two, choose a boat rod and a spinner, or a beach caster and a spinner – depending upon whether you boat fish or beach fish the more frequently. When you know precisely what you want and are certain it is a necessary piece of equipment, buy the best quality example of it you can afford.

Hooks

These hooks are actual sizes from No. 10 to 8/0. There are bigger hooks for shark, smaller ones for coarse fish, as well as a host of brand names and patterns. Some anglers won't use stainless steel hooks because escaped fish can't lose them. Cod take a heavy 5/0 or bigger; for bass a thin wire 5/0 Mustad 'Aberdeen' type is fine. Hone all hooks extra-sharp before use.

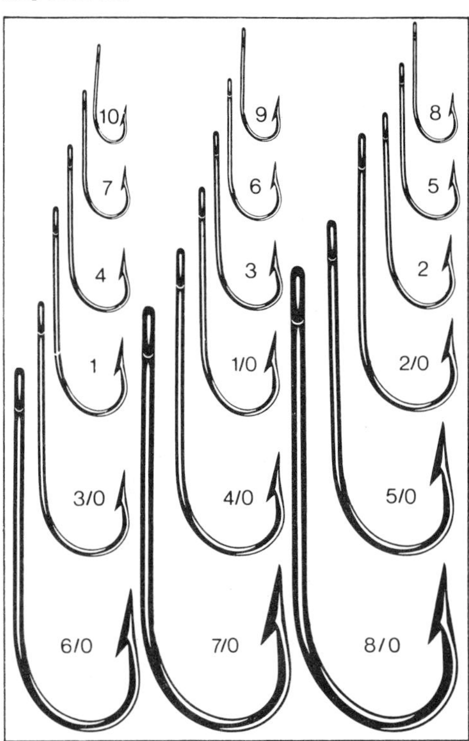

Lures and leads

Your tackle box won't be without a good range of leads, some bigger toby's (up to 30 grammes) and a German sprat for bass spinning. Pollack – and bass too – love the successor to the red rubber eel, the famous red gills, large and small size. Add a mackerel feather trace for jigging, a shorter stronger one for casting and a floating 'weight' made from a quarter of a candle for casting plastic eels over rough ground.

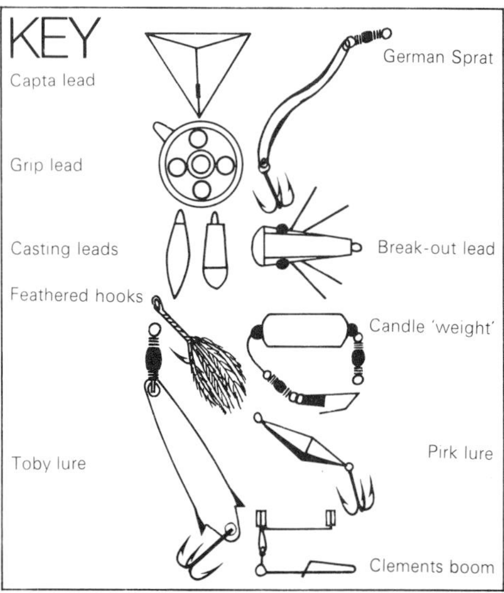

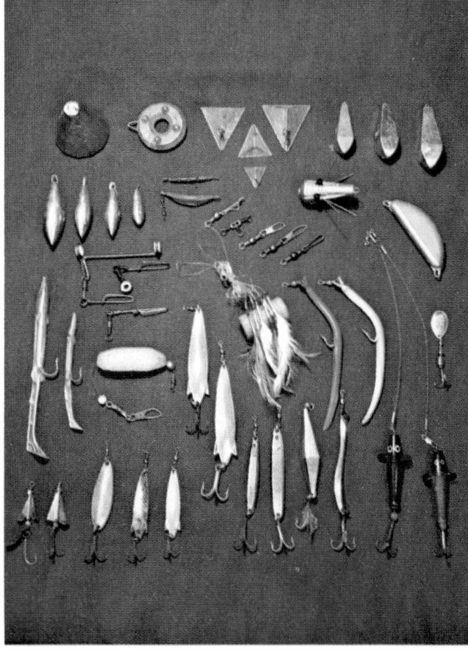

Equipment kindly loaned by A. Miles & Son, Anglers Supplies, 172 Penarth Road, Cardiff.

TACKLE GUIDE

Newcomers to sea angling sometimes fail to catch fish because they use the wrong tackle and bait. Here's a guide which will put you on the trail of a record fish – it's only a guide, for every successful fisherman has his own pet combination of rod, line, hook and bait.

FISH	ROD & REEL	LINE LBS	HOOK SIZE	BAIT OR LURE	WT. OZS
Bass	B E	15 10	5/0 2/0	Rag or crab White rubber eel	3 1
Red and Black Bream	E	10	Long Shank No. 4	Mackerel strip	2
Cod	A (shore) D (boat)	18 30	5/0 5/0	Lug Rag or squid	4 8
Conger	C	80	7/0	Fresh fish	6
L/S Dogfish and Bull Huss	D	18	3/0	Squid or mackerel	3
Flounders and Dabs	E	6	No. 4	Rag-baited 3 ins spoon trolled or long shank hook	1
Mackerel, Garfish & Scad	E or F	6	No. 5	Mackerel spinner, strip or feathers	1
Grey Mullet	F or E	6	No. 6	Cheese or bread paste	Shot
Plaice & Brill	B or E	10	Long shank No. 4	Lug or mussel	1
Pollack & Coalfish	D or E	15	4/0	Lure, sand eel or red gill	2
Rays & Ling	D	30	4/0	Mackerel strip	6
Shark (Blue and Porbeagle)	C	120	10/0	Fresh mackerel	1
Skate, Monkfish, Angler Fish	C	80–100	6/0–10/0	Mackerel fillet	6
Sole	E	6	No. 4	Lug	1
Tope and Smooth Hound	A (shore) D (boat)	20 20	6/0–10/0	Half mackerel or frozen herring	4–6
Turbot	D	35	5/0	Mackerel strip or sand-eel	6
Whiting & Pouting	E	10	No. 1	Lug	2
Wrasse & Rockling	E	20	2/0	Worms or limpet	2

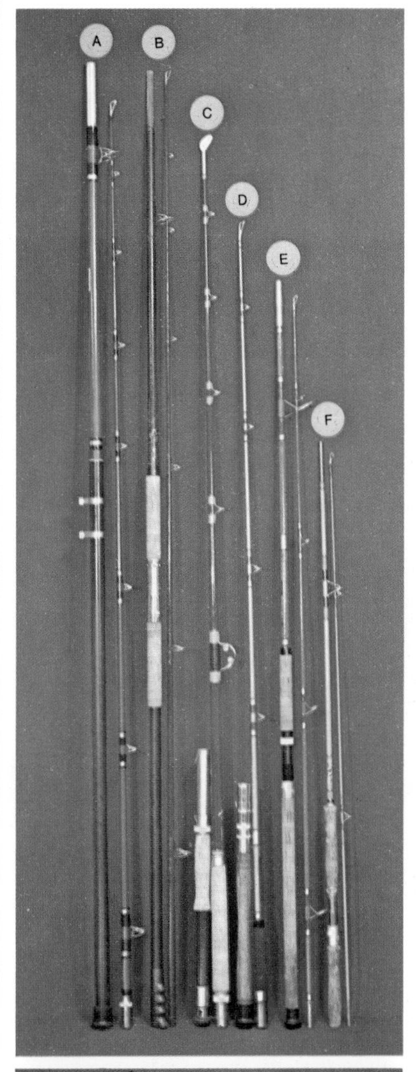

Clubs and trophies

Welsh sea angling clubs are affiliated to the Welsh Federation of Sea Anglers. The Federation gives good advice to all anglers through Regional Secretaries, particularly on competitions, where to fish and boat hire. Send a stamped and addressed envelope for information to one of the following:

President and Public Relations Officer:
Captain H. T. Evans, 'Kyrenia', Llanbedgoch, Isle of Anglesey. Tel. Pentraeth (024870) 658.

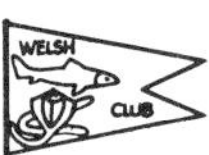

The Welsh Shark, Tope, Skate and Conger Club is a club open to associate and full members. These qualify for membership by catching one of the following species of fish in the sizes laid down in the club rules:

	Boat lb.	*Shore* lb.
Shark	60	60
Tope	30	30
Common Skate	37½	22½
Conger	22½	11¼
Thornback Ray	9	7½

The club organises the Welsh Cod Championship held at Swansea each year. *Secretary/Treasurer: Mr. Eric Woods, 1 Parc Glas, Skewen, Neath. Tel. Skewen* (0792) 2492.

Tope Angling Club of Great Britain Formed 1959; members qualify by catching a tope 30 lb or more on 35 lb b.s. line (boat), 45 lb b.s. line (shore). *Hon Sec.: Mr. J. D. Williams, 24 Church Walks, Llandudno. Tel.* (0492) 75105.

The Bass Anglers Sportfishing Society was formed in 1973 to protect the interests of this most important of our inshore species, and has a strong Welsh membership. It is always very pleased to help out with advice to members contemplating a bass fishing trip to Wales. *Sec.: Mr. J. Churchouse, Tel.* (03057) 71148.

The European Federation of Sea Anglers' 26 nation-members aim to further international competition in European countries. The Federation's tope championship has been held at Tenby in recent years. They also help individual members visiting Wales. *Hon. Sec. Mr. D. Williams, 21 Martin Road, Pen-y-Fan, Llanelli, Dyfed. Tel. Llanelli* (05542) 4501.

Competitions

Beach fishing competitions are rarely an opportunity of catching fish. It helps if your prepare beforehand, paying attention to the kind of detail that keeps the right bait in the best possible place open to you, as naturally and for as long as possible.

Equipment: Put aside your rod rest if it's a flounder or bass match and develop a lightweight kit reduced to essentials which you can carry on you. It saves walking back and forth into the surf. Unless you are absolutely certain in your handling of a multiplier, revert to a snag-free fixed spool reel.

Cefn Sidan Sands, venue for one of Wales' most popular angling competitions.

Members of the BP Chemicals (Baglan Bay) Sea Angling Club and their guests enjoy a day tope and ray fishing in Cardigan Bay with the Endeavour Deep Sea Club's boats under skippers Vic and Lee Haigh.

SAFETY AT SEA

Advice from Commander Charles Thomson of the National Coastal Rescue Training Centre, Aberavon

Before you go to sea check your boat for damage and from a check list make certain you have essential equipment:
● a bung and spare bung ● anchor with chain and rope attached to your boat ● flares ● simple first aid kit ● spare plugs and tools for engine repair ● a heaving line ● spare oar or paddle ● simple fire extinguisher ● bailer ● pump and repair kit for inflatable craft ● all your fishing tackle and gear.

Dry start your engine, stop as soon as it fires. When you launch your boat check for buoyancy, for leaks and depth for outboard engine. Look to your own clothing: cold is your worst enemy. Be warm, be comfortable and use light-weight anoraks, and trousers for protection against cold winds. Put on your life jacket and check for inflation. Telephone HM Coastguard. Tell him where you are going and when you expect to return. Ask for a forecast. Tell your family, or a friend where you are going and when you expect to return. If you don't know your proposed fishing area ask someone who does. Check a chart for tidal conditions and local hazards. Don't go out alone, but be one of, or take only, the number of passengers who can be safely accommodated and no more than the boat is licensed for. If they don't have warm clothing and life jackets don't go or don't take them.

AFLOAT

Keep away from shipping lanes. They are marked with fairway buoys. Anchor safely and watch for tidal drag. Observe from time to time any weather changes. Don't take chances with your boat, your equipment, your life or the lives of the people who will come to attempt to rescue you. If you doubt the future weather conditions head for home. Telephone coastguards, or contact your friends and tell them that you are safely ashore. Check your boat and engine, life jackets, etc.

DO YOU KNOW . . .

● There are few restrictions on bait digging in Wales. But do, please, always backfill.

● Almost every bay and estuary has a speed restriction of 6–8 nautical miles per hour.

● Government regulations stipulate maximum numbers of passengers and minimum standards in craft, safety equipment and crew. Walk off the boat – before it sails – if you find things are not as they should be.

● You should tell the nearest coastguard before doing anything out of the ordinary – like jigging bright lights about on craft or on lonely beaches at dead of night.

● The Ministry of Defence close large areas of sea to anglers from time-to-time – but not all the time – when experimental and training firing of bombs, guns and rockets takes place. Take care to brief yourself on firing times and warning signs from announcements in press and post offices local to your fishing area and from the maps in this guide.

● Sea-Fishing Industry (Immature Sea-Fish) Order, 1968, prescribes minimum size for certain fish:

	New size limit centimetres	*Equivalent in inches*
Brill	30	11.8
Cod	30	11.8
Dabs	15	5.9
Haddock	27	10.6
Hake	30	11.8
Lemon Soles	25	9.8
Megrims	25	9.8
Plaice	25	9.8
Soles	24	9.4
Turbot	30	11.8
Whiting	25	9.8
Witches	28	11.1

There is no minimum for ray, or mullet.

Bass

Legislation has been introduced adding bass to the above list. The minimum size is 10 inches (26 cm); the size of the fish shall be its length measured from the tip of snout to extreme end of tail fin. Though this is the statutory requirement, the Welsh Federation of sea anglers recommends anglers to return all bass to the sea if they are less than 15 inches from tip of snout to fork of the tail.

● River authorities have jurisdiction into esturial waters for salmon and sea trout.

Prestatyn and the Dee Estuary

Like its counterpart, the Severn Estuary at the other end of Wales, the Dee Estuary and its approaches has fish, but above average angling and boating skill and patience is needed to catch them. Estuary fish – flounders, mullet, and the occasional bass – are found here. Yet good tope and ray fishing is to be experienced simply by booking an angling trip from the Mostyn Dock.

I. **Prestatyn.** Two big holiday camps almost on the shore, plus a devoted holiday hotels clientele and active yachting and boating clubs operating from Barkby Beach, combine to make the sandy Prestatyn shore untenable for the daytime angler. Cross-beach tides swirl right to left on the ebb, for which reason a number of line-trapping groynes have been constructed on Ffrith beach, just west of the town. Concentrate on the area's rich shoals of flounders, occasional plaice and dabs; fish No. 6 long shanked hooks on fine snoods baited with small pieces of lugworm. You might even get a bass with tackle as light as that for they only rarely run bigger than 3 lbs.

II. **Point of Air.** Beyond the old lighthouse, reached through Talacre Village and a rough track to the dunes through shanty villas, is a wilderness of sand, lonely and desolate. The extreme spring tide low water mark

N

KEY

Buoy, Light or beacon, Shore mark, Boat mark, Slipway, Ragworm, Peeler crab, Lugworm, Razor fish, Sandy, Muddy, Stony, Rocky

R C L Z

Km 0 1 2 3 4 5 6 7 8

Mls 0 1 2 3 4 5

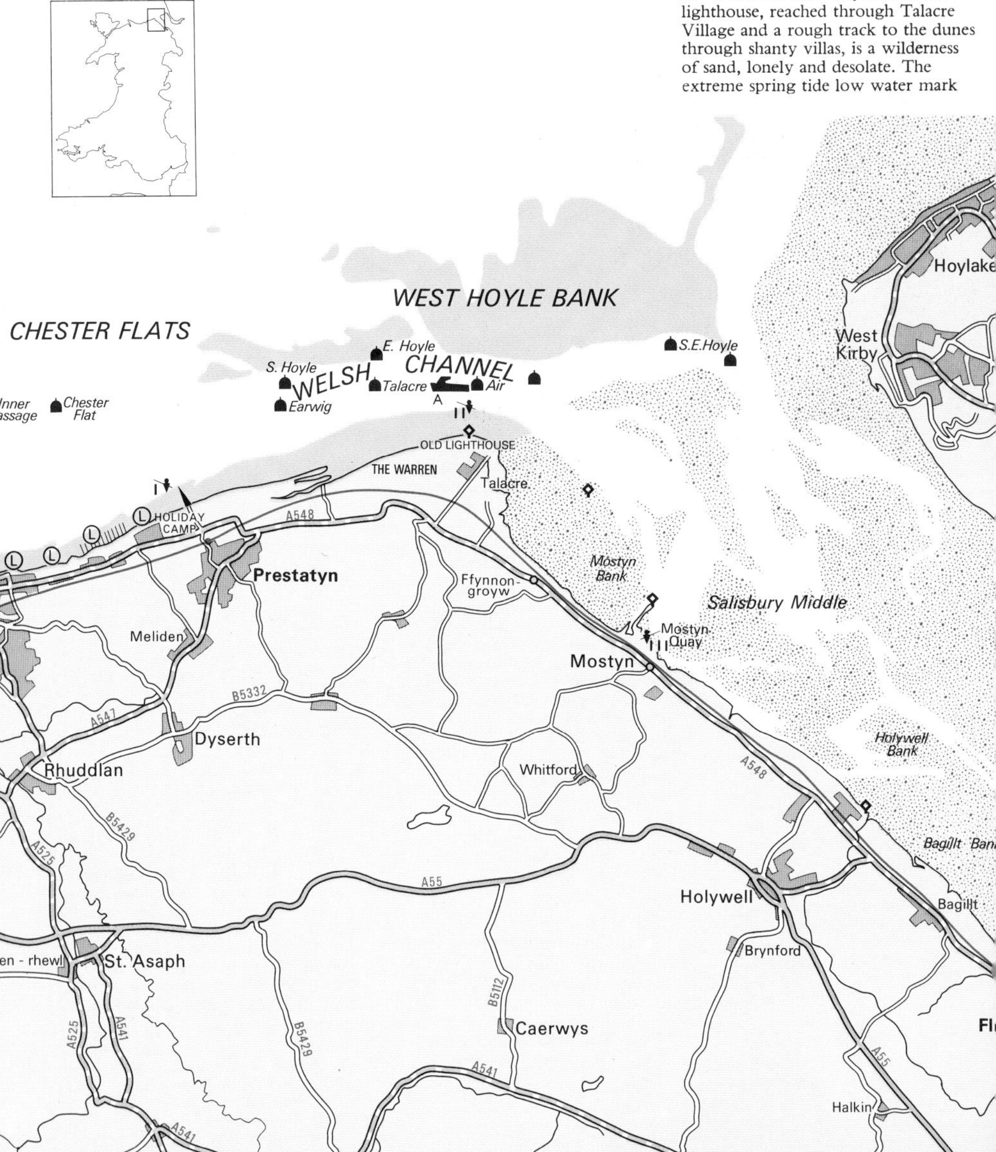

fronts a 13 fathoms deep channel – yes, almost 80 feet deep! – the Welsh Channel, ½-mile wide, separating the mainland sands from a veritable sahara, the West Hoyle Bank. Don't be tempted without sound local advice to venture too far when the tide is flooding, filling channels behind the angler with amazing speed. But followed down and well marked for danger, it's a mark that can give more than just silver eels. Big bass have been caught and others remain to be caught. Early season tope use the channel, travelling in small packs as in the Loughor Estuary of South Wales, looking for tasty flounders, a change from their normal mackerel diet. Fish light and get all your gear and bait into a small haversack.

III. **Mostyn.** The small dock of Mostyn is able to put angling boats to sea marginally longer than Rhyl. Mud laden waters in the immediate dock area are unlikely to inspire fish or fishermen but it can't be too bad, for Dee salmon continue to make their way through the sandy channels on their way towards Bala Lake. The beach is only lightly fished. Occasional small bass add to the customary bag of small dabs. Whiting and, less frequently, codling enliven the vigil of chillier moonlight nights with their insistent sharp knocks.

Boat fishing

The surge and depth of ebbing water pouring over constantly shifting sand banks of the Dee Estuary has the power to roll a small boat over without difficulty. Dinghy owners without a sound local knowledge of the area's tides, banks and danger points would be well advised to stay on the Prestatyn side of Point of Air.

A. **Welsh Channel.** Most of the charter and trip fishing from Mostyn Docks takes place alongside Rhyl boats (see following section, mark B.), but a sound boat and experienced crew looking for a change will pick up the challenge of successfully fishing the neaps and low springs flooding into the Welsh Channel. The Dee still holds some bigger bass simply because it's a big area and can't be fished efficiently from the bank or dinghy. Anchor solidly in the channel. Lug or ragworm bait ledgered lightly in the tide towards the fringes of the Channel are sometimes successful in landing them. Tope take to this kind of rapidly flooding water as we know very well, particularly where there's good depth, a narrow channel, plenty of flounders – and peace and quiet. To the normal light tope tackle of 250 yards – 300 yards of 15–20 lbs line add a Clements boom with 4 ozs weight, and a 4 feet wire trace baited with fresh mackerel or frozen herring – not stale slab stuff. But, and it's important, stop the Clements boom about 30 feet up the main line with a matchstick so as to give the bait freedom to behave just as a fish would in the tideway. You should get a few runs from June to early September.

Bait supply

The coast between Rhyl and Prestatyn has lug beds on low springs, but the digging is tough for the best black sewie lug. The approaches are from Rhyl, or Prestatyn Ffrith beach and Barkby beach entrances. A hard stint with a long-tined fork will collect enough in a small open wooden box for a 3-hour beach fishing expedition. Comparatively few are needed for boat fishing because of the low wastage.

Tackle shops

Connahs Quay. *Mrs. I. M. Williams, 316 High Street. Tel. Deeside* (0244) 813373. Fishing tackle supply; preserved bait, maggots and flies; advice on where to fish; *Angling Times* report station.

Prestatyn. *Sports Shop*, 4A *Meliden Road. Tel. Prestatyn* (07456) 2390. Tackle supply only.

Boat hire, trips or charter

Boat launching slipways

Prestatyn. Council-owned slipway at Barkby beach boating and yachting centre. Small charge.

Useful telephone numbers

In emergency
Dial 999 and ask for Coastguard.

At other times
RNLI, Flint. *Inshore rescue dinghy. Coxwain Tel.* (03526) 3320. **Coastguard,** *Rhyl Tel.* (0745) 53284. *(not constantly manned).* **Weather forecasts,** *Meteorological Office, RAF Station, Valley, Isle of Anglesey. Tel.* (0407) 2288.

Little Orme to Rhyl

Summer holidaymakers' use of the area's flat sandy, mainly featureless, beaches is intense, making shore fishing an early morning, evening or night-time occupation. Flatfish are common but bass begin to fade out east of Llandudno, except for odd big ones caught at Rhos-on-Sea and Colwyn Bay. The Colwyn Bay September Bass Fishing Festival has been won with specimens of 12 lbs 2 ozs fish and 9 lbs. 10½ ozs. Winter fishing is primarily for whiting and dabs, with the occasional codling for which the coast's lug beds come in handy. Many summer anglers prefer to go offshore in Rhyl-based boats for tope and rays which, though small, are abundant.

I. **Little Orme: Villa Marina and Arcadia Theatre.** Llandudno Bay's east end meets the abrupt wall of Little Orme Head. Near Villa Marina there is rocky ground which smoothes into shingle near Arcadia Theatre. Low water spinning with toby and white eel is always recommended over the rocks, but it would be foolish to ignore the ledgering potential – or float fishing just over the rocks – for bass, with bunched prawns or soft crab, which shouldn't be too difficult to get in June/July. Keep rag and lug for plaice and flounder higher up the tide in smoother ground and, late in the year, for the first arrivals of whiting, codling and dabs.

II. **Penrhyn Bay and Rhos-on-Sea.** In the words of a local angler – 'extremely graunchy ground', meaning, of course, rocky, weedy, with pools and depressions, interspersed with sandy spots and mussel patches. Bass, mullet, plaice and flounders are again in evidence but a longer cast, finding the sandy patches among the stones, give the chance of the odd ray and conger. Bass stay quite late in the year but are loath to return till June, though March arrivals have been recorded. Late summer is best, low water −1 to low water + 1½ and again for an hour up to high water. Being 'graunchy', anglers are not inhibited by summer-day activity. The beach's occasional king

continued on next page

rag on spring tides is choice bait, though soft and peeler crab, available here, will always do well in those conditions. Cayley promenade, where it turns into Colwyn Bay, and as far as the Bay of Colwyn Yacht Club slipway, is a favourite bass ledgering mark perhaps because it is crab-ridden. Rhos Point and the Little Orme end of the bay are good spots for spinning and many mackerel are taken.

III. **Colwyn Bay: The Victoria Pier.** Available in summer for angling 3 hours each side of high water, but holds few prospects other than small dabs and occasional whiting and small bass. Bait can be bought in a hut 100 yards west of the pier in summer. Winter fishing rights are vested in Colwyn Bay's Victoria Sea Angling Club who use it for whiting, codling and many small dabs.

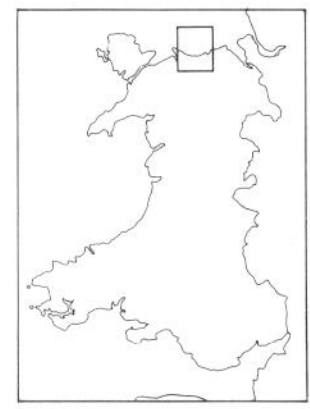

IV. **Old Colwyn.** The beach gives bass and flounders on lug or rag, and occasional beach tope if a good slice of fish or half a mackerel is used with plenty of light line to a wire trace.

V. **Tan Penmaen Head, Old Colwyn.** For comparative summer peace one can walk to Tan Penmaen Head, tunnelled by the railway, and fish as mark IV. Alternatively branch left (going east) a few hundred yards before the 70° hotel, dropping down towards the head through an old quarry. Heavy bass catches are made float fishing rag and crab. Tope fishing, too, is remarkably good.

VI & VII. **Quarry Jetties.** Llanddulas Quarries jetties (themselves out-of-bounds) at marks VI and VII are the starting point for summer casting. Again bass, flounders and tope are the quarry as at mark IV. Alternatively, drive onto the shingle bank at Llanddulas (access down road from big motorway-type roundabout) and fish straight out.

VIII. **Llanddulas and beaches east to Kinmel Bay.** A river-cut channel across sand is almost always a good point to start casting for bass and the mouth of the tiny Dulas river is no exception. Yet from Llanddulas east to Point of Air and Mostyn Quay, one would do better to concentrate on techniques of dab, flounder and plaice fishing, for these are by far the most prevalent species. The exception is Pensarn beach which fishes well for early and late season bass. Drive on to the shingle bank near Pensarn Station and along it, west, for 1 mile. Alternatively walk over the 'motorway' bridge from the old road layby opposite Gwrych Castle west exit. It smacks of long lining to adopt the big South Wales sand beach (Rhosili, Cefn Sidan, Pendine) technique of leaving two or three well baited traces (½-mackerel or leathery black lug) at low water cast mark, then walking back with your rod as the tide floods in. Yet from Llanddulas to Point of Air, 13 miles of beach, gullied deeply (and dangerously) parallel with the shore, it's a system that can give a tope and the odd big bass when other methods fail.

IX. **Rhyl.** Recent demolition of the pier has removed a popular if not particularly productive mark. The sea front's west side, reached easily at

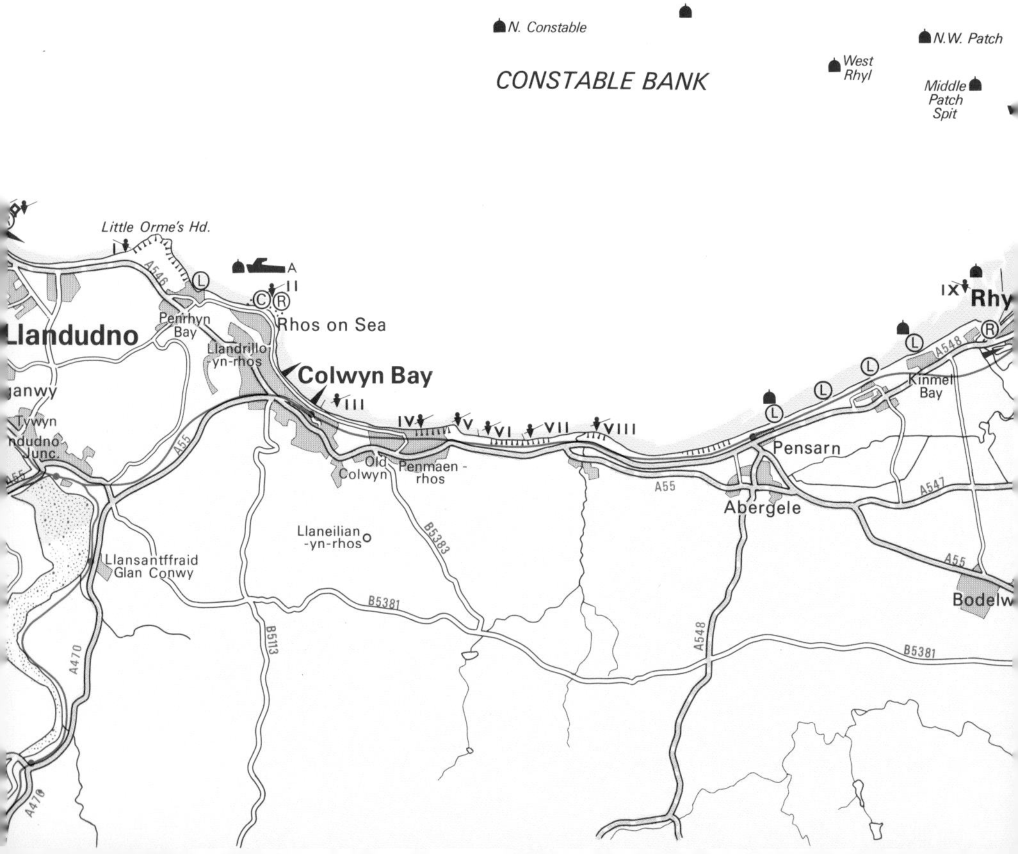

Tywyn and Kinmel Bay, ends abruptly in Foryd Harbour, base for several good deep water angling boats. The drying harbour's immediate approaches are a noted flounder mark and the occasional fresh water attracted bass will take ledgered black lug which can be bought at nearby Esso Marina petrol station (and tackle shop). Small harbour rag, easily gouged out of the Foryd, can be used for small flounders which stay in the Foryd's fresh water, the River Clwyd.

Boat fishing

With normal prudence, the owner of a solid little dinghy can increase enormously his chances of tope, ray and prime gurnard, even though forced to stay inside the 3-fathoms line. Stronger craft can reach 6 fathoms and Rhyl-based professional angling craft get as far as the 11 fathoms banks. Sea beds are sand or sand and stone mixtures and bait is plentiful.

A. **Colwyn Bay.** Launching is convenient for small craft and the 3-fathoms line comes close inshore off Penrhyn Bay and Rhos-on-Sea. Water skiers operating between Victoria Pier and Rhos Point. These and the tide race on the ebb around the Point are about the only dangers for small craft in fair weather. Go out from Rhos Point until Great Orme's Head comes well into view beyond the Little Orme; this line of view is virtually the 3-fathom line in this area and is not too deep for drop-netting for prawns and hermit crabs, used as bait. Tope – small but abundant – small rays and prime gurnard form the bulk of the summer catch, with whiting and codling in winter. Gurnard take fish baits and are worth fishing for. The distinctive red gurnard runs to over 4 lbs but the grey gurnard with spots on its grey back, is smaller. The tub gurnard is biggest of the three, but its brilliant blue pectoral fins are rarely seen hereabouts. Mackerel shoals run into the Bay of Colwyn with the flood and ebb, from early July till early September.

B. **Rhyl and the Bay of Colwyn.** Inside the 3 fathoms line – identified if you draw a line from Chester Flat Buoy to Rhos Point (Colwyn Bay) – and easily within the capacity of a good trailed angling boat in fine settled weather, there are small tope and skate, plenty of dogfish, dabs, plaice and the odd small conger. It is flatish, sandy terrain, difficult to find fish in quantity without an echo sounder. Fish on the ebb while slowly drifting on a dragging killick, from Chester Flat Buoy towards Middle Patch Spit Buoy, occasionally paying out small lumps of ground bait as the tide nears its last 2 hours down. Anchor up and drop over a sea bed rubby dubby of mackerel mash and cod liver oil for the new flood when you've hit a likely spot. Rhyl and Mostyn Quay's professionally skippered angling boats venture out more frequently than can the amateur angler, on 5 hour angling trips, with 8 hours-plus trips for seasoned anglers. One would do well to join them on board for very good tope, ray and gurnard fishing, monkfish, stingray and almost the whole range of flat fish, including small turbot and the somewhat similar but smaller brill.

Bait supply

Rhyl and Colwyn Bay's tackle shops are almost always well stocked with live and frozen bait. Here are several beaches with reasonably accessible bait:

Lug. The area's main bait stock, beds of good quality black lug, are found from Prestatyn, through Rhyl, Pensarn, Llanddulas, and Old Colwyn to Penrhyn Bay near Rhos-on-Sea. They are deep, need individual digging and a moderate to big spring tide is essential. It's easier for the visiting angler to buy from tackle shops.

Rag and crab. At Penrhyn Bay and towards the point at Rhos-on-Sea there is hard digging of king rag and picking of peeler crab on low springs. This beach also holds small fish and shrimps in weedy pools, as well as plenty of mussels. Offshore there is fairly abundant mackerel and drop netting for hermit crab and prawns.

Tackle shops

Abergele. *A. W. & V. Owen, 39 Market Street. Tel.* (0745) 823083.

Colwyn Bay. *T. S. Ronald, Tackle Box 50–52 Sea View Road. Tel.* (0492) 31104. Tackle supply and repair; fresh lug, rag, frozen baits, maggots, flies; advice given on where to fish; WWA river licences sold; permits sold for rivers and lakes; fishing trips bookable; *Angling Times* weighing station.

Rhyl. *Esso Marina Sea Fishing Trips, Harbour End, Wellington Road. Tel.* (0745) 2547. Tackle supply, fresh black lug, fresh fish, frozen baits; worms and flies, advice on where to fish; fishing trips bookable on charter or for individuals aboard *Welsh Lady, Rosina, North Star* and *Wendy Sue*, all over 32 ft.

Arthur H. Fogarty, 29 Queen Street. Tel. (0745) 54765. Tackle supply and repair; fresh lug and rag, maggots, worms and flies; advice on where to fish; WWA river licences sold; permits sold for River Elwy.

Wm. Roberts, 131 High Street. Tel. (0745) 53031. Tackle supply and repair; fresh lug and rag (when available), maggots, worms, flies; advice on where to fish, WWA river licences sold; *Angling Times* weighing station.

Mrs. Campini, Blue Shark, Quay Street, West Parade. Tel. (0745) 50267. Tackle supply, advice on where to fish.

Boat hire, trips or charter

As an added measure of safety, Rhyl Local Authority has a boating inspector who, as a condition of the granting of boat licences, has the final say as to whether the port's angling fleet may sail or not in unfavourable weather. Colwyn Bay has the only boat hire arrangement operated by a Welsh angling club.

Rhyl. *John Povah, Marina Sea Fishing Trips, Wellington Road, Rhyl. Tel. Rhyl* (0745) 2547. *Welsh Lady III, Rosina, North Star* and *Wendy Sue* – all over 32 ft long. Available all year at Rhyl. Pick up opposite Dolphinarium top of Sydenham Avenue. 2½ – 10 hour trips and charter. Tackle hire. Bait supplied.

Mrs. Campini, Blue Shark, Quay Street, Rhyl. Tel. (0745) 50267. All year trips. Correspondence to: Mrs. Campini, 9 Ronalds Way, Rhyl.

Boat launching slipways

Abergele. Beach launching.

Colwyn Bay. 1. West of the Promenade; **2.** Opposite the Dingle, bottom of Eirias Park; **3.** Left of Victoria Pier. **1–3** are all council-owned and may be used free by the public.

Llanddulas. Beach launching.

Rhos-on-Sea. Local council slipway on the Cayley embankment. Free use to public. Craft up to 18 ft. No winch.

Rhyl. Permission needed to use: *Rhyl motor boat slipway*, Foryd Harbour (just upstream of Foryd road bridge); *Rhyl Yacht Club slipway*, Foryd Harbour (just downstream of Foryd road bridge).

Fishing advice

Colwyn Bay Victoria Angling Club, Hon. Sec., Mr. Trevor Davies, Bryn Avenue, Colwyn Bay. Tel. (0492) 56366. Visiting anglers allowed temporary membership of club, (small fee) with licensed clubhouse. Club boats (see boat hire). The club organises the Welsh Open Bass

continued on next page

Competition held in the Bay of Colwyn on 2 days, end of September and Welsh All-Comers Small Boat One Day Championships in July.
Rhyl Angling Association, Hon. Sec., Howell Jones, 51 Pendyffryn Road, Rhyl. Tel. (0745) 50342.

Useful telephone numbers
In emergency
Dial 999 and ask for Coastguard.

At other times
RNLI Inshore Rescue. Rhyl. *Tel.* 4040. **Coastguard. Rhyl.** *Tel.* 53284. (*Not constantly manned*). **Weather forecasts.** *Meteorological Office, RAF Station, Valley, Isle of Anglesey. Tel.* (0407) 2288. *Colwyn Bay Post Office. Tel.* 8091.

Puffin Island to Llandudno Pier

Small inshore dinghies along this coast enjoy fishing equal to that of the Tenby/Saundersfoot area, in South Wales, which it resembles greatly. Both are prime holiday areas. Each has a comparatively protected bay, offshore islands, reefs and shallow waters, the home of many tope and first rate bass. In both areas the shore angler finds good bait and gets a good share of the catch.

Penmon – I. **Black Point**; II. **Priory Beach.** Anglesey's extreme eastern mainland point, reached by a short private road (small charge) from Penmon Priory, faces Ynys Seiriol (Puffin Island) across a narrow sound. From Penmon Priory around to the lighthouse there is excellent bass – and flatfish – fishing from just below bottom tide to well up the flood. Spinning for bass, pollack and mackerel from the rocks nearest the lighthouse is possible at most states of the tide. Bottom fishing, from shelving rock into the narrow sound itself is full of snags; fish the shingly beach just inside the lighthouse point for bass after a blow, tope when it's calm. Despite the fee, it's a popular summer trip for fishermen and friends.

III. **Llangoed – Aberlleiniog Beach.** Full of bait – crab, rag and mussel – this easily reached sandy (in its top reaches) beach off B5109, near Penmon TV mast, is also rich in bass and fat flounders. Fish from just before low water with ledgered soft crab or a quarter of one of the beach's giant ragworm. Hand hold and strike quickly on slack line or a tightening tug. Small tope take too, but you'll lose them on your light bass trace.

IV. **Llanfairfechan and Penmaenmawr.** Directly across Menai Strait from Aberlleiniog (mark III) are Lafan Sands – 3 miles from shore to outermost edge. Don't try walking them even for the excellent bass fishing into the channels, but two anglers can follow the tide out and in, in a good powered inflatable or dinghy and expect to have good catches on the new flood. On foot, fish at Penmaenmawr or Llanfairfechan. The low water mark curves sharply in towards Llanfairfechan from Lafan Sands; the town's east end beach has deeper water, those extending a mile west are shallower and demand a bit of path walking. It may be for this reason that occasionally more bass can be caught in the shallower water over the sands.

V. **Conwy Morfa.** Extends west of Conwy from the river to the headland of Penmaen-bach, and is fronted by the municipal camping site and a golf course. Mussel beds near the river give way to sand, bounded by rocks under the headland. Lug is plentiful and plaice and flounders arrive through the rising tide followed by bass. Long-liners from the camp-site often take plaice by crossing the first low water channel to set up tackle on the outer mussel bed fringes.

VI. **Llandudno – Black Rocks.** A noted spot for shoaling bass, $\frac{3}{4}$-mile from West Shore car park at Llandudno. Spinning tobys, red gills and German sprats either side of the rock outcrop 2 hours before high water and the first $\frac{1}{2}$-hour of the ebb is as effective as conventional ledgering with locally-found crab or with ragworm. Lugworm is least effective. A busy estuary at all times, it fishes best on evening tides in mid-autumn when there is a bit of turbulence. The lesser, early spring flush of bigger inshore fish, experienced in SW Wales, doesn't materialise here till June, by which time summer holiday activity is well into its stride. Conwy Bay dabs are a local delicacy, its dogfish a plague. Experienced locals, chest-wadered, wade for an hour's fishing at low water marks bordering deep channels north of the Conwy river's low water mouth opposite Penmaen-bach Head. The next British record bass could come from this mark, as a noted locally-based fishing writer hoped, before he had to be accompanied back to shore by the local inshore lifeboat.

VII and VIII. **Llandudno, Great Orme Head, town Pier and jetty.** As at most holiday piers, Llandudno's private pier (charge) properly restricts the fisherman's choice of mark to the landing stage end (Great Orme side) 8 am – 10 p.m After tripper boats have finished for the day and the crowds have thinned out, the jetty nearby can be used. In summer hefty plaice, dabs and flounders are taken, with the occasional bass; in winter, codling and whiting on crisp full tide nights. There are conger for stronger tackle from the rockier marks on Great Orme, or wrasse and small pollack with float tackle. There is no great change in the fishing all the way round the bay to Little Orme Head.

Boat fishing

Sheltered, though fast, inshore waters of great variety and fishing potential can be fished at many points from a solid little 12–14 footer. But no angler will ignore the excellent fishing farther afield, which he can enjoy with several excellent Conwy- and Deganwy-based boats.

A. **Ynys Seiriol (Puffin Island).** The waters around Puffin Island draw boats from Menai Bridge and Conwy. S and SE of the island they find scarcely 15 feet of water which funnels through a deep rift between Perch Rock and Black Point, levelling out to a 50 feet deep shingly plateau which plunges abruptly on to sand off the island's north west point, under 90 feet of water. Three such distinct habitats so close together add variety to the fishing. In summer, bass and mackerel shoal around the island. Tope and ray police the shallow plateau waters while conger and cod, pollack and coalfish haunt the rough and the rocky depths. The tide rips through Black Point narrows at up to 5 knots; rarely on springs can one avoid a 3 knot tide. Perch Rock and the rocky reef extending from it to Puffin Island are places boats avoid, but a closely controlled powered drift close to them through the navigable channel, alternately spinning and jigging feathers or perks, will take bass and cod, pollack and coalfish, of excellent quantity and quality. Winter time strengthens the cod and whiting shoals.

B. **Lafan Sands.** See remarks above (item IV) and Menai Strait boat fishing section, page 24.

C. **Conwy Bay.** From the northern lip of the Conwy Estuary's low water mouth, almost opposite Penmaenmawr, northwards to the western tip of Great Orme Headland, the rough sandy bed is outcropped with rock and overlayed with commercial mussel beds. By the end of June this area begins to give its annual crop of big bass taken on ledgered soft crab at low water over the shallow banks and rocks from anchored dinghies. When soft crab is not available – from Black Rock or Menai Strait – anglers turn to red gills and conventional slow trolling along the shallows between the estuary's red and white fairway buoy and Gogarth's red and yellow outfall buoy. As the bass spill over the sands, making for the estuary, and the water deepens in the bay, it pays to try a gently lifting rod, baited with mussel or ragworm, or slowly trolling a white spoon, for plaice and flounders which inhabit the bay in good numbers. Codling, whiting and delicious Conwy dabs are winter's fare.

D. **Great Orme Headland.** The 8 fathoms tableland extends from the steep walls of the Orme for 3 miles north, before dipping sharply then gently shelving in the 12–15 fathoms of Liverpool Bay approaches. Most of the deep water fishing is carried on beyond the Constable Bank. Inside it, within the range of a strong 14-footer in settled good weather, there is excellent fishing for small tope, thornback rays, flatfish and dogfish, for it is almost uniformly sand with shingle patches. 1973 saw the British red gurnard record broken time and time again along this coast. Though seemingly all head, it's an excellent fish for the pan when skinned; half-sever the head and then draw the distinctly red skin off sharply towards the tail like a sock. Tides are strong around the headland on ebb and flood and it is normally given a wide berth, but under the headland light, in slacks or neaps, there is sufficient settled water for feathering and spinning for small pollack.

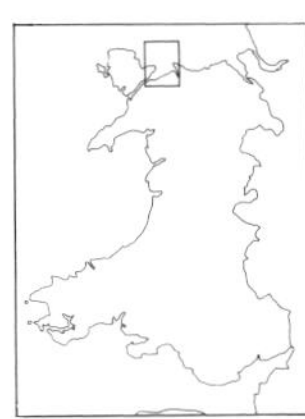

Menai Strait Several Order Area

Conwy Mussel Fishery Order Area
A bye-law prohibits the collection of mussels without permission within the area marked in mauve and also prohibits digging in any mussel bed in the Lancashire and Western Sea Fisheries Joint Committee area.

Bait supply

Digging is not permitted on Conwy Bay's mussel beds but this should prove no drawback as ample shop bait supplies, and picking and digging elsewhere, are available.

Crab. The shores from Beaumaris, east to Penmon have good soft and peeler crab on spring tides in summer. Aberlleiniog shore 1½ miles NE of Beaumaris, on Penmon side-road, is good (on right of stream in very low water weed). Some supplies (well picked) also at Black Rock towards Gogarth on Great Orme Head's west side.

Lug. Most mud/sand shores have pockets. Accessible, and easily dug individually, are good lug 100 yards due north of Conwy Morfa camping ground's slipway to beach. Llandudno's busy west shore has good supplies.

Rag. A little rag is found – though hard digging – at Aberlleiniog beach (1½ miles NE of Beaumaris) in individual blow holes near mussel beds both sides of beach stream. Hard digging at low water springs gives some near Llandudno Pier in rough ground and at very low springs near Black Rock on Llandudno's west shore. A heavy fine will be imposed for bait digging in the commercial mussel beds.

Shellfish and small fish, etc. Mussels abound throughout the area. (Commercial beds must be avoided). Shrimp and prawn can be netted almost everywhere.

Tackle shops

Conwy. *Cambrian Supplies, Castle Street. Tel.* (049263) 2275. Tackle supply, rag and preserved bait, flies, advice on where to fish.

continued on next page

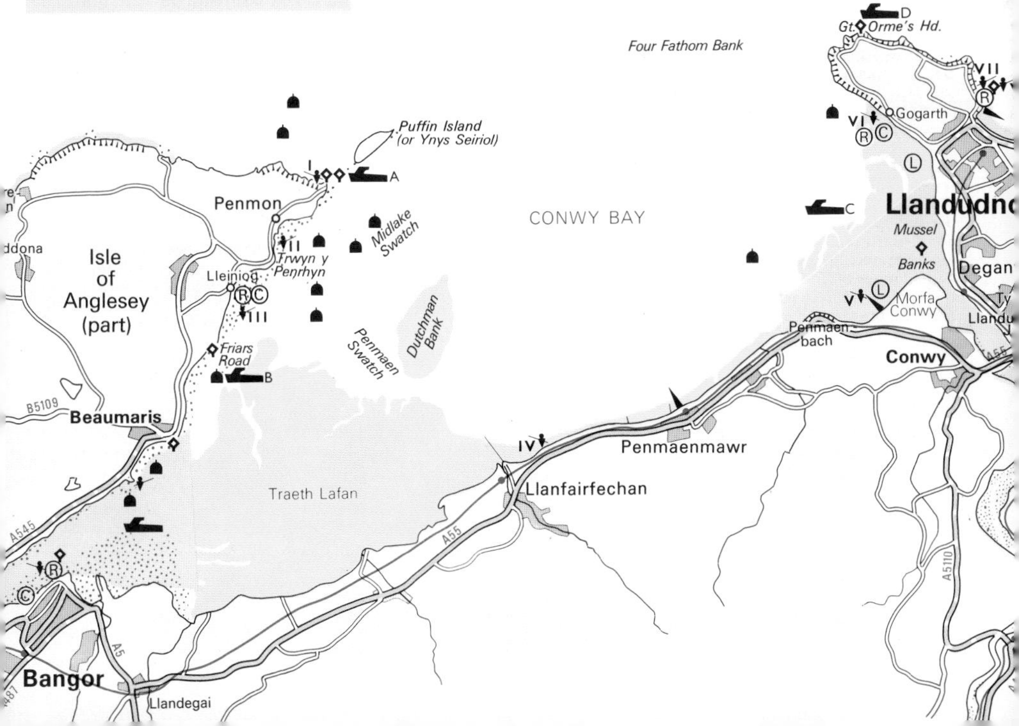

Conwy. *Conwy Angling Centre, 1 Rose Hill Street.* Tackle supply, sea bait, WWA river licences sold. *Angling Times* report station.

Deganwy. *H. L. Bayley Ltd, Ironmongers, 1 Victoria Buildings, Station Road. Tel. Deganwy* (0492) 83366. Tackle supply, preserved bait and advice on where to fish.

Llandudno. *Westmorlands, 19 Lloyd Street. Tel.* (0492) 77126. General fishing tackle supplies.; advice on where to fish.

Llandudno. *Mr. C. Bowen, Allsports & Hobbies, 18a Vaughan Street.*

Llandudno Junction. *North Wales Boat Shop and Anglers Corner, The Bridge Garage and Tackle Shop, Glan-Conwy Corner. Tel. Deganwy* (0492) 81073. Tackle supply, preserved bait, advice on where to fish. WWA river licences sold. *Angling Times* report station.

Penmaenmawr. *Mr. N. Evans, Sheffield House, Bangor Road.* Tackle supply, all sea baits, advice on where to fish.

Boat hire, trips or charter

Although Conwy's twin maritime interests of mussel-gathering and pleasure boat tripping for visitors cut down on the number of craft available for sea angling, there are still some experienced angling skippers for hire or charter at this picturesque little port. They know some excellent fishing grounds with shallow and deep water angling of real worth.

Conwy. *Castle Hotel. Tel.* 2235. Sea angling trips arranged locally for guests at the hotel, on request.

Conwy. *John C. Foulkes, Valley View, 62 Pengarth, Conwy. Tel.* (049263) 2880. *Michelle*, 40 ft, toilets, echo sounder. Daily summer and winter week-ends from Conwy jetty. Individual and charter day rates. No bait supplied. Tackle hire available.

Bryn Hughes, Hillview, Cadnant Park, Conwy. Tel. (049263) 2284/3795. **(a)** *Princess Christine*, 50 ft, toilets. Primarily pleasure cruises in summer from Conwy jetty. Charter by arrangement; **(b)** *Neptune*, 42 ft, toilets, echo sounder. April–October from Conwy Quay. Individual and charter day rates. Tackle hire.

Trevor Jones, 14 Penmaen Crescent, Conwy. Tel. 2499. *Emma B.J.* Daily from Conwy jetty. 12 persons. Tackle provided.

Starline Charter Fishing, B. H. Hughes, 12 Y Felin, Castle View, Conwy. Tel. Conwy 3795. *Conway Star* 32 ft, toilets, echo sounders, radar, ship/shore and ship/ship. Charter 5, 7 and 12 hours. Daily all year, from Conwy jetty.

Jack Williams, Dromod, 23 Cadnant Park, Conwy. Tel. (049263) 2216. *Topaz*, 31 ft, toilets, echo sounder, VHF. Daily April to November. Day trips and charter. Tackle hire.

Further information on Conwy boat and fishing services can be obtained from: *Conwy Riverboat and Musselmen Association, c/o Mr. J. C. Foulkes, 62 Pengarth, Conwy.* Tel. (049263) 2880.

Deganwy. *Meurig G. Davies, Pen-y-Berllan, Pentywyn Road, Deganwy. Tel.* (0492) 81983. *Lady Gwen*, 33 ft, Decca Navigator, graph sounder, liferafts, VHF ship to shore radio, toilet, tea supplied. Deganwy summer, Menai Bridge winter. Large heated wheel-house. Bait and fishing tackle for sale and hire. Daily sailings, individuals and parties catered for throughout the year.

Boat launching slipways

Conwy. Fishermen are advised to contact the Harbourmaster. Harbour Office, located on Town Quay. Tel. (049263) 3761, extension 51. Open every day except Monday and Friday.

Conwy Beacons Beach. Vessels to 30 ft long, from half-tide to high water.

Llandudno. **(a)** Llandudno lifeboat slipway; **(b)** Llandudno Sailing Club slipway. Free use of both for craft to 22 ft long. No winch – bollard only.

Llanfairfechan. Slipway to sands, for yacht club members.

Penmaenmawr. One 16 ft wide slipway opposite Yacht Club for club members and residents. Use free of charge.

Fishing advice

Royal Artillery Angling Section, Hon. Sec., Mr. Dave Bowen, Allsports, 18a Vaughan Street, Llandudno. Tel. (0492) 75978.

Useful telephone numbers

In emergency
Dial 999 and ask for Coastguard.

At other times
RNLI lifeboats. *Beaumaris. Tel.* (024883) 589. *Llandudno, Tel.* (0492) 75777. *Conwy (Inshore rescue) Tel. Deganwy* (0492) 83571.
Coastguard. *Llandudno. Tel.* (0492) 76214.
Weather forecasts. *Meteorological Office, RAF Station, Valley, Isle of Anglesey. Tel.* (0407) 2288.

Menai Strait

12 miles of pulsating water, ripping along at up to 5 knots in a channel barely ½ mile wide; it's tough fishing but has a reputation for being amongst the best in Britain. Tope in the western narrows, bass in the eastern funnel; both fish swim the treacherous Swellies of the middle Strait with conger, cod and pollack for company. May to November is the best general period with the autumn the best for bass. The last hour of the ebb and the first two of the flood – day or night – are the easiest to fish but not necessarily most productive. Menai Bridge, Beaumaris and Bangor suffer from summer boat activity, but not unduly.

Shore fishing marks

I. **Belan Point.** 1½ miles walk by dune path and soft sand from the end of Dinas Dinlle 'promenade'. Fish between low and high water marks to escape the wrath of Glynllifon Estate. Sand bottom with 5 knot tides at springs, 2½ knots at neaps. For one hour each side of low water, lighter leads can be used but crabs come out to play. Tope on fish baits, with bass, prime flounder and dabs, and dogfish, on lug, crab and rag. The best time is 2 hours after high tide down the ebb.

II. **Abermenai Point.** 2½ miles exhausting walk on soft sand from Forestry Commission car park at Newborough Warren. Sand with 5 knot tides (springs), 2½ knots (neaps). Good bass beach on crab, especially at low tide from the mussel bed on to the sand tail pointing up Menai Strait. Tope fishing excellent with frozen fish baits – particularly herring – or fresh mackerel. Prime flounders, dabs and whiting on lug. Bass spinning at low slack.

III. **Traeth Melynog.** 2 miles walk over dunes and hard lug-filled sand from Newborough village. Sand bottom. Fish the 8 feet deep gulleys on flooding tide with rag or crab. Beware the encircling water.

IV. **Caernarfon shore (between Ysgubor Isaf and Tŷ Calch (White House)).** By car from Caernarfon through Llanfaglan (swing bridge from castle not available). Sand and mud, rimmed with weed and stones. Shallow gullies fished on the making tide for bass with crab – plenty available in the weed in season. Tope in quantity come inshore to what is one of Menai Strait's best marks for this fish. Fast tides, so do not strand yourself on sandbanks. Nearby Foryd mud creek offers flounders and mullet as well as bass.

continued on next page

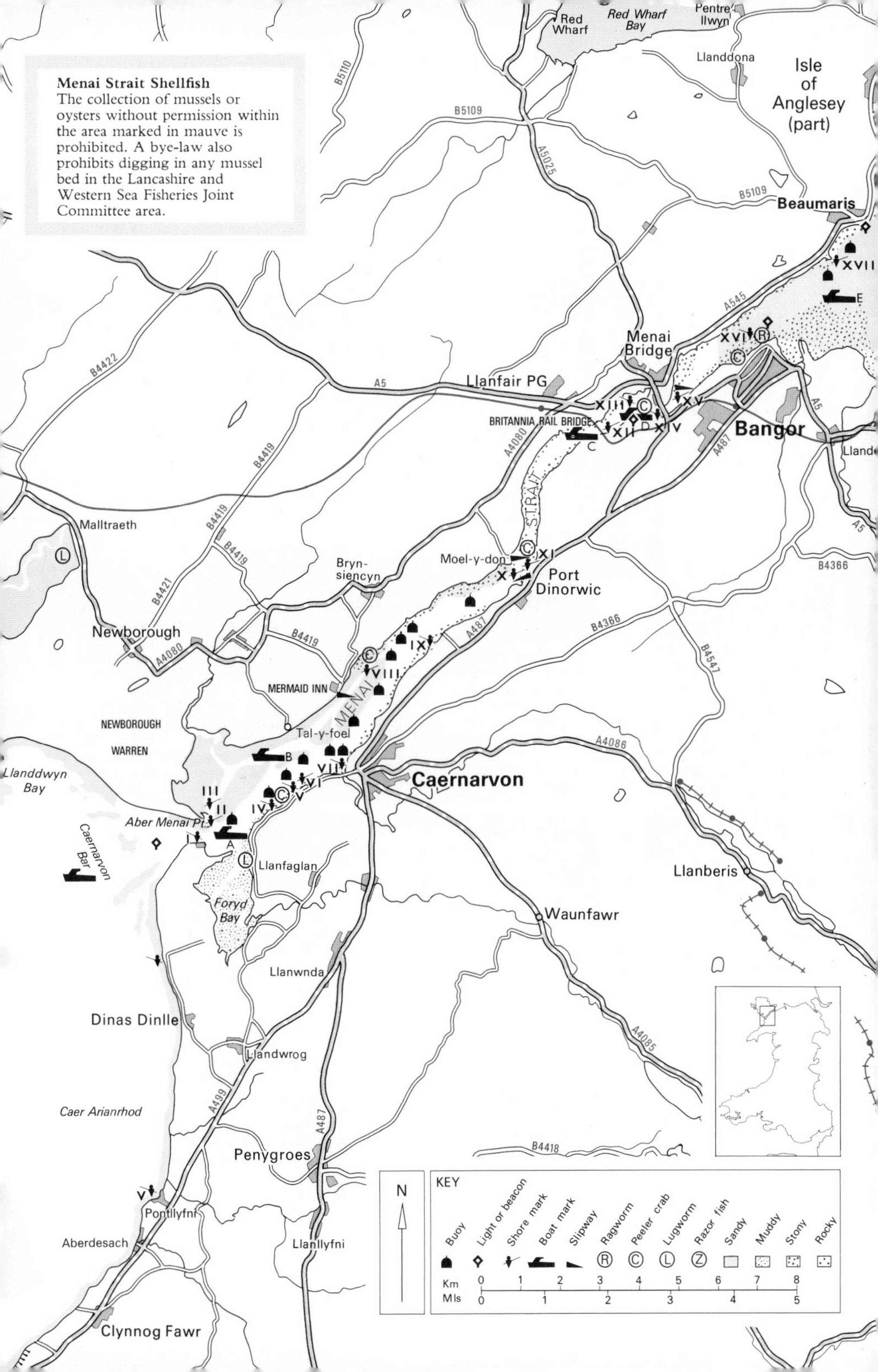
Menai Strait Shellfish
The collection of mussels or oysters without permission within the area marked in mauve is prohibited. A bye-law also prohibits digging in any mussel bed in the Lancashire and Western Sea Fisheries Joint Committee area.
Red Wharf
Red Wharf Bay
Pentre Llwyn
Llanddona
Isle of Anglesey (part)
Beaumaris
Menai Bridge
Llanfair PG
BRITANNIA RAIL BRIDGE
Bangor
STRAIT
MENAI
Malltraeth
Moel-y-don
Port Dinorwic
Bryn-siencyn
Newborough
MERMAID INN
NEWBOROUGH WARREN
Tal-y-foel
Llanddwyn Bay
Caernarvon
Aber Menai Pt.
Caernarvon Bar
Llanfaglan
Foryd Bay
Llanberis
Waunfawr
Llanwnda
Dinas Dinlle
Llandwrog
Caer Arianrhod
Penygroes
Pontllyfni
Aberdesach
Llanllyfni
Clynnog Fawr
Llande
B5110
B5109
A5025
B4422
A5
A545
A4080
B4419
B4421
A487
B4366
B4547
A4086
A4085
A499
B4418
KEY
N
Buoy
Light or beacon
Shore mark
Boat mark
Slipway
Ragworm
Peeler crab
Lugworm
Razor fish
Sandy
Muddy
Stony
Rocky
Km 0 1 2 3 4 5 6 7 8
Mls 0 1 2 3 4 5

V. **Caernarfon shore (golf course).** As mark IV. Between Ysgubor Isaf and the golf course are two buoys. Just right of the inner (black) buoy are 2 fathoms-plus of water giving good tope conditions. Some good winter codling and whiting fishing along this shore on lug baits.

VI. **Caernarfon shore (swimming pool).** As mark IV.

VII. **Caernarfon Quay Wall (Old Battery to Eagle Tower).** Mud at River Seiont mouth gives way to sand/stone mixture further out and towards Old Battery. Odd bass, flatfish – mainly flounders – and small eels. Mullet prolific. Some good prawns with a drop net. Tides 2 to 4 knots.

VIII. **Mermaid Inn, Brynsiencyn.** Limited parking on waterside road. Turn south off A4080, 3¾ miles west of Llanfair PG. Sand bars to SW of Inn, sand patches with stone and weed to NW. Casting and fishing hampered by old wooden piles and inshore buoys of water ski club. Good bass occasionally taken in low tide channels before tide spills over. Crab and rag best baits.

IX. **Caernarfon (Ferodo Works).** 1½ miles NE of the town turn towards Strait in Parciau. As mark VII but shoal bass will repay spinning with white electric-rubber eel or small red gill worked 2 ft behind a 2 in piece of candle used as a weight.

X. **Moel-y-don Old Ferry crossing.** 1 mile left off A4080, 2 miles SW of Llanfair PG junction with A5. Like Pwll Fannogl, 2 miles east along the Strait (car park), Moel-y-don has 20 feet of water in main channel reached from slipway. Crab on the bottom or floated gives good bass. Winter codling can be quite good with lug or crab baits.

XI. **Port Dinorwic.** (Car park near Marina). The Old Quay wall is flanked by rocky weed-covered banks rich in peeler crab. Small conger, plaice and abundant mullet. Some crafty big bass come close in on the high tide. The weedy rocks east towards Vaynol Estate are better than the wall but are snaggy in patches and difficult to reach.

XII. **Llanfair PG – Britannia Rail Bridge** (north side). 1 mile walk from Coed Cyrnol car park, Menai Bridge, or from Llanfair PG (leave A5 pull-in ¼ mile from Menai Bridge free for sightseers!). 2–5 knot maelstrom of snaggy mud and weed called The Swellies extend from the railway bridge to Telford's 100 ft above HW suspension road bridge. Mullet are big but difficult. Bass, the better one's 6–8 lbs, with floated crab or on the bottom. Smallish conger and odd pollack form the summer catch. Winter brings cod to 13 lbs and whiting which take lug and crab.

XIII. **Menai Bridge (Ynys Llandysilio).** A short downhill walk from Coed Cyrnol car park behind Anglesey Tourist Information Centre, Menai Bridge. The island accommodates a church and is linked by causeway to the mainland. Right and left of the causeway is thick mud with small impossible-to-dig lug. Weed-covered rock outcrops, sheltering a few peeler crab, almost surround the island itself. Fish the muddy patches between these rocks for bass as the tide floods in. At high tide, over the bigger mud patches, use a slowly moving trace baited with rag for flounders. These quiet lagoons are rewarding to the mullet enthusiast using ultra-light tackle and unconventional baits.

XIV. **Menai Bridge (at water level).** Approach as mark XIII but turn left for short way at start of island causeway. Fish near a little seated enclosure near a house but away from poles in the water. A roughish bottom and the full run of the narrowing Strait gives deeper water. Spinning and float fishing for bass is difficult to control except at slack water but can be productive. A solid, weighty, short-traced single hook ledger with a 3 ft long 'rotten bottom' is best for bass and for odd cod who choose to stay on from the good winter influx. Weed on the line is a real burden.

XV. **Menai Bridge.** St. George's Pier and the slipway (near Pochin's Yard (down Water Street), are two points used by the fisherman on a shore notoriously difficult to approach. Summer boat activity does not rule out a share of occasional bass. It's quieter and better for the cod in winter. Conger, dogfish and whiting take bait intended for better fry. Small pollack and wrasse make the same mistake with float-fished rag intended for big mullet. 3–5 knot tides are not uncommon, sweeping weights into frequent snags.

XVI. **Bangor.** The foreshore has to be fished now Bangor Pier is closed, probably for some time. Rag, from low springs stony ground, and crab, are the baits. Autumn whiting, winter cod and late summer bass form the mainstay of catches, though plaice wander towards the shore from the deep gulley opposite the old Bangor Baths. Make your way as far as possible towards the Menai Bridge for better marks into deeper water.

XVII. **Beaumaris.** Gallows Point yacht yard has parking nearby. At low water and for two hours afterwards, fish the main channel here onto sand. Otherwise the main beach is stony and fish are difficult to locate. The town's pier and sea wall are popular spots, but what you gain in convenience you lose in quality and quantity of fish.

Boat fishing

Caernarfon and Menai Bridge offer boat fishing trips and charter under experienced boatmen. Small boat owners would be well advised to take the hint and leave their own craft on land. If you venture into the Strait yourself, choose a calm day with a neap tide flooding; engine failure on an ebbing spring tide on a choppy day spells disaster. Use a dispensable anchor, or killick, for snagging is frequent in the middle Strait.

A. **Belan Narrows.** A trolled red gill is the classic bass technique in these conditions. For tope, anchor on the edge of the outgoing or incoming flood, just inside or outside Abermenai Point (as the case may be) is quiet enough in normal weather. Stream away a good half mackerel on a 5/0 to 8/0 hook ledgered on a wire trace and at least 300 yards of 20 lbs or more main line. A bottom hugging Capta lead weight on a Clements boom, stopped by matchstick a few yards up the main line, helps the deception. Lesser spotted dogfish can be a plague at times. Bull huss and thornback ray are less frequent additions to the catch. Prime flounders and dabs soon fill the pan.

B. **Traeth Melynog and Traeth Gwyllt (Aber Menai Point to the Mermaid Inn).** A boat is used for quick access and safety as beachcasting or bank spinning is impossible in the channelled outer fringes of Traeth Melynog sandbanks. Be quiet, and stream out soft crab on fine tackle. The catch of bass should be worth the effort if the netting boat from Belan Dock has not been there first. Row – not motor – eastwards just faster than the making tide, trolling a white spoon baited with rag, for specimen-sized flounders that shoal along on the advancing flood. Keep well outside the Mermaid's snare-ridden waters.

C. **Llanfair PG – Pwll Fannogl Deeps.** In the middle, opposite Pwll Fannogl car park and slipway, with the conspicuous mausoleum in Vaynol Park in line on the opposite bank, are 12 fathoms of water over a rocky bottom. Tide speeds at neaps of 3½ knots are bad enough but at springs they rise to over 5 knots. But it pays to persevere, for some good winter bags of cod have come out of this hole, and in the shute that rises from it to within 400 ft of the centre of the rail bridge. Summer tope and conger, and the species they prey on, can all be taken. For cod vary your methods: a bright metal lure of the Immelblinker or pirk types, large white feathers or Norwegian-type fish fags are not too expensive. Good quality black bream – fond of lugworm – are also taken, up to 3½ lbs. With a ledgered weight for conventional bottom feeders use a rotten bottom, for you will need to break out of it frequently. The *Endeavour* trace – stiff wire direct to the hook tied on to the main line swivel with heavy monofilament – prevents doggies and small conger knotting things up.

D. **Menai Bridge – The Swellies.** Shoals, fast currents and a merciless retribution for the careless and inexperienced – that's the Swellies. A sound boat and experienced waterman will find cod and conger, bass and pollack (summer). A trolled red rubber eel or large red gill is the favourite Swellies bass method. As in most boat fishing at anchor, you may have to move your mark three or four times in the brief slack water period to find fish. Start in the smoother 40 ft deeps, just east of Swelly Rock and 100 yards from the south bank, dropping back from time-to-time towards and beyond the centre of the road bridge – always under power – until an improvised anchor bites. Going in the opposite direction from Swelly Rock – towards the rail bridge – gives much shallower water. The deep gully opposite Bangor's old swimming baths gives large catches of plaice on cockle bait.

E. **Bangor – Traeth Lafan.** The extensive drying sands of Traeth Lafan are fringed with lagoons and channels which bass invade on the flooding tide. Too dangerous to fish on foot, a powered dinghy can explore them in comparative safety. Particularly prolific is the mouth of the Ogwen river when the tide begins to make. Spinning has given large catches of school bass. See remarks under mark B (Traeth Melynog and Traeth Gwyllt) on how to fish the bottom.

Bait supply

Crab, prawns and ragworm, with occasional lug patches form the backbone of the Strait's bait supply. It can be supplemented with local fresh-caught mackerel and herring in season.

Crab. In the weedy gullies between the Foryd and Seiont river at Caernarfon. Along the weedy rocks east of The Mermaid and around the dock of Port Dinorwic on each side of the Strait. Sparsely, underneath large stones on the rocky fringes south and west of the church on Ynys Llandysilio at Menai Bridge, and west of Bangor Pier. Extensively, amongst the weedy stones east of Beaumaris, particularly at Aberlleiniog.

Lug. Localised in The Foryd near Caernarfon and in great expanses opposite on Traeth Melynog reached from Newborough. Lug a bit high is more likely to catch bass than fresh lug.

Rag. Low springs at Beaumaris reveal stony areas with good rag, but hard digging. The area east of Beaumaris – especially. Aberlleiniog – has some rag but it is pretty well dug out. Look for individual blow holes amongst the mussel patches east of the stream or dig around the base of very large boulders on the beach.

Prawn and shrimp. Drop net from any convenient quay, pier or slipway. Caernarfon oil jetty has ample supplies.

Tackle shops

Bangor. *Ron Edwards, 6 Dean Street. Tel.* (0248) 2811. Tackle supply; preserved baits and flies; advice on where to fish; boat parties 8–10 persons arranged with J. Reegan; *Angling Times* report station.

Beaumaris. *Anglesey Boat Co., Gallows Point. Tel.* (0248) 810359 or 810652. Fishing trips by arrangement. Fishing tackle for sale.

Caernarfon. *Howard's Fishing Tackle, 72 Pool Street. Tel.* (0286) 2671. *Angling Times* report station.

Caernarfon. *D. Huxley-Jones, South Penrallt. Tel.* 23186. Tackle supply; frozen baits, maggots and flies; advice on where to fish. WWA river licences and permits for Seiont, Gwyrfai, Llyfni and lakes.

Menai Bridge. *Ken Johnson, Devon House, Water Street. Tel.* (0248) 714508. Tackle supply and flies; advice on where to fish; WWA river licences; *Angling Times* report station.

Boat hire, trips or charter

Beaumaris. *Plas Bodfa Hotel, Llangoed, near Beaumaris. Tel.* (024878) 249. Sea angling trips arranged locally.

Caernarfon. *Kusaka Sea Angling, Williams, Bryngwyn, Bontnewydd, Caernarfon. Tel. Caernarfon* 2666. 32 ft cruiser. Day or charter rates. 10 persons.

Caernarfon. *Harry Williams, Tre'r Gof, 22 Chapel Street, Caernarfon. Tel.* (0286) 4954. Two boats *Snowdon Queen* and *Seiont Queen*, 30 ft and 32 ft respectively. Toilets, radio, for hire or charter, for fishing or sightseeing. Day or charter rates.

Caernarfon. *John R. Jones, Pilot, 7 North Penrallt. Tel.* (0286) 2902. 3 charter boats for angling or pleasure trips. Also deep water moorings available.

Caernarfon. *Bryn Jones, Porth Lleidiog, Aber Foreshore.* Concrete slipway, boat park and moorings.

Menai Bridge. *Emlyn Oliver, Menai Ville Terrace. Tel.* (0248) 712456.

Menai Bridge. *J. Reegan,* 106 *Orme Road. Tel. Bangor* 4590. *Scotch Lass,* (A72) 40 ft, toilets, echo sounder. Daily summer and winter from Menai Bridge Pier. Tackle hire.

continued on next page

Gallows Point, Beaumaris

Increasingly, angling boats from other North Wales ports over-winter by fishing within the shelter of Menai Strait and Puffin Island from Menai Bridge Pier.

Boat launching slipways

Brynsiencyn. For light craft, near former Mermaid Inn. Turn off A4080 towards the Strait 3¾ miles west of Llanfair PG junction with A5.

Moel-y-Don. Turn towards Strait, off A4080 2 miles south west of Llanfair PG and continue for 1 mile. Apply to Plas Coch Caravan Park, Llanfairpwll.

Port Dinorwic, Turn towards Strait 50 yards from zebra crossing in the main street and follow road to boat sheds. Vessels up to 30 ft. Free use. No winch.

Menai Bridge. Concrete slipway at Porth Wrach, Water Street. Vessels up to 25 ft. Free use.

Beaumaris: Gallows Point. Private slipway. *Apply to D. Livingston. Anglesey Boat Co. Ltd. Gallows Point: Tel.* (0248) 810359. **Town.** Slipway used by Royal Anglesey Yacht Club (Tel. 810295) near inshore lifeboat station. Suitable for light craft.

Bangor. Private slipway and launching facilities. *Apply to Messrs. A. M. Dickie & Son, Garth Road, Bangor. Tel.* (0248) 51784.

Fishing advice

Ferodo (Caernarvon) Fishing Club, Sec., Mr. G. T. Jones, Ty-Gwyn, Saron, Bethel, Gwynedd.

Llanfairpwll and District Sea Angling Club, Mr. Steven Walburn, 97 *Tan y Bryn Road, Rhos on Sea, Colwyn Bay. Tel. Colwyn Bay* 46805.

Port Dinorwic Sea Angling Club, Sec., Mr. R. Rosser, 27 *Rhiwen, Rhiwlas, Bangor, Gwynedd. Tel.* 51963.

Useful telephone numbers

In emergency
Dial 999 *and ask for Coastguard.*

At other times
Lifeboat. *RNLI inshore rescue, Beaumaris. Tel.* (024883) 260. **Coastguard** *Holyhead Tel.* (0407) 2051.

Weather forecasts. *Meteorological Office, RAF Station, Valley, Isle of Anglesey. Tel. Holyhead* (0407) 2288.

Isle of Anglesey – Red Wharf Bay to Cemaes Bay

Telford's handsome suspension bridge links mainland Wales with the Isle of Anglesey, providing a way for the A5 road London to Holyhead. Menai Strait here is fast and vicious but makes up for it with good catches of big bass, winter cod and whiting.

Bass can be caught on this coast, but only when circumstances are just right – after a north-west blow at Red Wharf Bay, at Traeth Lligwy and at Dulas Bay, for example. The boat fisherman is rewarded most. Shallow gulleys of sand and shingle in 20 fathoms of water is the usual seabed pattern but depths reach 36 fathoms in isolated places. From points north of Wylfa Head and Cemlyn Bay lie the lucrative Archdeacon Reef, Coal Rock Reef, Ethel Rock Reef, whilst in a westerly direction lies the Victoria Bank. A new buoy recently laid warns of the Harry Furlough Reef – positioned approximately 300 yards NNE of the reef. However, the reef still remains very hazardous. Specimens caught include pollack, coalfish varying up to 10 lb and over. Alongside the reefs, and local fishing spots, spurdog, tope, bull huss, conger and skate lie in abundance. Further inshore, dabs, whiting, dogfish, etc., make good fishing.

I. **Cemaes Bay – National Trust headlands at Cemaes Bay and Llanbadrig.** Both headlands are accessible in a ½ mile walk from Cemaes Bay and Llanbadrig church respectively and are pretty well clear of most of the summer boating activity. Small conger, dabs and flounders, lesser spotted dogfish and pout whiting make up the bulk of the bottom fishing. Float fished rag or small slivers of mackerel bring moderately good wrasse on the feed, but light tackle is essential for sport. Whiting really come on in late October and continue throughout the early winter followed closely by cod. A night tide and big lug dug at Rhosneigr or Holy Island, on 4/0 – but sharp – hooks, is the best bait for them, for some run to a fair size for shore-caught fish.

II. **Amlwch Harbour and rocks.** The old harbour walls fill a cleft in the rocks. It is favoured by small boats including commercial and sporting fishing craft but although tidal, (improved with recent major dredging) 7–9 fathoms can be found on the rock marks about it. Small conger come close in near the harbour and to the rock marks. Remarks under mark I above apply.

III. **Point Lynas.** Anglesey's north-eastern tip is marked by a ½ mile lighthouse-tipped promontory, reached through the village of Llaneilian, 2½ miles east of Amlwch. Rock bound and rugged, Point Lynas offers ledge and rock fishing on its eastern face near the lighthouse into 40 ft and more of water on to a sand bottom between rocky patches. Though cod and whiting are its late autumn, winter and occasional spring residents, conger, ray, dogfish and pout offer summer interest to holidaying fishermen. The paternoster is efficient in these circumstances, especially as casting over 50 yards is not necessary and fish baits can be used.

IV. **Moelfre – Y Swnt (The Sound).** Ynys Moelfre, 250 yards offshore, creates a sound 40 ft deep which is the starting point of your casting; elsewhere intense water-sport activity will curb your own sport. There is scarcely an y soft crab in the weed-covered rocks along this part of the coast but this does not prevent a crab from being the best bait for these narrow-channel bass. Ledger a whole peeled crab on the making tide or float fish it on a big treble hook close in near the rocks at full tide. If you're in an experimental mood when the mackerel are around, catch one and ledger it alive for big bass on two very large trebles linked to each other by 9 in of monofilament. Tope range closely inshore for the dabs found in immense shallows of Red Wharf Bay, south, and Dulas Bay, north of the Island, and for the glut of mackerel which arrive in mid-July. Ledger a substantial belly slice of mackerel or a solid back half threaded on to a 6/0 hook attached to a 3 ft long light wire trace linked to 15–18 lbs line, but plenty of it. Cod and whiting are standard winter fare.

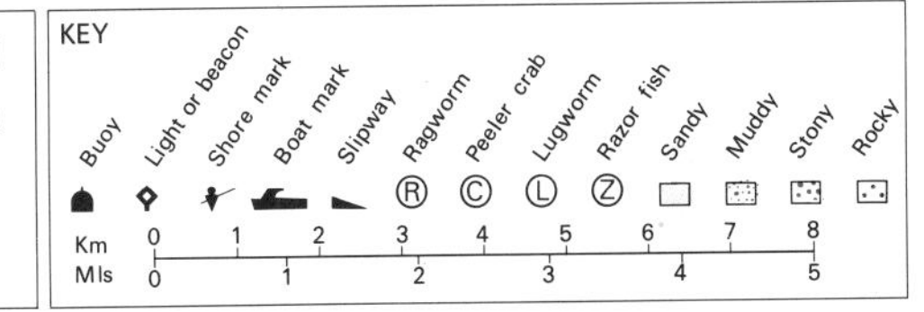

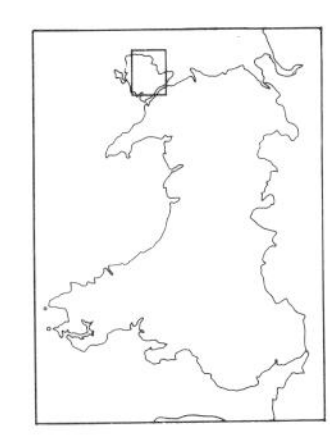

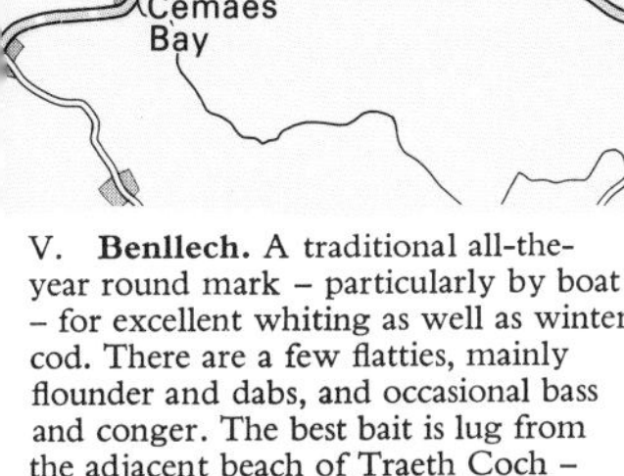

V. **Benllech.** A traditional all-the-year round mark – particularly by boat – for excellent whiting as well as winter cod. There are a few flatties, mainly flounder and dabs, and occasional bass and conger. The best bait is lug from the adjacent beach of Traeth Coch – Red Wharf Bay – the best time is a rising tide in the late evening, preferably in darkness. Mackerel are plentiful in summer.

Boat fishing

Moelfre's famous lifeboatmen have piled up a mint of medals for their bravery. It's a fact which holidaying fishermen would do well not to ignore, for though quiet and peaceful on a calm summer's day, the rocky, reef-ridden coast quickly becomes a graveyard for small craft when the wind veers around to the north and east. They are still picking up the bits from the *Royal Charter* which went aground there in 1859 with the loss of 459 lives. If you're well equipped, experienced and well advised by local experts, Cemaes Bay, Amlwch and Moelfre have both facilities and opportunities for good fishing. But watch the ebb tide. The skipper of the *Wygyr*, a regular sea angling boat based at Cemaes Bay on this coast writes: 'A powerful engine is very important, with plenty of fuel in reserve. Last season the *Wygyr* towed in no less than five boats, with occupants who had sailed out on the ebb tide, bombed along with the ebb, fished, and ran out of fuel on their return; no oars, no flares, no anchor or rope whatsoever!'

A. **Cemaes Bay – Ynys Badrig (Middle Mouse Island).** Just over 1 mile north east of Cemaes Bay lies minute Middle Mouse Island in 17 fathoms. For 1 mile due west of it there runs a 23 fathoms trench, with similar trenches north east and north west of the island by ½ mile. The bottom is sand and gravel with occasional rocky outcrops. But it is deep enough and clean enough for fishing the bottom on the drift. Cod and coalfish, ling and whiting will all take lasts of mackerel. Anchor up for rays and tope. You will find pollack nearer the rocks; sink and draw big red gills on a very long flowing trace with at least two intermediate swivels in it, attached to the main line by a French boom. A quick-release link at the bottom of your main line will enable you rapidly to change bottom tackle but use the same rod.

B. **Bull Bay – Ynys Amlwch (East Mouse Island).** East Mouse lies ¼ mile off the headland at Amlwch. Bull Bay curves away west and is intensely used by holidaymakers, but fishing outside is hindered only by the occasional high-speed water-skier. The bottom shelves abruptly from 5 to 12 fathoms and is then uneven for 1 mile or more, with odd pits of 27 fathoms. One such is one mile north west of East Mouse; Nebo wireless masts would then be directly behind Llam Carw headland just east of Amlwch. The tide race is fearsome on springs. Having regard to these hazards, fish it as mark A.

C. **Amlwch – Porth-yr-Ysgaw Bay and Point Lynas.** The sand and shingle 17 fathoms deep bottom off Point Lynas lighthouse is ridged by two 10 fathom high sandbanks running away from the point parallel with the mainland configuration. The banks start ½ mile out opposite recently dredged Amlwch harbour entrance and extends past Point Lynas to Trwyn Du Point. Watch for overfalls forming off the point in the full 3½ knots force of a spring tide. This area holds a variety of fish that will respond to all the conventional deep water mark tactics. Trot down and over the lip of the banks on the slower tides; anchor in the lee of the head in Porth-yr-Ysgaw Bay and fish the bottom or sink and draw. Skate, rays, conger, gurnard and dabs will take the ledgered mackerel strip, with pouting, whiting and cod replacing them in winter. Coalfish and pollack are not all that large but are locally abundant near rocky outcrops.

D. **Moelfre – Ynys Moelfre.** Moelfre Island rises from 4 fathoms, 250 yards off Moelfre Point. In some respects the dinghy-equipped fisherman will be much better placed than the shore-bound caster to exploit the sound between mainland and island. Beyond the Island the floor dips abruptly to 13 fathoms in little more than 300 yards and conventional bottom fishing methods can be used. But as we are here working the shallows round the island and treating the dinghy as a mobile piece of the shore, the remarks under mark IV above should suffice, if adapted to the new conditions. Trolling a red gill for bass will be the additional technique to use – but keep out of casting distance of the mainland or you will spoil the fishing of others.

E. *See remarks on previous page under item V.*

Bait supply

Menai Strait and Holyhead must remain the backbone of the Isle of Anglesey's bait supply. There is little between Red Wharf Bay and Cemaes Bay except:

Lug. Red Wharf Bay, the lower the tide the better, at Traeth Bychan and at Dulas Bay and Cemaes Bay.

Crab. Benllech has little crab – very little – in the weedy rocks that extend north of the pipe structure that crosses the sands. Amlwch offers the odd crab and rag worm at very low springs. (Climb down to a handkerchief-sized shore on the seaward side of the quay).

Tackle shops

Amlwch. *V. & M. Houghton, Fishing Tackle, 1–3 Mona Street, Amlwch Square. Tel.* (0407) 830267. Tackle supply, trout and advice on where to fish.

Cemaes Bay. *F. J. Hampson, Mona Stores, High Street.*

Cemaes Bay. *Anglesey Boat Centre, Beach Road, Cemaes Bay. Tel. Cemaes Bay* (040789) 510. 24-hour Ansafone service. Tackle supply and fresh lug-worm bait. Arrangements made for hourly, ½-day, day, weekend and charter angling trips. Advice on where to fish and chart of best fishing spots displayed.

Moelfre. *The Ship's Bell, Tel. Moelfre* (024888) 651. Sea fishing tackle and bait. Buoyancy aids and protective clothing.

Boat hire, trips or charter

Cemaes Bay. *Anglesey Boat Centre, Mr. David Wynne Williams, Beach Road, Cemaes Bay. Tel. Cemaes Bay* (040789) 510. 24-hour Ansafone service. mv *Wygyr*, 32 ft with toilets, echo sounder, radio. Available on day charter throughout the year. Arrangements can be made for angling weekends in conjunction with Harbour Hotel, Cemaes Bay (details on request).

Boat launching slipways

Amlwch Port. Suitable for craft up to about 36 ft. Unrestricted use, no charge.

Benllech. Slipway for light craft can be used.

Bull Bay. Slipway available, suitable for craft to about 36 ft. Unrestricted use, no charge.

Cemaes Bay. Harbour slipway for light craft controlled by harbour committee of local council. Apply to Secretary of Harbour Committee, Mr. D. W. Williams, (of Anglesey Boat Centre) 'Morglawdd', Cemaes Bay, for use and for moorings.

Moelfre. Slipway to beach for small craft. Unrestricted use, no charge.

Traeth Bychan. Slipway to beach for small craft. Unrestricted use, no charge.

Fishing advice

Amlwch Port Boat Club, Hon. Sec., Mr. Peter Williams, 11 Craig y Don, Amlwch Port.

Fishing trips and charter can be arranged at the Club House situated at Amlwch Harbour where visiting fishermen are welcomed on payment of a nominal admission fee.

Tackle supply and further advice on fishing, slipways and moorings, etc. are also available at the Club House.

Useful telephone numbers

In emergency

Dial 999 and ask for Coastguard.

At other times

Coastguard. *Holyhead. Tel.* (0407) 2051.

RAF Rescue Helicopter. *Valley near Holyhead. Tel.* (040784) 999.

Trinity House. *Point Lynas Lighthouse. Tel. Amlwch* (0407) 333.

Weather forecasts. *Meteorological Office, RAF Station, Valley, Isle of Anglesey. Tel.* (0407) 2288. Information on weather and tidal conditions also available from Anglesey Boat Centre, Beach Road, Cemaes Bay. Tel. Cemaes Bay 510.

Isle of Anglesey – Wylfa Head to Porth Trecastell and Holy Island

Sheltered Holyhead Harbour and its more turbulent approaches on the north west coast of Anglesey have excellent potential, so far only partially exploited by anglers. Holy Island forms muddy-sand lug banks where bass and mullet shoal. Outside the harbour – itself an excellent winter cod and bad weather summer fishing venue for conger and tope – assemble the whole army of summer visitors and predators, including blue shark, porbeagle and tope. Northwards, the reef and overfall-ridden channel around the Skerries fulfils the promise of good pollack and coalfish; southwards the bass lands extend in increasing value towards the Menai Strait. For variety there's excellent rock fishing around North Stack and South Stack lighthouse, including sizeable wrasse. You need never go short of bait – fine lug and moderately good rag is there pretty well for the digging.

I. **Cemlyn Bay.** Reached from a side road branching off Anglesey's A5025 ring road, 2 miles south west of Cemaes Bay. The strand, anchored on its eastern side, almost closes the sea from an extensive lagoon, now a nature reserve. Like all Isle of Anglesey beaches, it is best fished for bass in autumn and, facing north west, shares in the liking for a good blow from that quarter. Over the headland, Harry Furlough's Rocks extend ½ mile out to sea at low water. One can spin them for pollack of good size and coalfish, but they are very dangerous and lives have been lost here.

continued on page 32

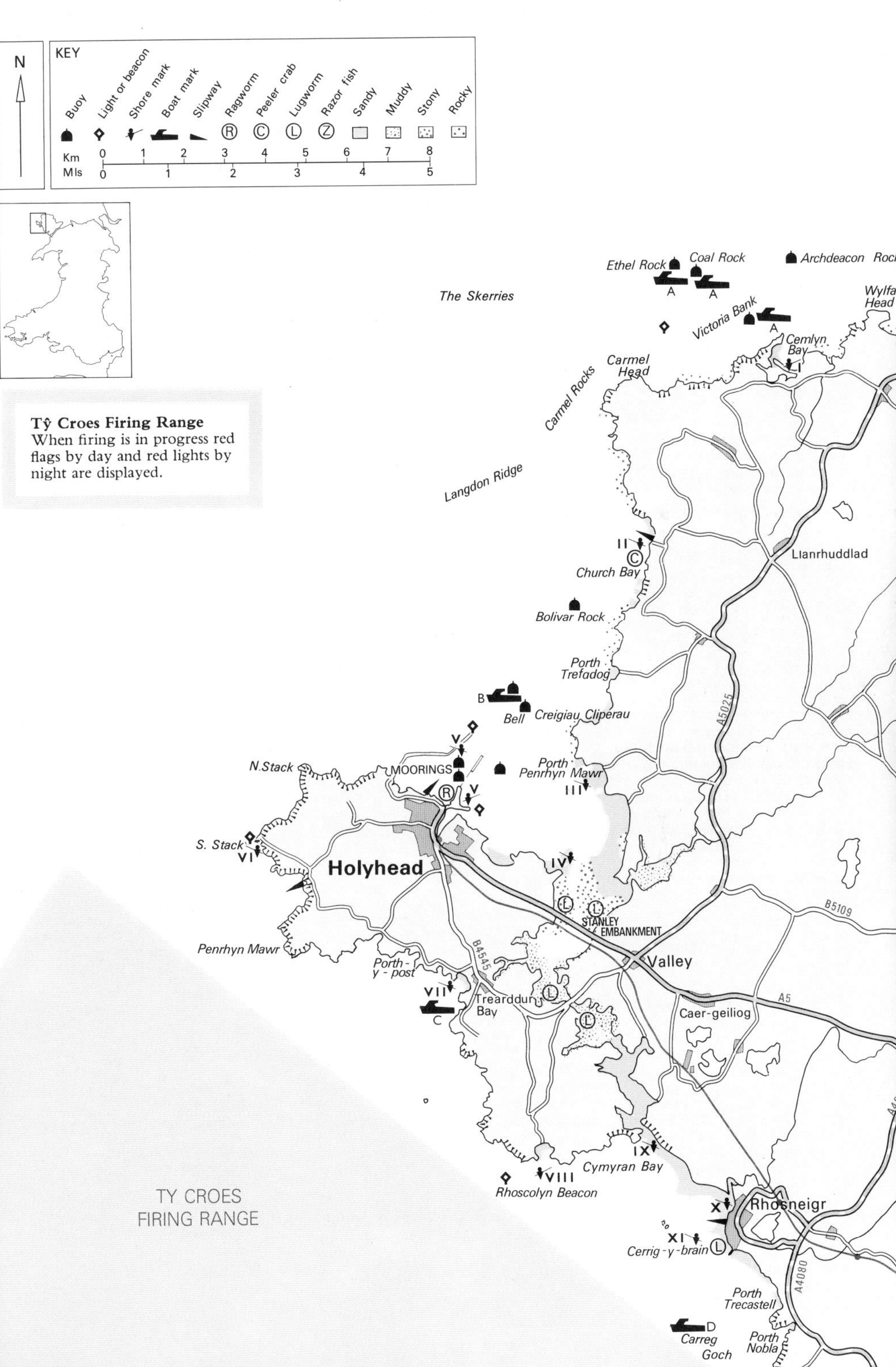
N
KEY
Buoy
Light or beacon
Shore mark
Boat mark
Slipway
Ragworm
Peeler crab
Lugworm
Razor fish
Sandy
Muddy
Stony
Rocky
Km 0 1 2 3 4 5 6 7 8
Mls 0 1 2 3 4 5
Tŷ Croes Firing Range
When firing is in progress red flags by day and red lights by night are displayed.
Ethel Rock
Coal Rock
Archdeacon Rock
The Skerries
Victoria Bank
Wylfa Head
Cemlyn Bay
Carmel Head
Carmel Rocks
Langdon Ridge
Church Bay
Llanrhuddlad
Bolivar Rock
Porth Trefadog
A5025
Bell
Creigiau Cliperau
N.Stack
MOORINGS
Porth Penrhyn Mawr
S. Stack
Holyhead
STANLEY EMBANKMENT
B5109
Penrhyn Mawr
B4545
Valley
Porth-y-post
Trearddur Bay
A5
Caer-geiliog
Cymyran Bay
Rhoscolyn Beacon
TY CROES FIRING RANGE
Rhosneigr
Cerrig-y-brain
A4080
Porth Trecastell
Carreg Goch
Porth Nobla

II. **Church Bay.** Approached by a $1\frac{1}{2}$ mile side road from the village of Llanrhyddlad, 5 miles north of Valley. The Lobster Pot restaurant near the beach has a name indicating the beach terrain you're going to find. A low tide inspection is essential. Anyway, a good search in the rocky gullies left of the small slipway and sandy bay will repay itself with some edible peeler crab. This is the northerly limit of the south west blow beaches. Crab, worked close in near the rocks just after low tide, is a favourite technique. Alternatively, try floating crab when the tide is pretty well in, then you'll be hunting over a great mass of weedy rock. A long cast into the sandy interstices between the rocks and into the open bay will attract rays, plaice and dabs, with cod and whiting very late in the year.

III. **Llanfachraeth – Porth Penrhyn Mawr and Traeth y Gribin.** A huge sickle of sand forming two south-western facing beaches on the mainland due east of Holyhead Harbour. Rarely heavily surfed because they fall in the harbour breakwater's protection, they nevertheless share in the fairly good bass fishing sustained by the extensive lug beds and lagoons north of Stanley Embankment. Holy Island's umbilical cord with the mainland. The bass expect to find lug, and lug they mainly get as bait, but rag is an excellent alternative.

IV. **Holyhead – Penrhos Beach.** Sandy patches, interspersed with extensive areas of muddy stone, border the great gully that leads south to Stanley Embankment at low tide. Penrhos Beach extends from Towyn Bay around the Penrhos headland to form its western side. The mark is approached on foot from the western end of the embankment or from Towyn Bay. Bass are the main quarry as in mark III, but don't ignore the dabs, flounders and mullet which abound on the flooding tide.

V. **Holyhead – British Rail Mail Pier and breakwater.** A permit from the booking office at Holyhead Station gives permission to fish the Mail Pier on Salt Island (the Irish boat terminal) on the territory of British Rail. The $1\frac{1}{2}$ miles long main breakwater, to which entry is unrestricted, gives access to 5 fathoms on its inner side with much of what that implies in terms of fish. At both marks a good strong terminal tackle and fish bait gives one a good chance of landing any conger, tope or ray hooked. Lighter gear can be used with lug and rag for a pretty wide range of fish, from lesser spotted dogfish to the roving bass and succulent dab. With the approach of frosty weather, fast and furious sport with whiting and cod is worth the effort of a late night.

South Stack Lighthouse, Holy Island

VI. **Holy Island – South Stack.** Two miles west of Holyhead town, the lighthouse crowned promontory of South Stack offers bass spinning and wrasse float fishing opportunities round the tide. Locals dig their medium sized rag in the gluey mess on the new harbour side of the small car park on the Salt Island causeway. They use it on a very light float from a number of rock platforms that extend round the coast from precipitous North Stack to the lighthouse at the South Stack. A long trudge of about a mile is necessary to reach the best spots.

VII. **Holy Island – Trearddur Bay.** Though a popular holiday and sailing beach, $1\frac{1}{2}$ miles south of Holyhead, its waters make an early morning or night trip in summer worthwhile. Mainly sandy, the bay has rocky fringes and isolated rocks that add variety to the conditions and to the fish. They lead to snagging if a low water reconnoitre is not made. Choose the south or north side; each has a minor road and rocky tracks near it that enable one to reach deeper water. Bass can be taken at low tide against the rocks with crab, or in the middle of the beach with lug or rag. With deepening water and the light failing, bigger species invade the bay: tope when the evening is still and warm, thornback ray – though small – dogfish and the flatfish, mainly flounders. The outer rocks are ideal summer mackerel vantage points.

VIII. **Holy Island – Rhoscolyn Bay.** Approached by a $1\frac{1}{2}$ mile long side road from Treaddur Bay or Four Mile Bridge, Rhoscolyn Bay is popular with holidaymakers in summer, though approach and parking is not easy. The right hand side of the bay disintegrates in a mass of rocks and islands which soon reappear as a beaconed shoal running almost a mile offshore. A mile to the left lies the Cymyran Strait; Rhoscolyn is therefore well placed for roving bass, flatfish and the occasional tope that feed on them. Survey at low tide when the children can enjoy the sands. Return at night or very early morning to place your crab or lug-baited hook unerringly in sandy havens between the rocks. A 4/0 or 5/0 thin wire Mustad Aberdeen-style hook, finely honed, on a 12 lbs trace is ideal for biggish bass.

IX. **Cymyran Bay and Sands.** A one mile trudge skirting RAF Valley on its west or across Crugyll Sands from Rhosneigr on the south of the airfield to the sandy southern exit of the Strait between Holy Island and mainland Anglesey, can be worth the effort. Alternatively – and there's not much difference in the effort involved – approach the Strait on Holy Island side by the Rhoscolyn road near Bryn-y-bar farm. Arrive at least an hour before low tide and fish the tide up with crab, lug or rag – in that order – making sure you hand-hold your rod for a quick strike. Spinning with a silver toby or red gill worked realistically as possible can be resorted to with more chance of success than usual when the tide run gets too much for a light bass rod. If you're broken up mystifyingly, change immediately to a tope rig, for the more adventurous of them will range on the flooding tide into the flattie-ridden strait, especially if the mackerel are a bit scarce. A packet of defrosting fish fillets could come in handy; you can always fry them yourself if you return empty-handed! Similar vantage points – most are difficult to reach – and methods can be exploited all the way up to Four Mile Bridge and beyond to the Stanley Embankment except on the Nature Reserve restricted area.

X. **Rhosneigr – Traeth Crugyll.** North of Rhosneigr, a popular holiday village, extend the sands firstly of Crugyll beach, then of Cymyran beach, for almost two miles. Afon Crugyll cuts a channel through the sand. Let it be your starting point for an evening session when other beach activity is over. Rely on the local lug as bait, for there is plenty of it. Alternate a simple 'wander tackle' for dabs and flounders with your conventional bass ledger. Some will fish the bass ledger with a smaller long-shanked flounder hook attached by a 9 in stiffish trace 18 in to 2 ft above the running lead so as to do the two jobs at once. That's all right as long as you don't want to cast a long distance.

XI. **Rhosneigr – the rocks.** A feature of this holiday village is a large rocky area 100 yards out on the sands. It is large enough and sufficiently high to afford harbourage in its sandy interior to a number of small craft. Though weedy, crab are rare, probably because it is continually picked over by an army of holidaying children. Crystal clear shallow water, with all the boating activity going on, make your daytime chances very poor. Choose an off-beat time when there's a bit of wind on the surface of the rising water. Bass search the weedy channels for stray crab, so a trip to the Menai Strait to collect some is the best way to avoid the activity of the day. Flatfish feed on the extensive lug beds. A good toss of a mackerel strip into the 8–12 feet of water found on the seaward side may well find the thornback ray and dogfish that come in closer on the tide.

Boat fishing

Holyhead harbour has launching facilities and three or four square miles of water protected from almost every blow. This harbour fishing is good, particularly in early winter for cod and whiting, and the dinghy man can venture into it in comparative safety. The north west cape of Anglesey is another affair. Rich in pollack and coalfish as well as tope, the area from Cemlyn Bay around to Church Bay is, nevertheless, a graveyard for small craft who have paid the supreme penalty for venturing out inadequately equipped and uninformed when conditions were not at their long-settled best. South of Holyhead, at Trearddur Bay and Rhosneigr, small craft regularly put out into the bay to find fish, away from the beach activity of high summer, but clear of headland tide rips.

A maximum speed of 8 nautical mph or lower applies in most bays mentioned in the text and should be self-applied at other bays used by bathers or light craft.

A. **The Islands between Cemlyn Bay and Carmel Head.** From ½ mile to 2 miles north west from Cemlyn Bay the tide-ripped craggy coast, turning the full force of the Irish Sea, offers excellent pollack and coalfish grounds to the venturesome. A three miles run west from Cemaes Bay is the best approach, for the Church Bay slipway is a little difficult for the bigger boat to reach the water. A low powered course set straight – Eddystone fashion – along the 10 fathom line near the bigger islands will take both species on whiffed red gills. Obviously an echo sounder will enhance the chances of finding suitable pinnacles and of avoiding the ensuing snags. A low powered slow drift, to beat the effect of 3–5 knot tides that sweep over the banks trailing away from Maen y Bugail (West Mouse Rock) in 7 fathoms of water, gives the bottom feeders a chance to catch up with the roving mackerel strip. Further out, with controlled drifts down the 17 fathoms channels between Archdeacon Rock, Coal Rock and the Ethel Rock, conger, ling, cod and turbot will come to feed. Anchored up in a slower run, with mackerel hunks dropping away on the tide, skate and ray, good tope and bull huss will be brought within range of your bait. These sophisticated methods obviously need a strong boat, power in reserve, good equipment and an attentive and knowledgeable skipper. If you and your boat don't measure up to these standards, charter a boat and skipper.

B. **Holyhead Harbour.** Book up with a local boat for the excellent deep sea fishing to be found 10 to 15 miles out from Holyhead. Within the harbour and its near approaches the comings and goings of Irish Mail and cargo boats and of aluminium ore carriers must take first place over your fishing. Yachting tuition also takes place in the New Harbour area, so choose a mark where you won't be disturbed. A pound or so spent on Holyhead Harbour chart, No. 2011, is worthwhile in this respect. Choose the buoyed rocky areas and the odd wreck – the outer Platters and Skinner rock in the New Harbour or out towards the Cliperau rocks; the 1½ mile long breakwater points almost directly at the Cliperau bell buoy and a green wreck buoy near it, both in 40–50 ft of water about ¾ mile off its end. In the winter, cod and whiting and in summer conger, rays, flats, dogfish and occasional tope, can be brought close at these marks with a bit of ground baiting mackerel and other scraps chopped up in an old meat grinder. The sand and shingle shallows along the eastern margin of the harbour – off Porth Penrhyn-mawr and Traeth y Gribin beaches – should be slowly trolled on the current with baited spoon for plump flounders. If you have a quiet engine giving low revs or an energetic rowing companion, switch to a trolled red gill for a bass search around the channel which leads to the Stanley Embankment.

C. **Trearddur Bay.** Launching a bigger craft can cause some problems if the slipway is not available, but the powered dinghy will have little difficulty launching off firm sand. The 10 fathom mark practically joins Penrhyn Mawr, north east to Raven's Point, just south west of Trearddur Bay. A rocky bottom a few hundred yards off Raven's Point gives way to sand and it is here that most fish are caught in the inshore waters. The normal habitants of the rocky terrain – bass, wrasse, small pollack – take float-fished mackerel strips, worms or crab. On the sand, rays, skate and tope give way later in the year to good catches of codling and whiting. Cod appreciate big baits, especially bunches of lugworm, or lugworm with a 3 inch sliver of squid left to flick about on the trace immediately above the attaching ring of a big hook.

D. **Rhosneigr.** Much the same conditions and remarks apply as at Trearddur Bay (mark C) except that the 10 fathom mark is pushed out more than 1 mile to Carreg Goch by a long shallow finger of shale and rock. Tope are increasingly numerous in the faster water near the tip. They are difficult to handle from a small craft for they can be heavy to tail in and thrash about inboard unmercifully. There's no sale for them and no large scale lobster baiting hereabouts, so the hope is that having played a catch to the side of the boat, a pair of wirecutters or pliers will release him to get rid of the hook – almost always in the lip – at his leisure. But be careful; their bite will amputate fingers easily.

Bait supply

Holyhead's tackle shops avoid bait like the plague but several diggers sell it as a sideline. A chat with local fishermen will soon reveal their addresses. Some put

continued on next page

bait for sale notices in their windows; one appears in the house at the mainland end of Stanley Embankment. If time, tide and age are on your side, there are opportunities of digging your own. Pack a garden fork – not a spade – with your fishing gear.

Lug. The drying expanses each side of Stanley Embankment and in the creeks around it have plenty of good lug, easily dug. Avoid the bird haunts of Penrhos Nature Reserve at all costs. At Rhosneigr, the gullies on each side of the neck of sand leading to the rocky island hold an abundance of small rag. Within the sandy confines of the rocks themselves there are several patches of much larger brown lug, easily trenched.

Rag. The limits of the New Harbour, just below the car park at the entrance to Salt Island, hold many medium-sized rag, though dirty to dig. Start on the right-hand side of the stream that cuts under the road. On springs, old diggings will indicate that you go down the beach as far as possible, and the rag get bigger accordingly.

Crab. There are few in the vicinity. The rocks at Church Bay hold the occasional edible peeler with some prawns and blennies. Elsewhere any patch of weedy stone is likely to have its small quota.

Tackle shops

Holyhead. *R. P. Owen, Stanley House, Old Market Square. Tel.* (0407) 2458. Preserved, packeted baits, worms and flies; advice on where to fish. WWA river licences sold.
Fishing tackle also available from: *Dorset Stores, Trearddur Bay Road, Kingsland, Holyhead.*

Holyhead. *R. V. Thomas, County Sports, County Buildings, Stanley Street. Tel.* (0407) 2059. Fishing tackle and sports equipment.

Boat hire, trips or charter

Holyhead. *Isle of Anglesey, Scimitar Club, Scimitar House, Porth-y-felin, Holyhead. Tel.* (0407) 2094 and 3178. Various craft 18 ft to 35 ft for hire. Sailing tuition, fishing and diving. Available all the year at Scimitar Sailing Club. Hour or day charter, with skipper. Bait available.

Boat launching slipways

Church Bay. Approach by narrow 1½ mile long road from Llanfaethlu or Llanrhyddlad on A5025 Valley-Cemaes Bay road. Slip suitable for small craft. Free use.

Holyhead. 1. *Yacht Club Slipway, Newry Beach. Tel.* (0407) 2496. Use by non-yacht club boats is not encouraged; **2.** Public slipway near old lifeboat station. No restriction on use for small craft.

Rhosneigr. Slipway to foreshore. No restrictions for small craft.

Trearddur Bay. *Yacht Club slipway. Tel.* (0407) 31311. Permission from Yacht Club or membership of a yacht club necessary – previous notice needed.

Fishing advice

Holyhead and District Angling Club, Mr. J. Lyons, 32 Holborn Road, Holyhead. Tel. (0407) 2656.

Visiting fishermen welcomed. Club boat. The club organises Holyhead and district Open Competition from the breakwater in October for prizes and trophies.

RAF Valley Sea Angling Club, Mr. Howl, RAF Valley. Tel. Holyhead (0407) 2241. *Ext.* 273.

Useful telephone numbers

In emergency
Dial 999 and ask for Coastguard.

At other times
Coastguard. *Holyhead Harbour. Tel.* 2051. **RNLI lifeboat.** *Holyhead. Tel.* 2596. **RAF Rescue Helicopter.** *Valley, near Holyhead. Tel.* (040784) 999. **Trinity House.** *South Stack lighthouse. Tel. Holyhead* 2042. **Weather forecasts.** *Meteorological Office, RAF Station, Valley, Isle of Anglesey. Tel.* (0407) 2288.

Aberffraw (Isle of Anglesey) to Porth Dinllaen (Lleyn Peninsula)

Broad sandy beaches and precipitous cliffs alternate on this part of the coast, renowned for its bass fishing. It includes Anglesey's productive south west corner – Aberffraw, Malltraeth Sands and Llanddwyn Beach with the 'island' at one end and Abermenai Point at the other. Across Menai Strait there's mainly sand from Dinas Dinlle to Trefor and again at Nefyn. Between lies Yr Eifl mountain range, whose seaward wall, though difficult to reach, offers excellent rock fishing. The tide funnels rapidly in and out of the Strait causing cross-beach currents on each flank. Depths inshore rarely exceed 2 to 3 fathoms.

I. **Aberffraw Beach.** Landing place of war galleys of Princes of Wales in the Dark Ages, Aberffraw beach is easily reached along the stream from the village on A4080. Surfcasting from an hour before low water or spinning on high water mark near the stream's mouth – for bass – is best when the popular beach's holiday visitors have left, in September.

II. **Malltraeth Sands.** In gullies of the extensive sandy bay, ledgering for bass or flounder with lugworm is restricted to the early hours of the flood, preferably in the twilight. To spin the narrows in late summer evenings for shoaling bass, or casting into the surf in the seaward bay, a mile-long walk is required from Newborough Warren Forestry Commission car park or along the north west bank from near Bodorgan.

III. **Llanddwyn Island.** See page 36. The ¾-mile long promontory of Llanddwyn, an island only at high water, can only be approached on foot from the nearby Forestry Commission car park in Newborough Warren. It is a nature reserve and the Gwynedd County Council Warden has been known to refuse permission to fish at high water. However, shoals of dogfish plague the bottom fisher, and few would make the trek for its mullet, but its shallow waters contain much more. Occasional bass will be contacted among the rocks about the neck of the island if crab is used. Lug, rag and fish baits attract whiting – great numbers in winter, of good size – codling, flounder and dab. Larger fish baits – from the island's waist towards the point – catch tope, ray and the odd skate. Small pollack and coalfish among the rocks take white feathers in the evening gloom. All hours of the tide give fish, the least responsive – as always – being the third and fourth hours of the ebb when the tide is running hardest. The nearer one fishes towards the beach the more it responds to fishing each side of slack low water.

IV. **Dinas Dinlle.** Belan Point has been dealt with in the Menai Strait chapter. Here we deal with the main western facing sand beach which extends from a half-submerged upside-down Army Dukw ½ mile south of Belan Point to Aberdesach, past Dinas Dinlle, a village 1 mile off the A499 south west of Caernarfon. Good bass are taken along its whole length but, because of summer holidaymakers, fishermen tend to congregate at the far end of the 'promenade' road where it makes a sharp right turn. It's quieter there. Few bass are taken before the middle of July and the late autumn is best. The sands are very narrow on neaps and between them and the pebble bank is a quickly filling deeper channel.

continued on page 36

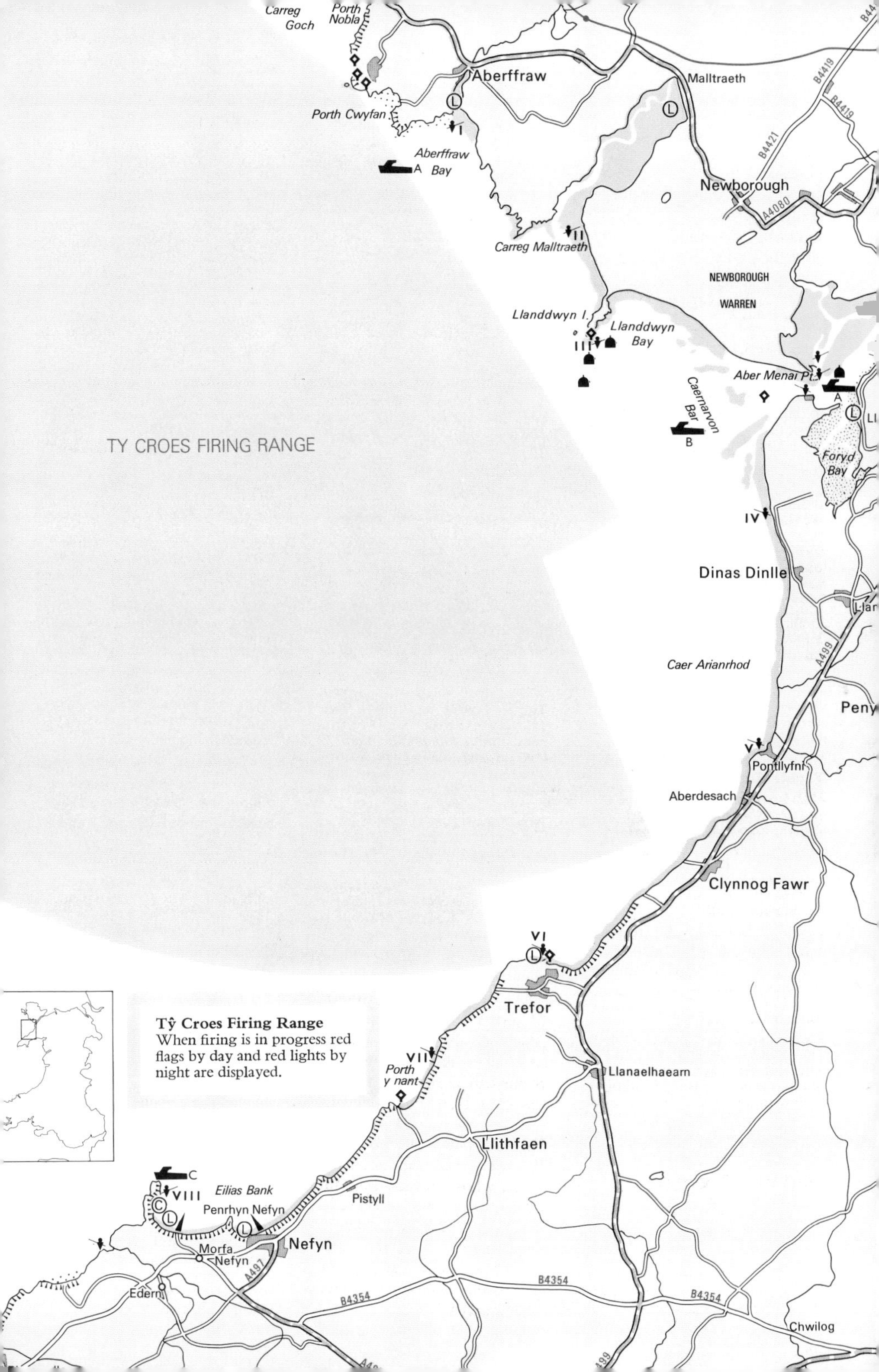

Tŷ Croes Firing Range
When firing is in progress red flags by day and red lights by night are displayed.

Ynys Llanddwyn, near Newborough

Aberffraw to Porth Dinllaen – continued

Drag is south to north on the making tide and the slightest blow makes quantities of fine green wood float around, so avoid a rod with a small diameter ring at the tip; it clogs quickly. Rag, lug and razor fish are equally efficient but crab should be saved for the more rocky areas towards Aberdesach end of the beach.

V. **Pontllyfni and Aberdesach.** Both villages lie on A499 Caernarvon-Pwllheli road. Each has a stream cutting the sand and shingle beach and both respond well to crab bait fished for bass in the gulleys, starting near the stream, in the late summer and throughout the autumn.

VI. **Trefor.** The quarrying village's little stub of cliff-bound quay is the last easy access to water before Nefyn. Easily accessible water hereabouts is shallow, demanding long-distance casting skill. Those who find themselves in this delightful area without beach equipment or casting skill will be grateful for the chance of deeper water close in. Flatfish, dogfish and roaming bass are regularly taken.

VII. **Porth y Nant (Nant Gwrtheyrn).** A mountain goat's climb and descent from the road's end at Llithfaen on Yr Eifl mountain (A499 Caernarvon-Nefyn road) leads to the derelict quarrying village of Nant Gwrtheyrn and then to Porth y Nant beach. Shelving, shingly, sliced by derelict piers and flanked by impossible cliffs, the 2 fathoms on the right give peaceful fishing for bass, dogfish and flatfish, with plenty of mackerel and whiting in season.

VIII. **Nefyn and Porth Dinllaen.** Both villages have a long association with fishing, particularly for herring, now rare in these waters. North facing and sheltered, both are the popular day resorts of holiday makers. Night fishing for bass, flatfish and lesser spotted dogfish is the only thing possible off the sand beach or its adjoining shingly, and stony outcrops, though bait is scarce. The best means of attack is with fish baits; cast boldly with rotten bottoms into very rough tide-ripped ground at the point of Porth Dinllaen beyond the lifeboat station. If you find a peeler crab, float fish it over this ground for bass. Near the lifeboat station are conger. The timid wait for mackerel and mullet to come into Porth Dinllaen on the evening tide. That's if the netters don't get there first.

Boat fishing

Plenty of fish, tides from $\frac{1}{2}$ knot to 1 knot, faster in the immediate vicinity of Menai Strait entrance, and inshore depths rarely exceeding 7 to 10 fathoms. These facts suggest bountiful catches but they are almost of academic interest, for launching a boat – even a dinghy – is difficult. Boat charter and fishing trips are an established feature at Caernarfon and give access to Caernarfon Bay's excellent fishing for blue and porbeagle shark and tope, conger and rays.

A. **Aberffraw Bay.** Boats line the creek at Aberffraw and dinghies can be launched without difficulty. Extend your range by 1 mile south west of Carreg-y-trai rock (the bay's right hand headland) and you're in long fingers of sand and shingle that hold tope, rays, dogfish, bull huss and plaice. Winter catches of whiting would be bigger if the bay did not cut up rough with a small south westerly blow.

B. **Caernarfon Bar and Llanddwyn Bay.** Boats strong enough to venture outside Menai Strait troll for bass with large red gills and rubber eels. When conditions are settled calm, go out from

Mussel Bank beacon to Caernarfon Bar black buoy in the ½-knot tides just before low slack and back in along the edge of South Sands (see Menai Strait boat fishing section).

C. **Porth Dinllaen.** Taking a dinghy ½-mile due north of the point puts 11 fathoms between you and the madding crowd; no mean feat on this coast of shallows and beach balls. The reward is vastly to extend your chances of a thornback ray, tope, more voracious dogfish, or a wide range of more appetising species who respond to fish baits.

(See also page 34 for: bait supplies; tackle shops; boat hire trips or charter; emergency services; launching slipways and fishing advice.)

Bait supply

Few beaches can be said to have no bait, but this stretch of coast has less than most, though Holy Island's lug and Menai Strait's crab and rag are close at hand.

Lug. Aberffraw Creek and Malltraeth Sands, with a few near the quay at Trefor and near the rocky promontory between the sands of Porth Dinllaen and Nefyn.

Crab. Rare, at Porth Cwyfan (Aberffraw), near Trefor and at Porth Dinllaen.

Mackerel. Plenty in Caernarfon Bay; sometimes even the dinghy man may have to buy them in Caernarfon.

Tackle shops (see also under Caernarfon in Menai Strait section).

Nefyn. *Mr. Brian Jones, Beach Shop, Nefyn. Tel.* (075882) 574. Tackle supply and preserved bait.

Newborough. *Newborough Tackle Centre, Mr. E. Owen, The Square, Newborough, Isle of Anglesey. (Tel.* (024879) 252. Tackle supply and repair, frozen bait and some fresh lug, local flies. Handy for Llanddwyn area. Specimen fish may be weighed on Llanfair PG SAC scales by arrangement through shop with club secretary.

Boats, hire, trips or charter.

Caernarfon. See Menai Strait section for information on boat fishing in Caernarfon Bay's deep water.

Boat launching slipways

Slipways are almost non-existent but a dinghy can be launched by hand on its trailer across the beach with some difficulty at:

Aberffraw, Dinas Dinlle, Aberdesach, Trefor, Nefyn and Porth Dinllaen.

Fishing advice

Seiont, Gwyrfai and Llyfni Angling Society, Hon. Sec., Mr. A. Roberts, 17 Castle Street, Caernarfon. Tel. (0286) 3512.

Useful telephone numbers

In emergency

Dial 999 and ask for coastguard.

At other times

RNLI lifeboat. *Porth Dinllaen. Tel. Nefyn* (075882) 288. **Coastguard.** *Porth Dinllaen. Tel. Nefyn* 204. *(Not constantly manned).* **Weather forecasts.** *Meteorological Office, RAF Station, Valley, Isle of Anglesey. Tel. Holyhead* (0407) 2288.

Lleyn Peninsula – Porth Dinllaen to Porth Neigwl (Hell's Mouth)

The long finger of Lleyn Peninsula probes deep into the Irish Sea. Its northern coast is rocky and the bays are small. Four excellent bass storm beaches brave the west wind. The rocks harbour good-sized pollack and wrasse. Big bass run the reef-ridden tide rips when brit and mackerel are about; in autumn they patrol the rolling surf shores. Virgin territories around tide-torn offshore reefs and island chains demand big boats and one or two far-sighted Abersoch skippers are aware of the potential in fish and fishermen. For the shore man, finding live bait is the biggest problem to be faced on Lleyn.

I. **Aber Geirch.** A ½-mile walk from Porth Dinllaen – or 1 mile west of Morfa Nefyn village – finds a creek bounded by rocks, the starting point of undersea cables. It fishes well for pollack and September and October bass. Spinning or float fishing close in conserves scarce bait from crabs and lobsters which haunt the rocky faces.

II. **Porth Towyn and Porth Ysgadan.** Towyn – a sand dune – and Ysgadan – a herring – are doubly rare on this coast. Turn off B4417 north or south of Tudweiliog village for a pincer movement on two sandy bays separated by a small bluff. Wrasse and pollack of good size are not the main quarry; bass are. A late evening session with spring tides at full ebb, or starting to flow up the rock gullies, will give a chance of good sized fish for about two or three hours. One also avoids the fairly heavy tripper use which Lleyn bays receive on fine days. If you're short of conventional bass baits try to get some bullocks liver from a butchers; bass sometimes go wild on it.

Porth Ychen and Porth Gwylan are two rocky coves 1¼ mile south west of Tudweiliog. Between Porth Ysgadan headland and Porth Ychen are rock platforms for evening fishing when pollack come out of their lobster-ridden hideaways in 25 ft of water. A white feather on a very light rod, fished as a reservoir trout fisherman would, gives good returns. Wives enjoy a visit to the 'Dive In' sea food restaurant on the cliffs near Porth Gwylan (Tel. Tudweiliog 246).

III. **Porth Golmon.** 1 mile north west of B4417, through Llangwnnadl, lies Porth Golmon with its sandy, rock-bordered beach called Traeth Penllech, extending north east for 1 mile – large by Lleyn north coast standards. Bass and tope fishing gradually improves in each bay from Nefyn to Bardsey Sound. Vary your tactics and quarry here and at Porth Oer, 3½ miles south west. In settled sunny calms, spin off the point for fresh mackerel. With it try a live-baited rein (i.e. no weight) for bass close in, or a large strip on ledger gear for tope. All you do is substitute a 4 ft wire trace and 6/0 steel hook for your 12 lbs bass trace and 5/0 wire hook. Provided you have plenty in reserve on the reel your main line can be as light as 18 lbs.

IV. **Porth Oer (Whistling Sands).** Sand beach, two miles west of Pen-y-groeslon, junction off B4413 and B4417 near Aberdaron; there is a car park 400 yards from the beach. This popular beach fragments on each side into reefs where the 3½ knot spring tides that spill over the Tripod rocks, 2 miles south west, exert a strong effect. In calms, fish it as you would mark III, but with stronger line in the rough. Prize your scarce Lleyn peeler crabs until a good westerly blow has fined down a bit at Porth Oer. Then you should do well towards the rocks.

V. **Bardsey Sound.** Impossibly cliff-bound for the most part, there are, nevertheless, a few rock platforms facing the Sound that give access to 10 fathoms or more of water. Approach them through Uwchmynydd; keep bearing left on the road out of Aberdaron, 1 mile away. Good pollack abound, as do wrasse, and it is an excellent spot for conventional bass float fishing.

VI. **Aberdaron Sands.** Earnest fishermen never fish here in the fever of summer-day activity, for it is very popular with holidaymakers. Come instead between mid-September and late April for the good bass – biggish schoolies and frequent 5 to 8-pounders which make this their headquarters in mild winters. Summer nights bring

continued on next page

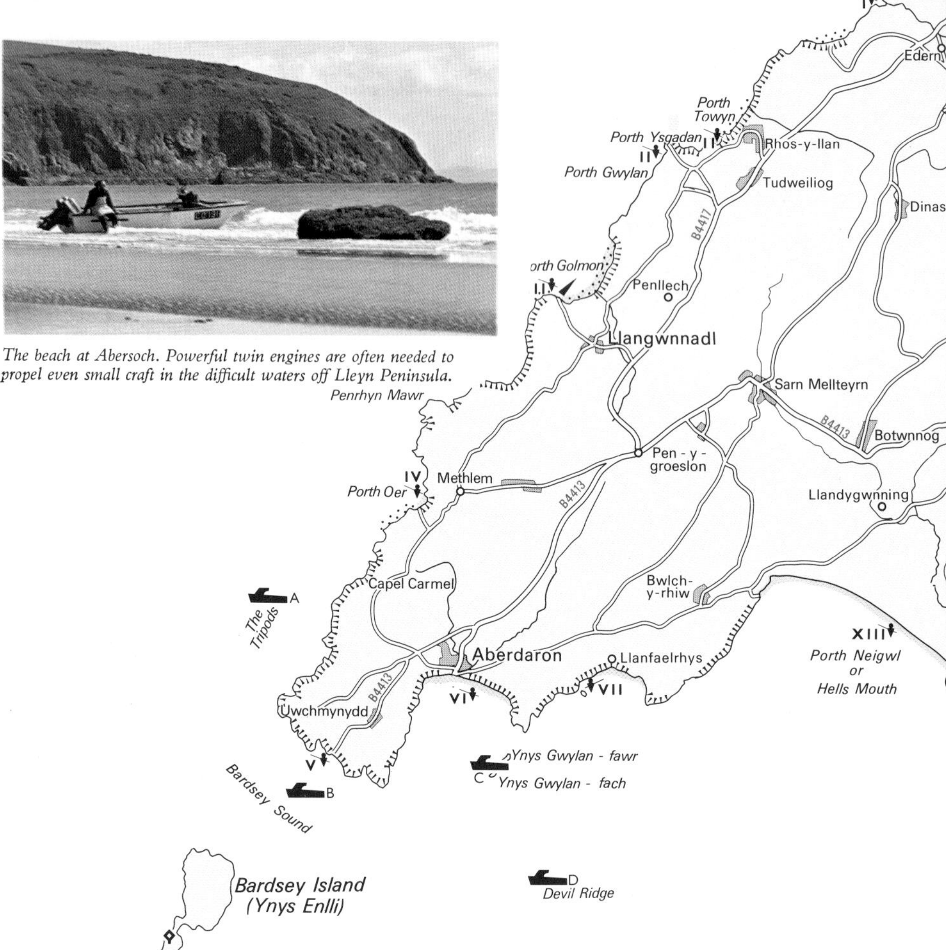

The beach at Abersoch. Powerful twin engines are often needed to propel even small craft in the difficult waters off Lleyn Peninsula.

Lleyn Peninsula – continued

them back temporarily, especially when, for a few days, a brisk – but not high – west wind and squalls have made the beach inhospitable to the sunlover. Fish the tide up, keeping mobile; start about the small group of rocks in the middle of the beach and move back, as the tide rises, towards the village and the small stream cutting across the beach.

VII. **Porth Cadlan.** Remote and difficult to reach, and probably the better for it, Porth Cadlan is a better beach than Aberdaron to bring off a daytime bass coup in summer. Clamber down from Llanfaelrhys, a village 2 miles east of Aberdaron. Choose a spot away from visitors who find even this idyllic spot; at low tide it's likely to be on the right where Maen Gwenonwy island forms a narrow channel with the land. Crab is best, if you can come by it. Ledgered mussels or a Californian squid may even be better in the fall of the year. Up grade or down grade hook sizes to suit the texture of the bait – with the size of fish well in mind, of course.

VIII. **Porth Neigwl (Hell's Mouth).** A glorious, classic 3½ miles of sand storm-beach, crystal clear, reached easily by a 250 yard level footpath from a pull-in near Tai Morfa, ½ mile south west of Llanengan, 2 miles south west of Abersoch. Even in settled fine weather a good surf runs; storms make it unfishable. But it can be very good for bass on razorfish, crag, rag or lug throughout autumn, winter and spring. In high summer, schoolies stay, but bigger bass are well off-shore. Keep any crab for the rocks on the left of the bay, a deceptive ½ mile from the footpath. A shallow beach, it well repays the expense of breast-high trousers-and-waders in one. Porth Neigwl has only one small cross-beach stream of note. Start here at near low water. Always carry your rod for bass tip and run frequently; try up-sizing or re-honing your hook if you can't make contact, alternatively scale down if you want to bring in the dabs or plaice who tend to pluck at the bigger-baited hooks. Don't try the Wessex ledger-paternoster combine here, otherwise you lose valuable casting distance.

Boat fishing

More and more Lleyn boatmen are realising the angling potential of waters impossible to trawl. Like West Country boats, several are switching in summer from time-honoured solo fishing to catering for clubs and groups. There's still a place in Lleyn's waters for the well equipped, sensible boat-owning amateur fisherman, but he will keep within his range of capability and fish the quieter bays.

A. **The Tripods.** From Braich y Pwll Head on Bardsey Sound, northwards for 3 miles, runs the underwater lobster-potted reef called The Tripods. Just a mile offshore for the most part, it rises to within 5 fathoms of the surface from a deep trough of 40 fathoms stretching away south west. Heavy overfalls rip the surface on flood and ebb when $2\frac{1}{2}$ to $3\frac{1}{2}$ knot tides ride over it; hardly the place for light craft which might be tempted to try to get out from adjacent Porth Oer beach. Its fish-rich fringes are similar to the Skerries shoals off Anglesey's north coast and the same how-to-fish comments apply (See Wylfa Head to Porth Trecastell and Holy Island, mark A). You fish it when conditions allow you to, as near as you can get to low and high slacks on neaps. There are red bream, turbot, plaice and brill – an uncommon flat fish – as well as the general run of a reef's bottom and middle water feeding fish. Aberdaron, 5 miles away, is the most accessible landing place. Here a tractor places lobster boats above high water mark. Porth Dinllaen and Abersoch are 14 miles and 18 miles one-way-only respectively, though both Aberdaron and Abersoch have to face Bardsey Sound's 5 knot furies.

B. **Bardsey Sound.** A wedge at 13-16 fathoms drives into the sound from the south east or the Aberdaron side, causing a W-shaped bank where it meets the general 24 fathoms bottom. 5 to 6 knot tides ensure no one lingers in the narrows on flood or ebb, but fishing on the drift, moving south east to north west over the lip of the wedge, is possible towards top and bottom slacks on smaller tides. Close in to the mainland cliff wall, and in the shelter of the $1\frac{3}{4}$ mile long island, there are excellent pollack, coalfish and – localised – bass. These are the kind of waters and fish all those pretty jigging lures were designed for – German sprats, tobys, pirks, flies and, of course, red gills.

C. **Ynys Gwylan Fawr, Ynys Gwylan Fach.** 1 mile south east of Aberdaron, the islands are within dinghy distance in fine weather. Mackerel spinning and pollack feathering give good catches of both. It's the kind of offshore sanctuary, away from the beaches and near the mackerel and brit, that bass take to in midsummer. Don't throw hardware at them; instead anchor up in 20 ft of water between the two islands ledgering soft or peeler crab, or a bunch of prawns, in the main stream. Smaller hardbacks instead of peelers will do at a push.

D. **Devil Ridge.** 2 miles beyond Ynys Gwylan Fach is Devil Ridge – 3 miles of sand and stone rising abruptly from 100 ft depth to within 30 ft of the surface. Overfalls are fearsome with

continued on next page

a bit of water about. Still, it's the kind of water in which real fish are found – pollack, skate, rays, tope, bull huss as well as cod and whiting in season – and fished sagely from Aberdaron or Abersoch by experienced skippers it repays handsomely. Take plenty of weights, at least 8 ozs to 1 lb; it's a bad bottom in spots.

Bait supply

Abersoch shops sometimes have supplies of bait. (See next coastal section). Mackerel are abundant in season but, without local knowledge and time, shore foraging can be disappointing. Very low tides will give:

Lug. Very patchy, even rare, in sheltered spots at Porth Ysgadan, Porth Golmon, Porth Oer and Aberdaron.

Razor fish. None now at Porth Neigwl on low springs. There are some at Abersoch beach, 2 miles east. A large sized table salt dispenser from your local shop normally gives enough to catch 60 to 80 razors though it would be a criminal waste to take so many. Take only those you are certain to use.

Sand eels. West Country sickle experts or Teignmouth netters would get a good haul at Porth Ceiriad and Porth Neigwl (Hell's Mouth). A quick rake and flick along the tide line in the right spot will throw up some.

Soft and peeler crabs. Very occasionally in weedy, rocky crevices at Porth Golmon and Porth Oer during June and early July.

Clams. An occasional one at Porth Ysgadan.

The lowly earthworm and limpet will both be taken by wrasse.

Tackle shops

See under Abersoch in next section.

Boat hire, trips or charter.

(See under Abersoch in next section.)

Boat launching slipways

Aberdaron. Light trailed dinghies can be manhandled over high water mark, soft sand to hard sand. On occasions a tractor service operates for pulling heavier trailed boats above high water mark or on to the road. Enquiries to *Mr. Stanley Harrison, Pendref, Aberdaron. Tel.* (075 886) 209.

Porth Oer (Whistling Sands). Launching from beach not encouraged. Car park 400 yards away and almost impossible to manhandle craft to tide line.

Porth Ysgadan: Launch from beach.

Fishing advice.

(See next coastal section)

Useful telephone numbers

In emergency
Dial 999 and ask for Coastguard.

At other times
RNLI lifeboat. *Porth Dinllaen. Tel. Nefyn* (075882) 288. **Coastguard.** *Porth Dinllaen. Tel. Nefyn* 204. (*Not constantly manned*). **Trinity House.** *Lighthouse, Bardsey Island. Radio linked. Lighthouse, St. Tudwal's Island West. Radio linked.*
Weather forecasts. *Meteorological Office, RAF Station, Valley, Isle of Anglesey. Tel. Holyhead* (0407) 2288.

Lleyn Peninsula – Porth Ceiriad to Criccieth

A broad, shallow, 2 fathoms shelf extends well off shore and competition from other water users is high in summer. Spring, autumn and early winter bass fishing can be first class. Mackerel return each year in fair quantities and offshore reefs, islands and hollows give excellent bottom fishing. In a typical year's fishing, Brian Jones' boat (see Abersoch) has caught tope to 65 lbs (best catch one day 27 fish), thornback ray to 23 lbs, 10 lbs turbot, bull huss to 16 lbs, spurdog of 12 lbs and 9 lbs pollack. Here too, high summer brings porbeagle and blue shark for those with the gear and application to catch them and autumn is never without its monkfish. Tides are comfortably fast, but rarely impossible, except, of course, on the ridges and in sounds.

I. **Porth Ceiriad and Trwyn Cilan.** 2 miles south of Abersoch through Bwlchtocyn. Park at Pantybranner Farm for Porth Ceiriad. Trwyn Cilan – a dangerous rock station – is reached by parking at Cilan Fawr Farm and walking ½ mile. Both marks are much less frequented than most Lleyn beaches in summer. A long cast into 16 to 20 ft of water will contact thornback ray, skate, dogfish, flounder and winter whiting, according to the kind of bait and how it's presented. Big fish baits are easiest to come by in summer. Rag and lug fished on a small long shanked hook – No. 4 – slowly moved from time to time, are best for flat fish particularly winter dabs.

II. **Abersoch.** A strong freshwater stream cuts the main sands. There's a stub of quay, anchored boats, bathers, yachts and water-ski boats. It's not promising. At night and early morning, fish the main beach from an hour before low water. There is plenty of whiting in winter at night by the Sailing Club using lug, also some flatfish and bass on the rising tide at night from the small quay into the river channel. Beyond Bennar headland, by the golf course, lies a wider beach with better fishing. Fish on the opposite end to the clubhouse. Razor, found on the beach, is the best bait for bass and plaice. Catches of bass improve in quantity and quality as autumn wears on and dabs are caught by the score in early winter. Though difficult of access from a point on A4999, ¾ mile north of Warren Caravan Park entrance, the Old Quarry beach under Mynydd Tiry-cwmwd has given some good bass on the flood.

III. **Llanbedrog – Carreg y Defaid.** Below the village is a small sand beach protected by a wooded headland. Heavily used by holidaymakers and netters, it is much better to turn to Carreg y Defaid, 1 mile north west, where there is a limited parking cul-de-sac 50 yards from the beach. Flounder, plaice and frequently bass, respond to Abersoch's razor or lug, fished at night.

IV. **Pwllheli – Carreg yr Ymbil (Gimblet Rock).** The seafront promenade extends by way of Morfa Garreg housing estate to the promontory caravan site, boatyards and yacht club. Seaward of this unpromising agglomeration of activity is a large rock, Carreg yr Ymbil, where a limited and often crowded, mark is found. It's a bit awkward at night but well worth the effort of reaching it in daytime in September and late April for bass and flounder.

V. **Pwllheli Harbour mouth.** A drying waste of a harbour where a marina was planned, but haunted now by mullet and the occasional bass, funnels out into Abererch Bay. Fish the bottom at the harbour mouth (but out of the boat channel) from Glan y Don, the northern side, reached from ½ mile east of town (free car park closing early, and short walk). Walk to the stony southern point for some spinning or float fishing for shoaling school bass. Here, it's shallow, weedy and beacons stand out of the water near the bank. A good spinning rod is needed to get distance on the rising tide.

VI. **Abererch Strand.** Approached from A497, 1 mile east of Pwllheli, or by a ½ mile walk down a lane by the side of Butlin's Camp main gate. Extensive and only frequented in parts by holidaymakers, it can give some big bass after a strong blow. Plaice and flounder take a bait gently moved from time-to-time. Nearer Butlins, at Penychain, the water is deeper, rockier and faster. Late evening is a good time here, when camp children and parents have deserted the shore.

VII. **Llanystumdwy.** For 4 miles from Penychain to Criccieth the beach shallows, with great clumps of stone terspersed with sand and pools, cut one point by Afon Dwyfor. It's vast, serted, difficult to fish. As a bait fering it has few crabs, but many ennies and small eels. It must have uch more. The bass expert wanting get away from the routine of known aches would almost certainly discover emadog Bay's biggest bass. It is a easant ½ mile walk past Dwyfor ver's trout pools from Bont Fechan A box, ½ mile west of Llanystumdwy.

II. **Criccieth.** Busy by day, the aches are fishable only in late evening the summer. Between the stone quay d castle headland is a cove. Cast aight out where the bottom is clean; holds plaice of about 1½ lbs as well as ss. The pier end is stepped down and protected by railings. Due south and uth west finds snags but is a good ot to float-fish soft crab for bass. A uth east cast finds broken ground and racious tiny flatfish. Persevere with ab, for bass are about.

oat fishing

nly on the area's western end – ound the islands of St. Tudwal d in the 14–20 fathom waters uth west of Porth Ceiriad – is ious boat fishing possible. sewhere a boat simply gains cast- g distance; one has to go a long ay to get beyond 4 fathoms, ough for the strong dinghy there always some rays and dabs. unching is difficult except at bersoch, which is geared to nateur boating with facilities and ow-how. Pwllheli had plans to crease its extensive yachting and otor boat facilities by develop- ent of a marina in the harbour.

St. Tudwal's Island East and est and Carreg y Trai. Saint dwal, commemorated here, at nstadwell on Milford Haven, and at eguier on the Brittany Coast, must ve liked his fishing. East Island and lighthoused West Island make a small angle with Carreg y Trai. All three ve 7 or 8 fathoms off their south east ak and a mere two fathoms on their rthern trailing edges. Though lobster hermen grumble of falling catches, all pollack are sufficiently abundant make a trip worthwhile to the West and despite the depredations of a ge seal colony which basks on nearby rreg y Trai at low water. Choose a ap tide to anchor up near the Sand- t Buoy off Penrhyn Head. Here ornback rays run from 12 to 15 lbs. gfish and bull huss are about in their al bait-stealing numbers. ersoch, 1½ miles north west of the ands, is conveniently near and for smaller boat based here there is a od bank in about 20 ft of water (low), some ½ mile SE of Llanbedrog headland, where springtime thornbacks and summer tope are always a possibility.

B. **Cillan Gutter.** (C) **Muddy Hollow.** Tremadog Bay's general 7–8 fathoms deep table-like bottom is split up the middle by a valley of water much deeper. Cillan Gutter, 250 ft deep, is its broader seaward end; Muddy Hollow is the narrower, slightly shallower at 120 ft, east end of the undersea valley. An echo sounder finds the best fishing positions along the sides of the valley and used in the hollows comes upon strange pits 50–60 ft deeper than the general depression. 6–7 miles out from Abersoch, the marks escape any headland's effect on tides, which run about 1 knot. Tope, taken on ledgered live mackerel, thornback ray and monkfish feed here as well as plaice and other flatfish. Significant runs of whiting and occasional codling arrive in waves from November.

D. **Pwllheli.** The two fathoms line snakes its way across the bay from Abersoch's Bennar headland to Butlin's Penychain Camp headland. One significant off-shoot points from Pwllheli's Carreg yr Ymbil (Gimblet Rock), finger-like, straight out into deeper water to the Gimblet Shoals. Inshore fishing takes two forms. Firstly, slow trolling of a rubber eel for bass, or baited spoon for flounder, between the harbour mouth's outer black buoy and Abererch beach. Secondly, after the turn of the tide, bottom fishing from Carreg yr Ymbil out to the Gimblet Shoals, in summer for ray, flatfish, dogfish and small pollack as well as the occasional roaming tope, autumn monkfish, and in winter for whiting and codling. 2–4 ozs will keep bottom. Take care to avoid chains of lobster pots. A bass troll along the Abererch shore to Penychain should be followed by some bottom fishing at anchor in 20 ft, ¼ mile off the point. Mackerel shoals dodge in and out from mid-July to provide bait. More and more fishermen are deep freezing summer surpluses for winter fishing bait supplies.

Bait supply

Mackerel are not difficult to obtain from July to early September, but other bait is at a premium. Gather no more than is necessary; a medium capacity cool box will help it last longer.

Lug. Abersoch's small river estuary has lug patches. The sands below Abersoch golf course hold good lug, high up the beach. Pwllheli harbour's lug is small and sparse on the north side of the harbour entrance channel. A little further up the harbour, on the east side near a car park, there are a few more, but disappointing.

Razor fish. Found on low springs at Abersoch's golf course beach. Table salt, a razor fish spear or just plain trenching with a fork is needed to get them.

Crab. Singularly lacking. A few remain in the rocks at the south entrance to Pwllheli harbour and in the weed along the north side of the harbour entrance channel.

Small fish. There are great numbers of blennies and other small fish under weedy rocks between Penychain head and Criccieth.

Tackle shops

Abersoch. *Brian Jones, Gift & Fishing Tackle Shop, The Harbour.* Fishing trips on *Silver Queen* arranged. *Tel.* (075881) 2646.

Mr. Lewthwaite, Trade Winds, Abersoch. Tel. (075881) 2530. Tackle supply; fresh lug, mackerel, shellfish, mussels, preserved baits, flies; WWA river licences.

Criccieth. *R. T. Pritchard & Son, Sheffield House, High Street, Tel.* (076671) 2116. Tackle supply and preserved bait. WWA river licences; permits for local waters.

Morgan's Newsagents, 1 High Street, Criccieth. Tel. (076671) 2557. Tackle supply, etc., preserved bait, maggots and local flies; advice on where to fish; WWA licences and local permits sold.

Pwllheli. *D. & E. Hughes, 24 Penlan Street. Tel.* (0758) 3291. Tackle supply and repair, frozen baits, maggots, worms and flies. Advice on where to fish. WWA river licences sold. Permits sold for Pwllheli & District Angling Association waters.

C. W. Martin, Sports Dealers, The Maes. Tel. (0758) 2414 or 2762. Tackle supply and repair. Lug, rag, fresh fish, frozen baits, maggots, worms, flies. Advice on where to fish. WWA river licences sold. Permits for local stretches. Fishing trips bookable.

Boat hire, trips or charter

Abersoch. *Mr. Brian Jones, Abersoch Angling Services, Cemlyn, Abersoch. Tel.* (075 881) 2646. *Silver Queen,* 31 ft, toilet, echo sounder, ship-to-shore radio. Daily summer and part of winter. Pick up Abersoch harbour. Bait provided. Tackle hire.

A. H. Lewthwaite, Trade Winds, Boat Hire, The Harbour, Abersoch. Tel. (075881) 2530. *Trade Winds* and *Blue Dolphin.* 20–25 ft. Elsan toilets. Available 1 May to end of October. Trips and fishing arranged. Bait provided. Tackle extra.

H. F. and M. A. Grimes, Pleasure Craft Hire, The Boat House, Warren Beach, Abersoch. Tel. (075881) 2988. Pleasure craft hire boats *Belamda* 23 ft,

continued on next page

ferrograph. Available May – October from beach opposite Warren Camp, Abersoch for tope and mackerel fishing, trips or full boat charter. Bait provided when possible, tackle for hire. Also 10 ft 6 in self-drive boats with 2½ hp outboards available for hourly hire.
Pwllheli. *Mr. R. Roberts, Argraig, Penrallt, Deneio. Tel.* (0758) 2916. *Isabella*, 30 ft. with toilets, ferrograph, available for hire or charter. 1st April to 30th October, picking up Lifeboat House Pwllheli Harbour. Bait provided. Tackle for hire locally by prior arrangement.

Boat launching slipways

Abersoch. *Yacht Club slipway near pier. Club members only.*
Abersoch. Council slipway (small fee) reached off Lon Golff.
Hooks Marine, Abersoch. Storage, launching and tractor hauling services.
Abersoch Land and Sea Ltd, Abersoch. Tel. (075881) 2957. Boat sales, Boat storage, launching and tractor hauling. Fishing Tackle for sale.
Criccieth. Public slipway to foreshore near Pier.
Llanbedrog. Dinghies can be launched over the beach.
Pwllheli. Public slipway alongside R. W. Vowell's boatyard. Free use. Also slipways and launching facilities at
1. *Marine Boat Club, Marinaland, Outer Harbour. Tel.* (0785) 2271.
2. *Wm. Partington Marine Ltd, The Harbour. Tel.* (0785) 2808. Private slipway, small charge to public.
3. *Pwllheli Sailing Club.* Slipway to inner harbour and another facing sea. *Tel.* (0785) 2219.
4. *R. W. Vowell, Yacht Services, The Harbour. Tel.* (0785) 2251. One public slipway, one private slipway.

Fishing advice

Pwllheli and District Angling Association, Hon. Sec., Mr. G. W. Pritchard, Edwyfed, 30 *Lon Ceredigion, Pwllheli. Tel.* (0785) 3531. *Criccieth, Llanystumdwy and District Angling Association, Hon. Sec., Mr. G. Hamilton, Morawel, Llanystumdwy, Criccieth, Gwynedd. Tel. Criccieth* 2251.

Useful telephone numbers

In emergency
Dial 999 *and ask for Coastguard.*

At other times
RNLI Abersoch. *Inshore lifeboat.*
RNLI Pwllheli. *Sea-going lifeboat and inshore rescue craft. Tel.* (0785) 2229 *coxwain:* 2314 *mechanic:* 2200 *lifeboat.*
Coastguard. *Nefyn* (075882) 204. (*Not constantly manned*) **Trinity House.** *Lighthouse, St. Tudwal's Island West. Radio contact.*
Weather forecasts. *Meteorological Office, RAF Station, Valley, Isle of Anglesey. Tel.* (0407) 2288.

Black Rock Sands to Llwyngwril

Though extremely beautiful, this coastline has little that interferes with the enjoyment of the fisherman. Holidaymakers concentrate at established points – at Criccieth, at Black Rock Sands, for a mile along the vast Harlech Strand, again from Talybont to Fairbourne and a little at Llwyngwril. This leaves vast expanses almost untouched. Sandy, with shallow water almost throughout, you will have to master the twin bass-fishing techniques of gully fishing in estuaries and long distance casting into a rolling surf. There are plenty of fish; bait is the problem.

I. **Black Rock Sands.** An extension of Morfa Bychan, reached through Porthmadog, or Wern on A497. Cars fill the sands by day. Evening twilight brings anglers to fish with Porthmadog lug, or clams, for bass homing in on Traeth Bach estuary. Two hours before low water to well up the tide, early and late in the year, is advocated.

II. **Morfa Bychan.** The western side of the channel leading into Traeth Bach estuary comes in close to the land between Morfa Bychan and Borth-y-gest. Fish the tide in for bass, with crab or lug, till the water spills over the sand flats. Then switch to a wandering tackle for plaice, flounder and dabs. A white plastic baited spoon is also useful here.

III. **Llanfihangel y Traethau.** The village is at the northern end of B4573, near Talsarnau. Drive through the village to the beach. Fish the gullies up from as low as possible with large baits of crab, clam (found here) razor fish or lug, for good bass. Always – always – stay on the south bank of the main stream and its large tributaries or be certain of a line of retreat. A very small dinghy or inflatable anchored near the stream would be reassuring. Mullet abound – as well as bass and flounders – but a technique to catch them in these conditions has to be invented!

IV. **Harlech Sands.** From the entrance to the beach, alongside Royal St. David's golf course, to Harlech Point and back is a round trip of 6 miles. Short of taking an old bike, few make the effort. Yet from the top of the beach the main entrance to Traeth Bach estuary can easily be fished. Every bass, flatfish and tope that decides to explore this wilderness of sand gullies – and many do – must get a whiff of your bait.

V. **Mochras or Shell Island.** Turn west in Llanbedr, 2½ miles south of Harlech, crossing the 'causeway' in a lagoon to the promontory 'island' south of the Artro's estuary. Private property, it is a popular camp site in summer. Owner: George G. Workman, Shell Island, Llanbedr, Meirionnydd. Tel. 217. The estuary can also be fished from the northern spit at Llandanwg. Bass, flounder and mullet invade the lagoon on the rising tide,. The outer beach, though stony, can also be fished conventionally in the heavy surf which builds up with a westerly or south westerly blow.

VI. **Talybont.** From Mochras Point to Barmouth Bridge is 8 miles of uninterrupted, featureless, straight sand storm-beach. Extensive caravan sites border it, but it's virtually unfished when fish are really there, mainly because appropriate baits are difficult to find. But if armed with salted-down or frozen razor fish, squid, a few crabs out of the deep freeze and what lug there is about in late spring or autumn, you will be well satisfied with your catch of bass and flatfish. Let Afon Ysgethin at Talybont be your starting place.

VII and VIII. **Barmouth.** Though busy, Barmouth has two spots that can be fished even in high summer. If you can get over to Ynys y Brawd, just 100 yards offshore, fish for bass on the extreme western point of the island. It's best when the tide is turning and rising. If this is impractical at the time, go to mark VIII, Barmouth railway bridge, which straddles Mawddach estuary. It is open to fishermen for a small fee. Keep to the Barmouth end, ledgering in the fast run. A free-lined live sand eel would be ideal, but few know the secret of where to find such a bass delicacy hereabouts. Spinning is practised in the first 1½ hours of a tide into a holding pool from the low water spit just west of the bridge. As you're more likely to get sea trout here, buy a licence first to make your catch legal. Otherwise, concentrate on the big and plentiful mullet which frequent the quay.

IX. **Fairbourne.** A car can reach almost to Penrhyn Point facing Barmouth. Where you choose to fish on this shallow, sandy 1½ miles stretch depends on weather, tide and time. In a good spring or autumn surf, fish the open beach. A quiet, warm and still summer evening, with the tide beginning to trickle up the gullies, would indicate a position towards Penrhyn Point to catch the bass and flatfish shoals coming into the Mawddach estuary.

X. **Llwyngwril.** A much rockier coast with stones and weed being uncovered at low tide. Several water gullies tumble precipitously to the beach under the main road, A493, from towering 800 ft high hills. The hardy try their luck in these conditions and are often rewarded with good bass, which are soft on peeler crab or a big live blennie. Other baits just vanish under the onslaught of crabs and small fry.

continued on page 45

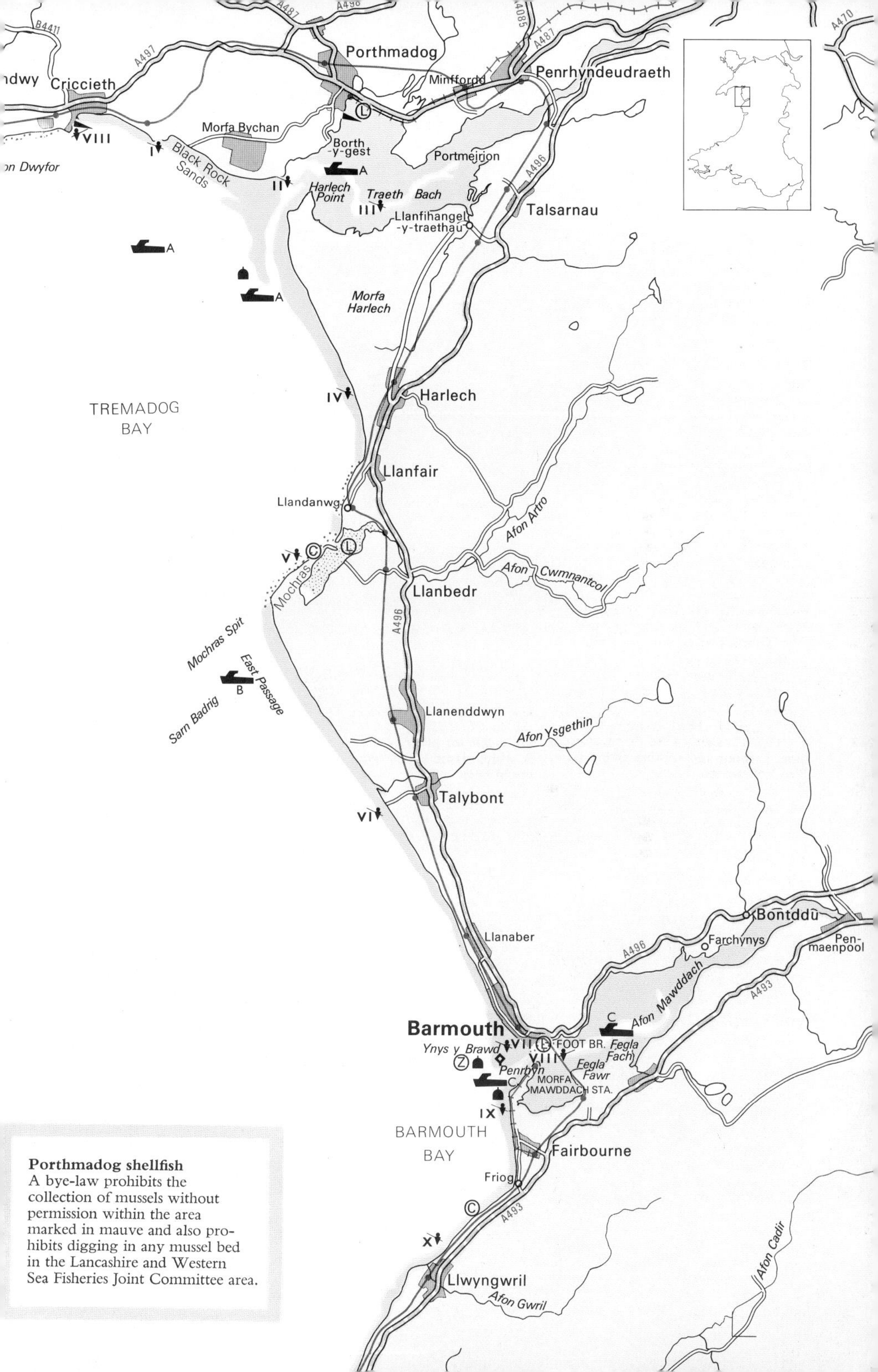

Porthmadog shellfish
A bye-law prohibits the collection of mussels without permission within the area marked in mauve and also prohibits digging in any mussel bed in the Lancashire and Western Sea Fisheries Joint Committee area.

oat fishing

orthmadog and Barmouth are both ble to cater for any size of angling oat, from dinghy to 35 footer or nore. Tiny Llanbedr Creek is deally placed to explore the area's nost interesting feature, the range 14 miles long Sarn Badrig – t. Patrick's Causeway. Heavy hoals of mackerel bring blue shark, orbeagle and tope. Yet, though orth Cardigan Bay is heavily ished commercially, the larger porting specimens are comparatively untouched.

. **Criccieth and Porthmadog.** A onstant 50 ft of water over a wilderess of mud, Tremadog Bay scarcely eems exciting to contemplate. Yet, vith Traeth Bach estuary near, conditions are more varied that they seem t first sight. Off Criccieth, cover as nuch ground as you can on a slow drift, shing the bottom in 8 fathoms or nore. Flatfish, including plump plaice, ogfish, occasional rays, skate and tope re all taken. Vary the tactics; patrol the hore and the bar before entering the stuary. Troll with rubber eels for bass r, much slower, and along with the ide, with baited spoon, to let the ounder shoals catch up with you. Stake ut a claim in a remote gulley deep in he estuary and fish it for a couple f hours on the flooding tide, changing our tackle with the conditions. Keep verything light and fine and when edgering, cast well away from you, or its exceedingly clear and shallow.

. **Sarn Badrig.** This phenomenon f marine geography runs from Aochras, or Shell Island, south west or 14 miles into Cardigan Bay, breaking surface almost along its length on ow tides. Too far from Barmouth or Criccieth for amateur fishing, it can owever be reached from the Artro stuary and Mochras. The area harbours eef-loving specimens and attracts their redators. Strangely enough the land nd of the causeway falls into 30 ft of vater. Here, in the east passage, and in s immediate vicinity, is the point to tart drift bottom fishing for tope and urnard, bass trolling and spinning prays for pollack along the trailing dge of the reef. Mid-reef, and south thereof, there is bottom fishing for red gurnard, monk and skate, plaice and dabs. The south west tip of the Sarn attracts tope, and porbeagle shark have been landed recently.

C. **Barmouth Bay and Mawddach Estuary.** The area is of a similar configuration to the Traeth Bach estuary and its approaches in shape, depth and conditions. Barmouth is home port of a small fleet of fishing vessels, professional and sporting. A broad table-land of sand in 4–5 fathoms extends for at least 6 miles due west from Barmouth Outer black buoy and it is a well-fished area, being comparatively safe in settled weather. It gives skate, ray and, in the odd patch of rough, pollack; mackerel bait is plentiful. A variation of tactics as at mark A above gives the best returns for smaller vessels restricted to fine weather fishing 5 miles, at the most, from the shore. A 5 knot restriction applies within the harbour limits.

The castle of Harlech seen across the ay from Mochras – or Shell Island a peninsula popular with camping nglers. Northwards lie the Harlech Sands extending to the mouth of Traeth Bach estuary while to the South nile after glorious mile of sand beach uns away to the Mawddach Estuary.

Bait supply

This is a difficult coast for bait. A cool box – at least – filled every three days on bait forages to the Isle of Anglesey will repay the effort.

Lug. On Porthmadog esturial sands beyond the Glaslyn river – but do not dig in mussel beds – and at Mochras lagoon near Llanbedr. There are scarcely any at Barmouth or in the Mawddach estuary.

Clams. Along damp declivities in the sand near Llanfihangel y Traethau. These are large cockle-type shellfish with a siphon of creamy white flesh, something like razorfish in substance. Neat holes, the size of a new half penny, betray their hiding places, 1½ spits down.

Crab. A few, with blennies, in rocky patches at Mochras and Llwyngwril.

Tackle shops

Barmouth. *All Sports & Hobbies, Beach Road. Tel.* (0341) 280240. Advice on where to fish; *Angling Times* report station.

Dolgellau. '*Celfi Diddan*', *Eldon Square, Dolgellau, Gwynedd. Tel. Dolgellau* (0341) 388. *Angling Times* report station.

Harlech. *S. & C. Wilby, Newsagents, Rosslyn House, Harlech. Tel. Harlech* (076673) 460. Tackle supply, flies, advice on where to fish.

Porthmadog. *J. & R. T. Davies, Angling Centre,* 11/13 *High Street. Tel.* (0766) 2464. Tackle supply and repair; fresh lug, rag and fish when available, also maggots, worms and flies; advice on where to fish; *Angling Times* report station.

Porthmadog. *Pugh's Tackle Shop,* 94 *High Street. Tel.* (0766) 2392. Tackle supply and permits for local rivers.

Boat hire, trips or charter

Barmouth. *Mrs. J. M. Irvine,* 4 *Aelfor Terrace, King Edward Street, Barmouth. Tel.* (0341) 280248. *Viking* 47½ ft, toilets, Fishfinder, radio. Also 32 ft. GRP twin screw angling vessel. Daily March to October. Pick-up opposite Yacht Club, Barmouth Quay. Trips and charter. Bait when available. Tackle free.

Porthmadog. *E. Roberts,* 33 *Chapel Street.* Various craft, 14 ft, 10 ft and 9 ft, for hire at hour, day and weekly rates. Book at above address or at 'Minafon', Borth-y-Gest.

Boat launching slipways

Barmouth. Public slipway at harbour; launching possible 2½ hours each side of high water only. Launching fee. Contact *Mr. E. D. Jones, Harbour Master. Tel.* (0341) 280671.

Llanbedr. (*Shell Island*). *Pensarn Sailing Club. Private Slipway.*

Porthmadog. Slipway for public use operated by *Cyngor Dosbarth Dwyfor* (*Dwyfor District Council*). *Tel.* (0758) 3131.
For launching and landing fee contact Harbour Master at Porthmadog.

Enterprise Sailing Limited Dealing with coastal cruising courses, delivery service, yacht charters.

N. Wales Yachting Company. Yacht Brokerage.

Porthmadog Power Boat Company. Sales and Marine Engineers Service.

E. & M. Mills Limited. Yacht design and construction. Full supporting boatyard facilities.

Talybont. Launching across beach only.

Fishing advice

Talsarnau & District Angling Association, Hon. Sec., Mr. M. Owen, Hafod Wen, Penrhyndeudraeth, Merioneth.
Artro Angling Association, Mr. E. Hoyle, Plas-y-Bryn, Llanbedr.

Useful telephone numbers

In emergency
Dial 999 and ask for Coastguard.

At other times:
RNLI lifeboat. *Barmouth. Tel. Coxwain: House* (0341) 280485 *or Quay* (0341) 280671. **Coastguard.** *Barmouth. Tel.* (0341) 500. **Weather forecasts.** *Local forecast available from Barmouth auxiliary Coastguard. Tel.* (0341) 500.

Tywyn to Aberystwyth

A varied coast with well established deep sea angling facilities which continue to develop. The shore down to and including Aberystwyth gives first class bass catches but south of the town the coast becomes inaccessible.

I. **Tywyn – Aber Dysynni.** The River Dysynni is renowned for brown and sea trout. Its esturial lagoon, 2 miles north of Tywyn, is reached by the Sandilands Road. Park by the river and walk along the bank under the rail bridge to the track leading to the river mouth which has been diverted to form a wide canal. The river's clear waters funnel out across the beach near Sarn-y-bwch, another causeway reef, which stabs 3 miles south west into Cardigan Bay, leaving a trail of isolated rocks near the shore. Bass sometimes shoal around these rocks, attracted by the estuary, to be picked off with spinner and float-fished crab on the rising tide. In autumn – mid-October – ledger what bait you can get for the bigger bass, keeping your casts straight down the wall of large slate slabs if you want to be free of snags.

II. **Tywyn Sands.** The time to fish is when a west wind clears the popular sands of holidaymakers. It brings the surf and bass in. ¼ mile below the promenade, large boulders on the sands protect a river's outfall from the dunes. Here a year or two ago an 11 lbs bass fell to mussel, but there are many more in the schoolies class. The last quarter of the rising tide should be the high point of your session, with mid-October being the peak period for quality fish.

III. **Aberdovey Golf Course.** The golf course mark – a walk through the dunes – takes one away from the crowded estuary. Fish it for bass when the surf has a bit of life. Otherwise fish at mark IV.

IV. **Aberdovey: channel and quay.** Low water rising in the channel and high water on the quay gives a handy succession of marks that can be fished only in spring, autumn and at night; at other times the water is hammered by competing water sports. Bass in the 4 to 6 lbs range are met with. Floated soft crab conserves rare local supplies. Second best is spinning – tobies and red gills – but they take a fair number of fish, more than at most places. Flatfish are numerous; withdraw up the estuary a little further for them.

V. **Ynyslas Dunes.** The Dovey river's south bank is a noted flatfish mark. Locals just toss into deeper water along the narrowest part of the channel, facing Aberdovey or into the Afon Leri outfall with mackerel strip or lugworm for good flounder – though crabs abound. The mud is very soft in parts and the tide strong so exercise extreme caution. Low water to high water fishing on the northern end of the outer shore is often more productive and bass in the 6 to 8 lbs range have been reported, though uncommon. Varying baits is usually out of the question here; you fish with what you can get.

VI. **Borth beach and Craig yr Wylfa.** Thoroughly netted and also well scoured by skin divers, but still a classic storm-beach, occasionally fishing well late in summer after a south westerly or north westerly moderate breeze. There are occasional ray in summer and monkfish up to 45 lbs come very close in. South from Borth the coast is rocky and sometimes inaccessible. Near the village, interesting water can be reached in the rock fall near the base of the cliffs. Flounders, dabs and even small turbot, as well as bass, are caught.

VII. **Sarn Wallog.** Being the shoreward end of Sarn Gynfelyn, this wall of boulders dries for 300 yards on springs. It can be approached by a ¾ mile rough footpath from B4572, 2 miles south of Borth, or by the cliffs from Clarach, and offers mackerel spinning, the occasional small pollack and gurnard and – let it be said – dogfish and eels. Local anglers fear the bass have deserted this mark because of overfishing.

VIII. **Aberystwyth.** Alternating belts of sand bottoms and rocky reefs, as well as the muddy harbour and river mouths, give an interesting choice of conditions at all states of the tide. From rocks in summer soft crab ledgered or float-fished attracts occasional large specimens. Best spots are channels or breakwater at Constitution Hill end, on flood −4 to −1 before high in evening light, also on the Castle Rocks and breakwater. The promenade opposite Cor-y-Castell shelter onto rocky ground – 2 to +2 high water, has also been productive. Clear ground fishing is available from Constitution Hill rocks south side, at low water when dogfish and dabs will be contacted – whiting in winter. The only other clear ground is found opposite the north end of the promenade and midway between Castle Point and the Harbour. Spinning is an evening activity on summer high tides when mackerel, small pollack and bass are taken. The harbour is mainly mud and shingle where mullet feed. Bread, harbour rag, cockles – even mackerel strips – might take this very elusive but strong fighter. The wooden jetty on the harbour mouth's north side is now closed but was a good flounder mark, casting 90° seaward more than 40 yards. The stone jetty on south side of the harbour is a very much fished mark in summer with high water spinning and float fishing on the seaward side for pollack up to 3 lbs on artificial sandeel and prawn respectively. Very occasional bass are taken on spinners here, though often of good size. Bottom fishing with a cast of 70 yards to clear boulders will give a variety of fish, though the biggest bass are caught right up against the wall, the classical spot when fishing from quays, walls and piers. In summer there are catches of dabs, dogs, pouting, poor cod, pollack with occasional gurnard, ray, conger and bass, and in winter dabs, dogs, pouting, poor cod, whiting. Care is needed when a heavy swell is running as it creeps up the side of the jetty with considerable force. The beach sweeping south from the stone jetty, known as Tanybwlch beach, is a fair bet for occasional large bass in summer, both ledgering and spinning, as well as dogs, flounder, dabs, pollack and good mackerel spinning on summer evenings with dogs, flounders, dabs and whiting in winter. It is a reasonably snag-free area but keep away from northern and southern ends. The rocks south from Tanybwlch are very difficult to fish but have good potential as bass and pollack areas as there is a great deal of food here. Rocks are low lying with no really clear areas to cast a bait onto, except about 1 mile south of the Morfa Bychan Caravan Camp where sandy patches between boulders offer a fair chance of a bass.

Boat fishing

Cardigan Bay has first class tope, ray and shark grounds in 20 fathoms, knowledgeably explored by the Endeavour Deep Sea Group's three Aberystwyth-based 36 ft long deep sea boats. Even the 7 fathoms table-land closer inshore, frequented by more modest boats, has its share of fish and there's variety – including black bream – on Cynfelyn Patches.

A. **Tywyn – Sarn-y-bwch.** Less obvious than the other causeways, Sarn-y-bwch extends over 3½ miles from Tonfannau near Tywyn. Its head shows as a dangerous swirl of water, its feet being planted firmly in four fathoms. Bass shoal at the shore end. In deeper water every species of rock-loving fish this coast possesses finds a home, mainly pollack and bream, wrasse, small conger, whiting and pouting. Towards Sarn-y-bwch black buoy and just north of the Sarn and ¾ to 1 mile out from the mainland, ray, tope, bull huss, monkfish and gurnard appear.

B. **Aberdovey: estuary and bar.** As it is similar in marine geography, fish and fishing, to the Traeth Bach estuary and Mawddach estuary, the comments under marks A and C in the previous section apply.

C & D. **Sarn Cynfelyn** – (known as the Causeway). In the first mile or so bass may be taken on artificial trolled sandeel as well as small pollack. From

.ere most of the way along the cause- vay to the Patches Buoy 7 miles out lack bream abound from June – Sept- mber, sizes getting larger further from hore. Immature specimens should be eturned to the water and a very low eel limit set to let them remain well stablished. To find the bream, anchor ptide from the boil (the tide rising to et over the causeway) and let the bait rot down onto the shallower ground. 'ollack, poor cod, dogfish, tub and red urnard are also found from 1 mile out n the causeway with a possible bass. About 3 miles out a 'Gap' appears in he causeway with patches of clean round which hold good size thorn- ack, huss, gurnard with possibly a ting ray, tope or monkfish in summer. 'rom the Cynfelyn Patches buoy for bout 3 or 4 miles in a general NW lirection deeper water and varied rounds hold a good variety of species. 'here are excellent rocky mounds that n summer produce good black bream, ollack up to 3 lbs, pouting, poor cod, logfish, huss, cuckoo wrasse and allan wrasse, large mackerel, tub and ed gurnard and occasional small ling, odling and conger. The softer ground etween the rough areas holds dabs, hornback, huss, tope, the three species of gurnard and dogfish. A good hornback area lies roughly ½–1 mile SW of the buoy with weever often in ttendance in summer. Anywhere from bout 10 miles on a general westerly lirection from Aberystwyth tope are easonably common June – early- September with porbeagle and some lue shark July – September.

E. **Aberystwyth – Cardigan Bay.** The Endeavour Deep Sea Angling Club boats hunt with great precision, n pairs or triplets May to October, 15–18 miles out on a direct 255° (true) ourse from Aberystwyth, along the 20 athoms line. They bring upper water fish towards the boat with rubby dubby, and bottom feeders, including all the dogfish and bull huss in creation, with a tempting trail of tasty morsels left to run free with the tide. Less well- equipped boats stay inshore, drifting along the 8 fathoms sandy table-land, down into 'The Gutter', marked 'Trawl- ing Grounds' on the chart, looking for slight depressions holding a wide range of species. In Cardigan Bay, thornback ray are predominant, running 12 to 14 lbs, but as high as 22 lbs. Tope are numerous but small, mainly males, of 25 to 30 lbs, though *Endeavour's* record is 63½ lbs. Porbeagle and blue shark are sometimes fished for in earnest, and they run to 130 lbs and 93 lbs respectively. Conger, ling and cod are comparatively rare at the depths normally fished in Cardigan Bay and are 'minnows': cod to 14 lbs, conger to 26 lbs and ling of 18 lbs. Turbot run small, *Endeavour's* 14½ lbs record has stood for some time now but monkfish, autumn visitors to the bay, run to a

continued on next page

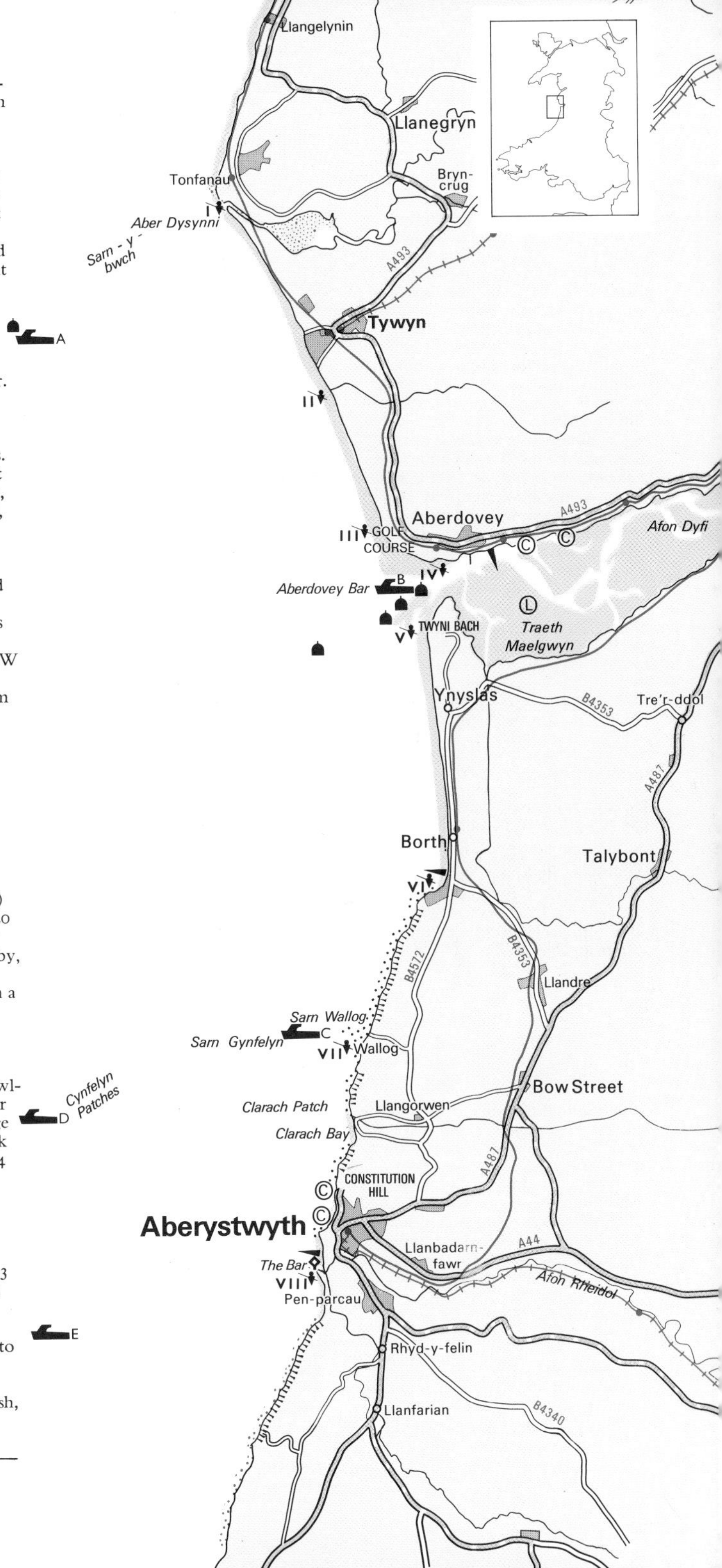

good 56 lbs. With the three gurnards, plump black bream and a Welsh Record John Dory, with the odd weever, there's always variety in the catch. Nearer Aberystwyth the ground holds dogfish, tub and grey gurnard, dabs, thornback and homelyn rays, greater weever and some huss. Some nice pollack up to 8 lbs can be taken over the rocks a matter of a couple of hundred yards from the shore at Aberystwyth, the rocks between the Pier and Castle are especially productive more particularly on calm summer evenings around dusk. Trolled artificial sandeel or float fished prawn both take pollack, with occasional coalfish and bass as variety. This type of fishing must only be undertaken with a very experienced skipper who knows the area well. Whiting are plentiful from September to January and get gradually thinner on the ground until by May few are left. However, the further one goes offshore the longer the whiting stay around and are of a much bigger average size than inshore. They seem to prefer areas of fairly clean ground and are much more difficult to find on the rough areas. They don't grow big by British standards, a fish over 2 lbs is a very good one off Aberystwyth.

Bait supply

Harbour ragworm. Plentiful in Aberystwyth harbour's mud.

Crab. In weedy rocks and walls for ½ mile along the estuary's Roman road at Aberdovey, from a small seafront public garden ¼ mile east of the pier and in reasonable quantity all the way south from Borth rocks to 5 miles south of Aberystwyth, except in short sandy and pebbly regions.

Lug. Dovey estuary's south beach at Ynyslas (sand carries a car for about 200 yards out) has many casts but lug are small and difficult to dig.

Prawns and shrimps. Catch in a drop net baited with mackerel lowered from a pier, rock or dinghy at anchor. Between May and September reef rockpools between Porth and Wallog, Clarach and Aberystwyth – north and south of the main promenade beach and especially south of Aberystwyth – hold quantities, and from Llanrhystud southwards. Have a handnet handy.

Razor fish. At very low springs very rare in sand between Tywyn and Aberdovey.

Whelks. Small dog whelks common on rocks are good bait for whiting and particularly wrasse, occasionally bass.

Tywyn. *Fish Shop, National Street. Tel.* 710937. Squid and mackerel for bait.

Tackle shops

Aberdovey. *W. D. Evans & Son, London House, Seaview Terrace. Tel.* (065472) 353. Sea bait and all tackle.

Aberystwyth. *J. E. Rosser, 3 Queen Street. Tel.* (0970) 7451. Tackle supply and repair; preserved lug, rag, sandeels and squid, large fly and lure selection; advice on where to fish; permits for Aberystwyth and Llanilar waters. WWA river licences sold; assistance given for booking fishing trips and advice given on freshwater fishing.

Canolfan Chwaraeon (Sports Centre), North Parade. Tel. 617565. Tackle supply, preserved bait, permits for local rivers and WWA river licences sold.

Tywyn. *Mr. John J. Roberts, Trefellyn, High Street. Tel.* (0654) 710697. Advice on where to fish; WWA river licences; permits for rivers and lakes sold; fishing trips bookable.

F. R. Porter, The Sports' Shop, 6 College Green. Tel. (0654) 710772. Tackle supply and repair; frozen baits, maggots, worms and flies; advice on where to fish. WWA river licences sold; permits for Dysynni river; fishing trips bookable; *Angling Times* report station.

Boat hire, trips or charter

Aberdovey. *Mr. C. W. Bartlett, The Garth, Tywyn. Tel. Tywyn* (0654) 710 869. MFV. *Ceffyl Mor*, 26 ft, toilet, echo sounder, 10 rods. All year. Pick up Aberdovey Pier. Bait provided. Tackle hire. Charter or trips by arrangement.

Aberdovey. *Trefeddian Hotel. Tel.* (065472) 213. Sea angling trips arranged locally for guests at the hotel, on request.

Aberdovey. *Panteinion Hall Guesthouse, Fairbourne, Meirionnydd. Tel. Fairbourne* 475. 40 ft. fishing cruiser *Memette*, from Aberdovey. Tel. Tywyn 710898 or Fairbourne 475 for arrangements.

Aberystwyth. *Endeavour Deep Sea Centre, Schooners Landing, St. David's Wharf, Pen yr Anchor. Tel.* (0970) 612818. Long range load line exempt fleet. Certified to 20 miles. Class VIIIA Survival equipment. Subscriptions for personal members and visitors (nominal). Day boat, individual rates, day charter for clubs and groups. Available all year. *Endeavour I, Endeavour II*, former with echo sounder, and *Endeavour III*. Each 36 ft. 11½ tons fully equipped. Concessionary rates (33⅓% reduction) on Dinas and Nant-y-moch trout lakes 12 miles from Aberystwyth, for Endeavour Club personal members.

Aberystwyth. *'Ofanto', Skipper Lee Haigh. Licenced for 12 passengers inshore. Tel. Aberystwyth* (0790) 617782. Bed and breakfast accommodation available ashore.

Boat launching slipways

Aberdovey. Near Dovey Hotel. Charge in and out plus storage.

Aberystwyth. North side of harbour on quay near mouth. Council owned. Free use. Takes dinghies only, up to 18 ft. long. New slipway of loose gravel between inner basin and main harbour. Large boats can be launched 2–3 hours each side of high water. Apply to Harbourmaster. Tel. (0970) 612078.

Borth. None. Beach launching.

Clarach. None. Beach launching.

Tywyn. Promenade. Free use to public.

Fishing advice

Aberystwyth Sea Angling and Yacht Club, Angling Section, Club House, The Harbour, Aberystwyth. Visiting membership arranged; enquiries to *Mr. M. James, 52 Maesceinau, Waun Fawr, Aberystwyth.*

Useful telephone numbers

In emergency
Dial 999 *and ask for Coastguard.*

At other times:
RNLI Lifeboat. *Aberdovey. Tel.* (065472) 464; *Aberystwyth. Tel.* (0970) 2456. **Coastguard.** *Aberdovey. Tel.* 327. *New Quay. Tel.* (054552) 212. (*Not constantly manned*). **Outward Bound Sea School.** *Aberdovey. Tel. Aberdovey* 464. **Weather forecasts.** *Aberporth Royal Aircraft Establishment, Meteorological Station. Tel.* (0239) 810117

Llanrhystud to Ceibwr

A coast which is difficult to approach has its good points; day fishing in the summer, a most pleasant occupation, can be practised by those energetic enough to make the trek. This section of Cardigan Bay has few conventional bass sand beaches. Its northern half is shallow and stony, costly on tackle and temper. The southern half is rockbound almost the whole way. Cardigan estuary adds variety to the conditions and, with New Quay, shares a good name as a profitable fishing holiday centre.

I. **Llanrhystud;** II. **Llansantffraid (Llanon).** Both beaches are essentially the same; a small river or stream cuts across a shallow beach of stones and weed, interspersed with small patches of sand, increasing in size recently at Llanrhystud. Apart from the obvious starting points of the river outfalls, both marks, and the miles of similar featureless beaches that extend south of them, are difficult to fish. With wrong end tackle, snagging is frequent and a surf makes it doubly difficult. If you

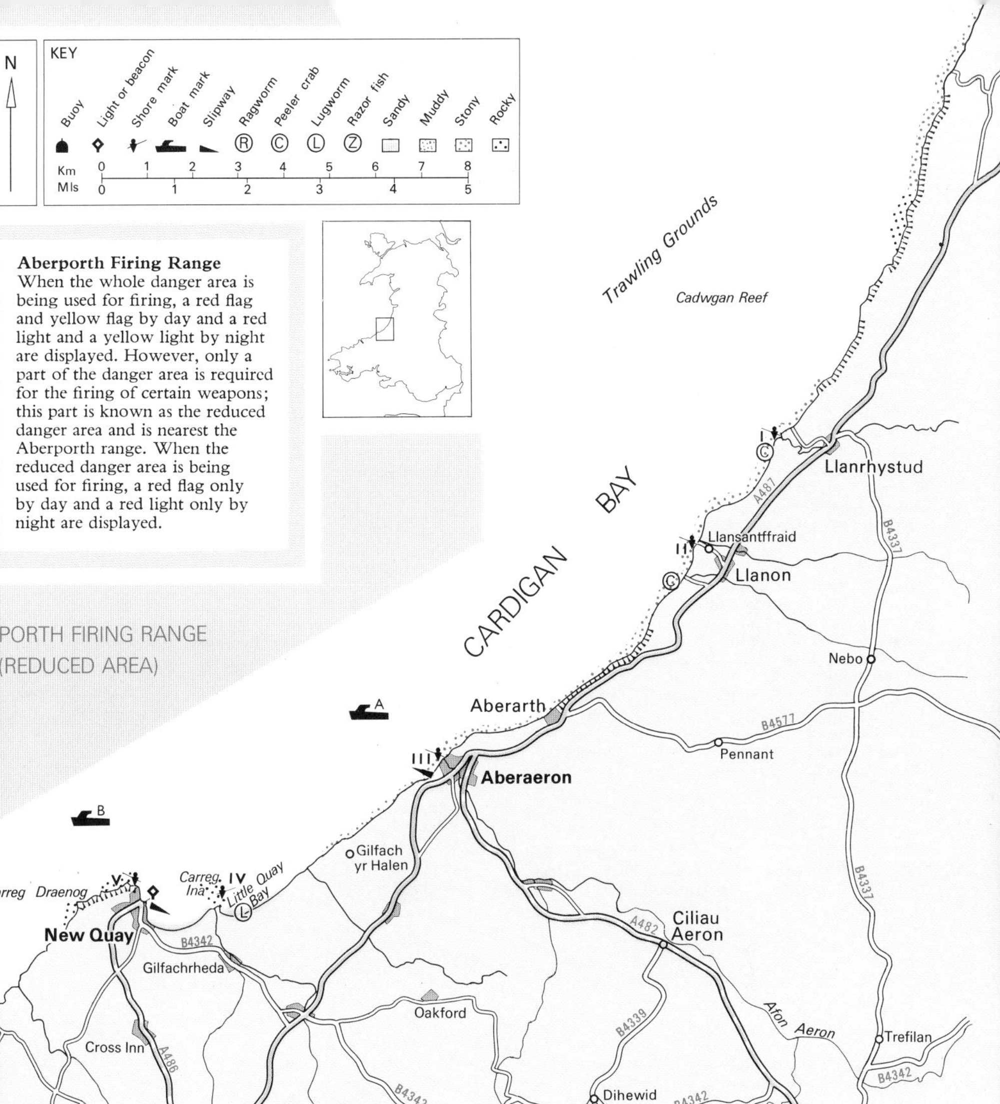

have to use a heavy beach caster, go for 25 lbs main lines with 2½ ft of 20 lbs line securing the 4 ozs lead and the hook on a short 15 lbs trace. This will give a useful 60 yards cast and the ability to pull out of most weed and stone situations safely. Keep your rod high and wind in like fury when rebaiting. Best of all use a light bass rod. A streamlined 2 ozs weight with 15 lbs line is more than adequate for it and rarely snags up. The reward for perseverance can be a good bass.

III. **Aberaeron.** Differs from marks II and III only in that it has a small 'promenade' structure, a harbour mouth ending in stone piers and a groyne-like structure which funnels vessels into the harbour. Fishing, limited in space, is only possible in and from the harbour wall from half tide up. Southwards to Gilfach yr Halen it's all rough and hard to reach with no outstanding features to concentrate fish or attention.

IV. **Llanina (Cei Bach or Little Quay).** A promontory thrusts into the bay as a rocky finger, ending in Carreg Ina. Stream fed, it is a noted bass spot on both sides. Approach the point by a 200 yards walk from Cei Bach car park. Lug, on the spot, is the staple bait, with local crab being the real killer.

V. **New Quay headland.** An arbitrary location for several good rocky platforms extending south west from the headland approached by the cliff path from New Quay. Float fishing and spinning in the vicinity of Carreg Ddraenog sometimes known as Bird's Rock, for mackerel and pollack – very close in for wrasse – alternates with brave casting into rough ground for the odd bass (very occasionally) and dogfish. Weevers abound, so be careful. The town's harbour and quay is much too busy at all times for serious summer fishing by day.

VI. **Llangrannog – Ynys Lochtyn (Pen y Badell).** Skin-divers work this coast of clear waters and convenient

continued on next page

rocky shores, like Ynys Lochtyn's eastern face. Large spider crabs abound. A National Trust cliff path north from crowded Llangrannog beach – take the steps on the beach's north end – reaches the headland in 15 strenuous minutes. On the headland, are rock platforms convenient for casting but which can be exceedingly dangerous. The eastern side has rough ground with good wrasse, conger, bass, mackerel, rockling, pollack and huss. The northern point has rough patches up to 50 yards out, then sand; dogs, the three gurnard species, huss, conger, pollack, bass, dabs, pouting, poor cod, thornback and homelyn ray, conger, mackerel, rockling and whiting, nearly all on fish bait except wrasse which go for crab, lug or whelk. Western ledges have clean ground with dabs, whiting, dogs, bass and mackerel. Float fishing will avoid the spider crabs and catch all but the very bottom feeders.

VII. **Traeth Penbryn and Tresaith.** Two extensive sandy beaches linked by rocky outcrops, two miles east of Aberporth. Very similar to the bays of Lleyn's north coast (see Porth Dinllaen to Porth Neigwl section), they are fished the same way. Bass are taken in spring and autumn near the rocky outcrops on each side of the bays. Start an hour before low water and fish the tide up. Evening is best, for every bay has a generous share of seclusion-seeking holidaymakers. A larger fish bait will take tope, small rays and dogfish.

VIII. **Cardigan – Traeth y Mwnt.** Immensely popular, though constricted, the sandy bay has a large car park on grass near a conspicuous church. Forego the beach. Fish the rocks on the right hand headland except when a heavy swell makes it a very dangerous place to be. Mackerel shoal within spinning range and pollack of about $1\frac{1}{2}$ to $2\frac{1}{2}$ lbs will take a lure of feathers meant for the mackerel. For the best evening sport, wind solder wire on to a single white down-feathered No. 1 hook and cover the wire with silver cigarette paper or silver milk bottle top. It casts remarkably well alone on a very light rod with 6 lbs or lighter line.

IX. **Cardigan – Gwbert and Poppit Sands.** Though parking is limited at Gwbert, there are excellent marks in the vicinity. Cardigan Island, reached by cliff path from near the Cliff Hotel – itself a convenient and comfortable base for fishing holidays – leads one mile along low cliffs to the rocky shore opposite the island, 250 yards offshore. The intervening channel spins well for mackerel and pollack. The Teifi river spills into the sea near the Cliff Hotel. A convenient rock position here chosen at low tide gives first class spinning as the tide floods in, with bass often in the 5 lbs or more class. A red gill or silver toby is best. A large blue or green Mepps will take sea trout at this spot. Poppit Sands, south of the river mouth, is almost a holding ground for bass and mullet waiting to ascend the river as far as the salt water lagoon above Cardigan Bridge, past the convenient marks along the walk near the town bridge. A bass well over the British record 18 lbs 2 ozs was taken in the saltwater lagoon but unfortunately never verified and accepted. The last twists of the river, winding over lug beds just inside the river mouth and the final estuary formed when the tide goes out over Poppit Sands all produce prime bass on a lure or with razor fish, lug or rag, fished on the bottom, and flatfish, mainly flounders. Take out a River Division licence and you can vary an evening's bass fishing with spinning for sea trout.

X. **Moylgrove – Ceibwr Bay.** 3 miles west of Cardigan Bridge, Moylgrove is almost a mile from the quiet cove of Ceibwr, a rock enclosed bay where mackerel and small pollack abound at full tide.

Boat fishing

Though slight variations, well known to the regular boats, occur in the pattern of distribution of Cardigan Bay fish, for all practical purposes the general remarks under the Aberystwyth section apply also to this area as far south as Cardigan Island, particularly along the 10 fathom mark, roughly one mile out. An echo sounder is essential to pick particular features out of the

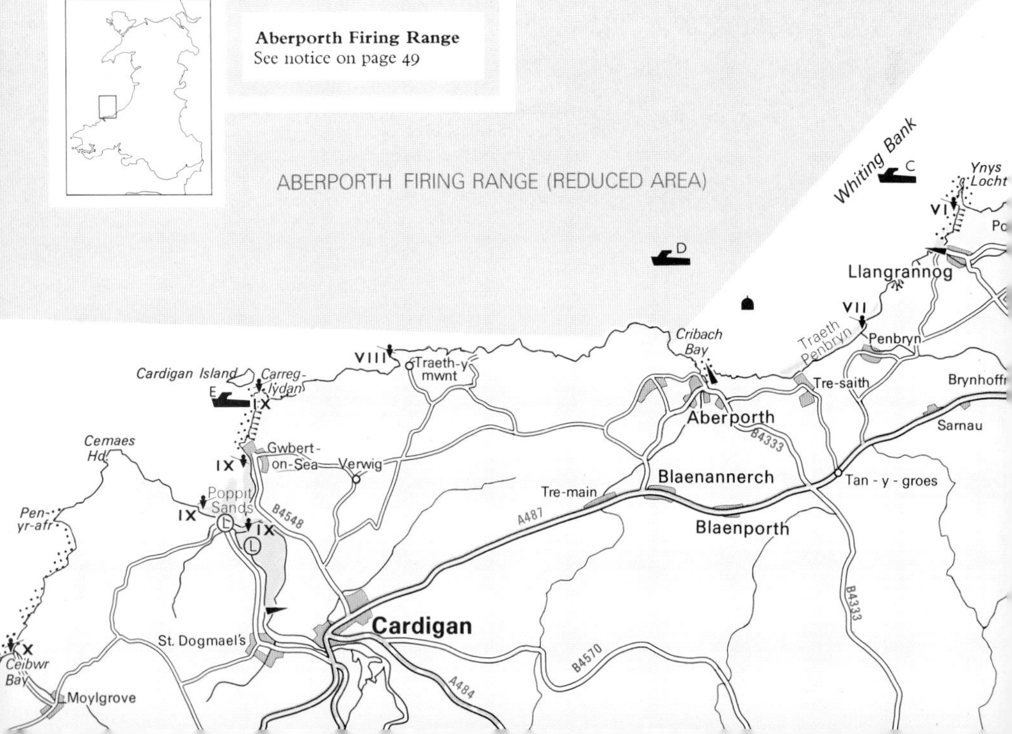

'angrannog beach and the cliffs towards ıys Lochtyn. The left margin cuts the ea where rock platforms are found.

eneral 10 to 14 fathoms table-land .at extends further out, deep into ıe Aberporth rocket sea-ranges. everal boatmen, particularly at ew Quay, and at Cardigan, ecialise in sea fishing trips. The termittent closure, over many ears, of the area affected by Aber- orth experimental rocket range ıs created what is almost a fish serve and good catches are hieved when firing is not taking ace. Scallops in great numbers e trawled in and about the fringes the rocket range but you would ıve to be very persuasive to get a allop fisher to part with one or o for you to commit the cardinal ı of using them as bait. They will course, take a bait themselves.

Aberaeron; B. **New Quay; Llangrannog – Whiting Bank;** . **Aberporth.** Each of these four liday centres has small boat launching cilities. Mackerel are plentiful, giving an advantage to the boat fisherman along a coast infamous for its paucity of home grown or imported worm and crab. For general bottom fishing see the remarks under Aberystwyth. The change in the general pattern concerns pollack; numerically stronger, they increase in size southwards.

E. **Cardigan Island and Estuary.** With so much quality salmon and sea trout fishing available to local people, sea fishing is a neglected art. Trolling and feathering for bass and pollack, for example, much practised in West of England estuaries, such as the Torridge and Taw from Appledore, and the Yealm from Newton Ferrers, finds few real adepts in Wales. The Teifi estuary's funnel-shaped approaches – with Cardigan Island nearby, but inaccessible to the public – provides the kind of conditions where a study of the method's finer points would pay off handsomely. Bass run big in this area; an over 18-pounder has been caught. A large red gill trolled – or whiffed – along a course set around the island, in along the rocky shore to the mouth of the estuary and out towards Cemaes Head, and back again, executed properly, will take bass. Another West Country favourite, a drift lined mackerel strip, allowed to run away on the in- or out-going tide near the bar, or in the island's strait, will give bass and pollack.

Bait supply

Adapt your methods to the use of blennies, shrimps and prawns, for there are plenty beneath stones from Llanrhystud to Gilfach yr Halen. Peeler crab are surprisingly rare.

Crab. Some in rocky ground at Llanina Point and in rocks south of Poppit Sands, Cardigan.

Lug. New Quay's Llanina beach (Cei Bach or Little Quay) and Cardigan's Teifi estuary south bank near Poppit have good lug.

Mackerel come in very close at Mwnt and Ceibwr Bay.

Tackle shops

Aberaeron. *John Evans, 1 Alban Square. Tel.* (054553) 356. Tackle supply, frozen baits, advice on where to fish. WWA licences sold. *Angling Times* weighing station.

Aberporth. *E. T. Davies & Co., Electric Shop. Tel.* (0239) 810278. Tackle, advice on where to fish, and preserved bait.

Cardigan. *M. & A. Williams, 10A Pendre. Tel.* (0239) 2038. Tackle supply and repair; preserved bait; advice on

continued on next page

where to fish; WWA licences sold; permits for lakes and rivers; *Angling Times* weighing station.

Boat hire, trips or charter

Cardigan. *Bowen Bros, Boat Hirers, Greenacre, Tel.* (0239) 3176 and (0239) 3368. Self drive motor and rowing boats, day or week. Mackerel fishing in *Wanderer* 27 ft boat. Embark: St. Dogmael's.

Gwbert. *Mr. Gareth Williams, The Dolphins, Gwbert. Tel. Cardigan* (0239) 2832. 26ft *Aquastar 'Celtic Mariner'* with toilet. Available summer. Embark: Gwbert. Mackerel trips per hour. Other trips by arrangement.

New Quay. Boat fishing trips arranged by *Mr. Clive Davies,* 19 *Hill Street, New Quay. 'Iolanthe'*, 32 ft, sleeping accommodation for 2, toilets, echo sounder.

Mr. D. Stones, c/o Beach Cafe, Dersanjo, 31 ft, echo sounder, toilets, fully equipped. Available all year. Bait provided. 2-hour fishing trips.

Boat launching slipway

Aberaeron. Harbour slipway. Free use by arrangement with harbourmaster.

Cardigan. *Glanteifion, St. Dogmael's.* Free access from road to river. Craft up to about 30 ft.

New Quay. Free use of slipway to harbour by arrangement with harbourmaster. Tel. (054 552) 275.

Aberporth; Ceibwr Bay (Moylgrove); Llangrannog; Llanrhystud; Tresaith. Access available to the beach for dinghies.

Fishing advice

Aberaeron Angling Association, Hon. Sec., Mr. H. Evans, 1 *Alban Square. New Quay & District Angling Club, Hon. Sec.,* Can be contacted through local tackle shops.

Useful telephone numbers

In emergency
Dial 999 and ask for Coastguard.

At other times:
RNLI inshore rescue lifeboat. *New Quay. Hon. Sec. Tel.* (054 552) 521 *or* 311. **Coastguard.** *New Quay. Tel.* 212. (*not constantly manned*). **Weather forecasts.** *Gloucester Meteorological Office. Tel.* (0452) 23122. *Aberporth Royal Aircraft Establishment, Meteorological Station. Tel.* (0239) 810117.

Newport to Strumble Head

The estuaries of the Nyfer and Gwaun rivers add a softer touch to a region of tough rocky peninsulas. Bass are not numerous, but to make up for it, pollack and wrasse increase in size and number. Inshore waters are sheltered at Newport Bay and Fishguard Bay with good bottom fishing mid summer to late autumn. Deep sea angling, centred on Fishguard, is as yet scarcely tapped, but has great potential.

I. **Newport – Trwyn y Bwa to Pen y Bal.** Pembrokeshire coast footpath – 167 miles long from the Teifi to Amroth – affords access to most parts of the west Dyfed peninsula. Park near Newport golf course and walk north along the signposted path. Pollack spinning, and float fishing close in to the rocks for wrasse, is possible at a number of points in fine weather. Mackerel strip on a long flowing trace will also catch bass who like the fast rips and rugged bottoms extending from the mainland just north of Pen y Bal towards the rock of Carreg y Drowy.

II. **Newport Sands.** Go north of the Nyfer (Nevern) river towards Newport golf course and walk down the sands towards the river. From an hour before low water to well up the tide, fish on the bottom with lug or rag – crab if you can get it – for bass who search the estuary. Chances are better when a north west breeze has given the water some life, in spring or autumn. On still evenings when the tide is getting towards full, dusk is setting fast and busy young holidaymakers have left, spin here, or on the town side of the river, for shoaling bass, varying your choice of lure between small and large tobies, Mepp's spoons and small metal Devon minnows. for this is a good sea trout river. You will need a River licence from the nearest tackle shop to take sea trout, even in the estuary or sea.

III. **Fishguard Lower Town.** 'Under Milk Wood' village of the screen version of Dylan Thomas's famous play, the little harbour of bobbing boats is the yachting and fishing centre of the locality. There is little daytime fishing in and about the tidal harbour wall because of landward and seaward boat activity; as Dylan Thomas puts it – 'herring gulls heckling down to the harbour where the fishermen spit and prop the morning up'. Walk beyond the harbour to the fort on Castle Point, for 17 to 20 ft of water, rough ground in the gullied eastern side and an opportunity to fish the sandy interstices for the odd ray and conger, pouting and stray bass. If you have little faith in fresh fish baits cast from the shore, available locally are lug and mussel (on tides other than poor neaps) and some razor fish (spring tides).

IV. **Fishguard Harbour – Green Light and Red Light.** East breakwater thrusts ½ mile from Goodwick Sands promenade into a disappointing 2 fathoms. Tipped by a green light platform, it faces the red light of the main ½ mile long seaward breakwater, reached through Fishguard harbour station and its marine installations. There is no hindrance to fishing the green light – except, of course, the light platform at the end – but for the red light breakwater, which reaches a more respectable 5½ fathoms along its inner length, you must have a permit from the Marine Superintendent's office. The harbour is used by cross-channel Irish ferries. Plaice and dabs take ledgered lugworm on the sand and mud mixture bottom, but it's very rough around the breakwaters themselves. Conger, with the odd ray and lesser and greater dogfish – nurse hounds hereabouts – are caught on the edge of this rougher ground. Small pouting, pollack and wrasse take a narrow mackerel strip floated over their hiding places among the large sea protection rocks at the bases of the breakwaters.

V. **Strumble Head Lighthouse.** This is almost the only easy access to a fishable position on the craggy, sea-lashed Pencaer peninsula lying west of Fishguard and Goodwick. 29 fathoms of water lie just off the lighthouse, depths characteristic of the coast down to St. David's and sufficient to bring the bigger bottom feeders close in. Those who are masters of spinning techniques over really rough ground find excellent sport with pollack and bass. If you possess the quicksilver reactions of the float-fishing coarse fisherman, there are big wrasse. Those who want a sea-bed a little less craggy, will fish into deep water below the coastguard's watch station.

Boat fishing

Only Newport, tiny Cwm yr Eglwys creek and Fishguard's Lower Town, are really suited to the visiting boatman. Their waters, well protected from prevailing west and south west winds, are comparatively deep: 10 fathoms are reached in little over a mile and 15 fathoms in just over 2 miles.

Newport – A. **Trwyn y Bwa;** B. **Dinas Head.** Trwyn y Bwa headland has a 2-3 knot tide on springs, Dinas ead something similar. Both have a ıttom shelving steeply north west from ft to 100 ft deep. Sparsely populated ith anglers at the best of times, winter hing is almost ignored, north Dyfed's astal waters have only been explored full or part-time netters and lobster-en who, naturally are reticent about ecise fishing marks. We know that uth Cardigan Bay, partly preserved it is by Aberporth Range activities, s rich grounds. This is true of their tension south west towards Newport d Fishguard. Tope, skate and ray, gfish and huss, as well as monkfish, bot and red gurnard, are all found by hing mackerel lasts on the bottom. At ıst two species of shark – blues and rbeagle – are common enough to ırrant expeditions solely for them. ey came close inshore, over rocky ound, where pollack and coalfish run wards the 5 lbs mark. Mackerel, of urse, are extremely common.

Fishguard Bay. Sheltered, nveniently reached by dinghy from wer Town harbour, the outer fringe the bay is an excellent sea fishing nue. The inner harbour is almost ind and tide free. Just beyond the ain red light breakwater (see beach hing section IV above) there are 50 ft water, and ½ mile further out the sea bed drops abruptly into 13 to 18 fathoms. Several conger and pollack wrecks and rocky areas litter the approaches but their location demands at least an echo sounder. Though only ¼ to ½ knot in the centre of the bay, tides race around headlands – particularly Pen Anglas – much faster. Cod and whiting are winter visitors, but there's little fishing for them as most local anglers hibernate from November to March, except for the late autumn bass hunt; knowing their winter gales this is understandable. Summer, from late June, to well into autumn, makes up for it with tope, skate and ray, conger, small ling and gurnard, as well as reasonable pollack.

Bait supply

Crabs. Rare, under stones and weed at Newport Parrog beach, Cwm yr Eglwys, Pwllgwaelod (each side of the neck of Dinas promontory) and Fishguard (Goodwick and Lower Town).

Lug. Newport sands, near the river mouth has limited quantities. The sands of Goodwick, historic surrender place of the French in the last invasion of Britain in 1797, will give up its lug from about half tide down, except on extreme neaps. There are some razor fish here, too, which can be salted out on spring tides.

Tackle shops

Fishguard. *Marine Chandlery, Cwm Boat Stores, 19 Quay Street, Lower Fishguard. Tel.* (0348) 873604. *Angling Times* report station.

W. E. Collins, 40 West Street, Fishguard. Tel. (0348) 873652.

Newport (Dyfed). *Beynon's Fishing Tackle, Temple House, Upper West Street. Tel. Newport* (0239) 820265. Tackle supply and repairs, frozen baits, worms, flies, advice on where to fish. WWA river licences for sale. Information given on fishing trips. *Angling Times* report station. Newport and District Angling Association water angling permits on sale.

Boat hire, trips or charter

Many small boat owners take out anglers, as guests, from Lower Town, Fishguard. Arrangements can be made through The Angling Club Secretary. (See section below.)

Fishguard. *Mr. B. Brooks, Quay Road, Lower Town. Miss Kelsey,* 30 ft. Available summer. Contact on the quay.

Newport. *W. Beynon Williams, Fishing Tackle, West Street, Newport, Dyfed. Tel. Newport* (0239) 820265.

continued on next page

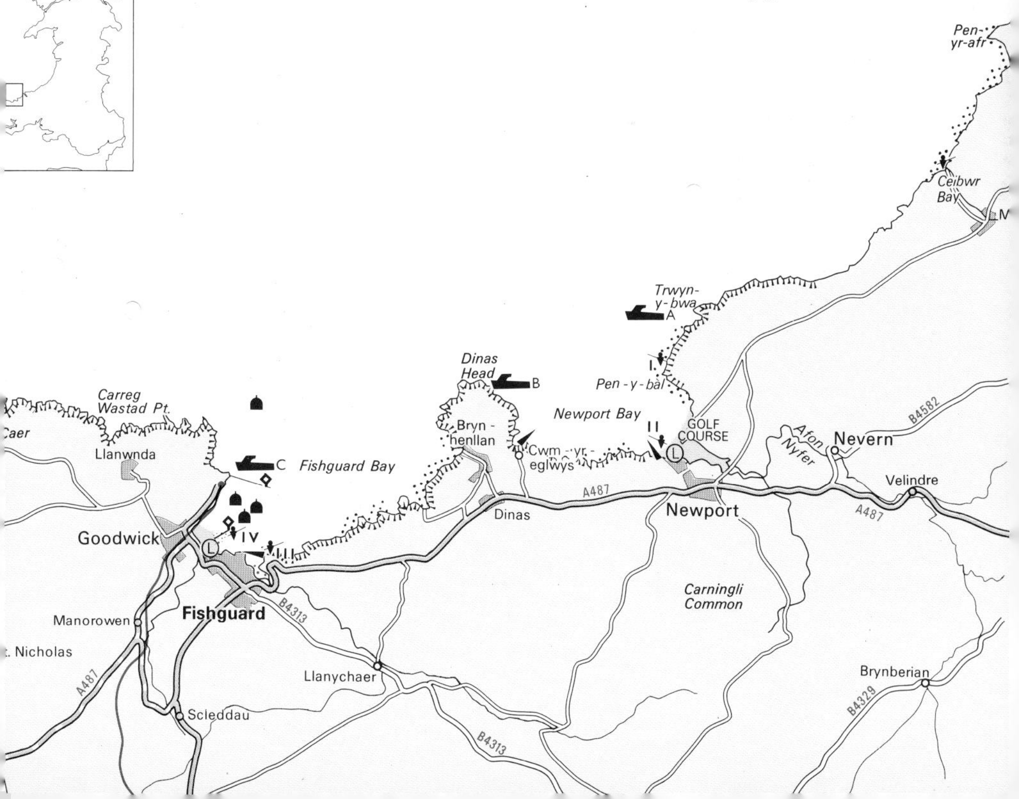

Boat launching slipways

Cwm yr Eglwys. Access to the beach for dinghies.

Fishguard. Free use of facilities for boats up to 30 ft at: *Lower Town:* 2 slipways from quay (1 with winch), 1 slipway from car park; *Goodwick Sands:* 1 slipway from car park.

Newport. 4 slipways on the Parrog (town side) of Nevern river estuary. Free access for dinghies.

Fishing advice

Fishguard and Goodwick Sea Anglers, Hon. Sec., Mr. Brian James, 8 Allt-y-Carne, Goodwick, Fishguard, Dyfed.

Useful telephone numbers

In emergency
Dial 999 and ask for Coastguard.

At other times:
RNLI deep sea lifeboat. *Fishguard Harbour. Tel. 2266.* **Coastguard.** *Fishguard. Tel. 3449. Strumble Head. Tel. St. Nicholas (03485) 258.* **Nearest Helicopter.** *Contact coastguard who will call in RAF Brawdy.* **Weather forecasts.** *Gloucester Meteorological Office. Tel. Churchdown (0452) 855566.* **Aberporth Royal Aircraft Establishment.** *Meteorological Station. Tel. (0239) 810117.*

St. David's Peninsula – Aberbach to Nolton Haven

Remote, rocky, with deep clear water, the peninsula of St. David's crumbles into an archipelago of islands: Ramsey – the largest – and the Bishops and Clerks. It's pollack ground all the way, with tope not far behind in quantity. Rock platforms predominate but Whitesand Bay and the 2 miles long Newgale Sands give a taste of the extensive West Wales bass storm beaches which are found to the south, linked by the coast path.

I. **Abermawr and Aberbach.** Turn north to Granston and Tregwynt from A487, 3 miles south west of Fishguard, for the short walk to Abermawr beach. Shelving steeply, the bay has 40 ft of water fairly close in. Bass, mackerel and pollack spinning into rough ground on the outcrops towards Aberbach, and ledgering on to the sandy bottom of the bay for bass, plaice and flounder, is often rewarded with good fish.

II. **Porthgain;** III. **Abereiddi;** IV. **St. David's Head.** In Porthgain creek's cosy little pub, lobster men and crabbing men mix with holidaymakers for

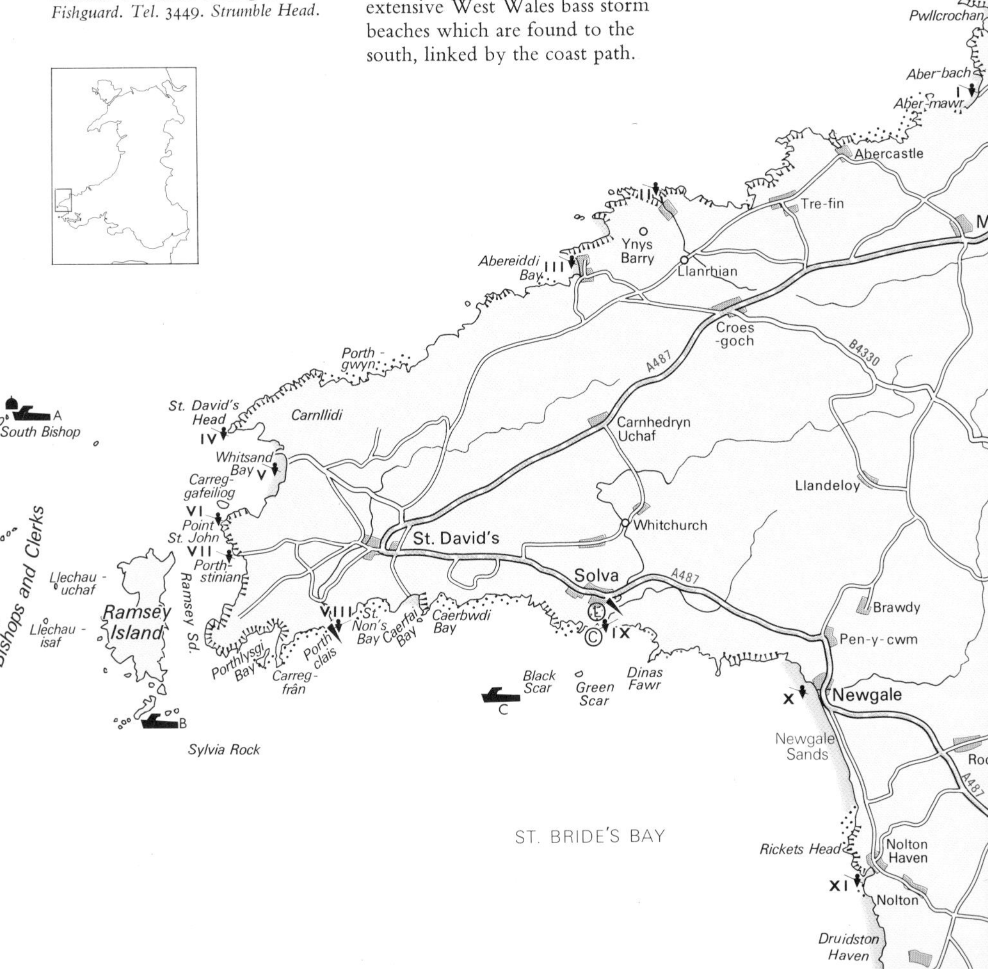

refreshment and might be persuaded to chat about the coast's great fishing potential. Like Abereiddi beach, Porthgain is reached from the secondary coast road linking Mathry with St. David's. St. David's Head is a little more difficult to reach; it's a 20 minute trek by coast path from Whitesand Bay car park. Pollack and mackerel are the main quarry, caught from rock positions into deep water. Red rubber eels and an assortment of metal and plastic lures make the early catches from convenient ledges of rock. With mackerel in the bag it's possible to widen the range of fishing: floating a strip on a long trace over the lairs of pollack and wrasse or ledgering a sizeable strip of belly or free lining a mackerel for bass, tope and even bigger fry.

V. **Whitesand Bay.** Picturesque and popular, this wide expanse of sand is the largest stretch of beach available to visitors in the immediate St. David's area. There is a convenient car park (charge) just above the beach and nearby hotels and caravan sites for those wanting to fish this coast at all states of the tide. The constant run of surf at Whitesand Bay attracts many malibu board experts which tends to detract from the fishing. Bass take ledgered lug and ragworm, though both have to be dug elsewhere – at Fishguard, Solva or in the Milford Haven. It's a beach well worth fishing early in the day, or when the last visitor has gone in the evening, particularly in late March, April and May and at the tail end of the year, up to mid-November.

VI. **St. David's – Point St. John.**
VII. **St. David's – Porth Stinian.**
VIII. **St. David's – Porth Clais.**
Mark VII is reached by a short road leading due west from St. David's. Parking above St. Justinian's lifeboat station is limited. Walk north along the cliff path through National Trust coastline to several convenient deep water marks, or carry on to Point St. John, an excellent mark. Porth Clais is a narrow, fjord-like harbour, full of boats, whose steep sides funnel out to form rocky ledges. All three marks – and dozens between – offer first rate shore pollack fishing (not to be confused with first rate boat pollack fishing which, as it were, is a different kettle of fish). The spinning rod is vitally important as a mackerel bait-gatherer. Take your heavy tackle as well, for conger increase in number and size, sustained as they are by an unlimited food larder and rocky lairs. Caerfai Bay has a car park and is another convenient access to the coast path. Keep your spinning rod at the ready whenever you're near the open sea rock ledges for mackerel and school bass come close in mornings and evenings when the sea is calm.

IX. **Solva.** The ¼ mile long creek of Solva is mainly sand and mud, flanked by rocks and hemmed in by high green banks. The southern bank widens to form a small sea-facing beach. High tide sets many boats a'bobbing. A small quay on the north bank and a rock promontory on the south bank at a sharp turn in the fjord are two float fishing marks suitable for mullet and bass. The odd soft crab found on the south side near the harbour mouth at low tide, should be kept for float fishing close in over the stones. Ledger big brown harbour lug onto sand nearer the fjord mouth for flatfish and bass.

X. **Newgale.** A classic shallow storm beach curving 2 miles south to Rickets Head, with a fine run of surf after the slightest breeze, it has resident school bass shoals, plus the occasional bigger bass. There are also plaice and flounder and, frequently in winter, small whiting and codling. The main A487 road runs beside the beach behind a wall of storm-thrown pebbles. At the south end, where the main road approaches the beach down a steep hill, there is a very convenient car park. Near the rocky and precipitous north end a small stream winds its way across the beach in a bed of stones covered with a green slimy weed; many bass have been taken on it, but fish are taken anyway along the beach. Some favour a point ¼ mile south of the car park, near a caravan site, where Bathesland Water brook spills over the beach. The last two hours of the flood and first hour of the ebb are best, particularly at night. Low water periods give pleasant fishing but are not particularly fruitful.

XI. **Nolton Haven.** The haven sits in a narrow defile in the middle of St. Bride's Bay. Northwards the coast is rocky with access to the water around Rickets Head limited by the cliffs and steep grass slopes; southwards lie the sands of Druidston – pronounced Drews'n locally. Here you're likely to get more peace fishing on a summer's day than at Broad Haven or at Newgale, provided you're willing to search out rock ledges by walking the strenuous Pembrokeshire Coast Path. Parking as near Druidston Head as possible, ¼ mile NW of the actual village of Druidston, is still not very near the beach, and can be difficult to find, leaving a ½-mile trudge on foot. The headland is very good for bass, 4–6 lbs, and flounders.

Boat fishing

The numerous island chains off the western tip of Wales are rich in fish. Every creek around St. David's shelters its quota of lobster and crab boats and from time to time skin divers have incurred the wrath of conservationists who accuse them of raping the sea bed. But the area is almost untouched by sea anglers. The fish are there, and plenty of them; Idwal Chapman's *Mizpah* has had excellent catches with tope to 48 lbs, conger to 30 lbs, pollack of 11 lbs and bull huss of 15 lbs. But make no mistake about it, these waters can be dangerous for boats of all sizes, particularly in the 6 and 7 knot tide races between the islands and between Ramsey and the mainland. Stick to bays sheltered by headlands, or offshore dry rocks. Keep off the reefs and out of the runs. The rewards warrant the effort of launching from the area's infrequent slipways.

A. **Bishops and Clerks Rocks.** 3 miles due west of St. David's Head lie the Bishops Rocks of which 120 ft high North Bishop is by far the biggest. The ridge, 1½ miles long, with wrecks at both ends, is heavily ribbed by overfalls and eddies at the extremities. Close in to the central, more sheltered group of rocks, in 10 to 17 fathoms of water, are excellent pollack marks. The extremities of the reef can only be fished in relatively calm conditions, in short slack periods which occur 2 to 3 hours after high water. In the 25–30 fathom channels on each side of the North Bishop reef, and particularly on the western side, tope and blue shark are abundant. Similar conditions, all of which demand a sound boat and considerable local knowledge, are found along the ridges of the Bishops and Clerks – Carreg Rhoson ridge and the shoals that extend from Ramsey to South Bishop lighthouse. Porth Clais and Solva creeks offer protection from high seas and winds.

B. **Ramsey and the Sound.** Only a powerful and reliable engine should be used in this strait of 6 knot tides and cascading water. Suitably equipped, shore-hugging small boat anglers – it's at least a two man job – will find excellent sport from Carreg Gafeiliog all the way around to Carreg Frân, south of Porth Lyski. Besides the mackerel, small skate and plaice of Whitesand Bay, there are sizeable pollack in the rockier spots and some bass. Anyone able to venture to the wreck-riddled islands south of Ramsey will find excellent pollack marks in 7 fathoms along the south west shore of Ynys Bery and around the submerged Sylvia Rock where 3–5 fathom shallows dip suddenly to over 23 fathoms.

C. **St. Bride's Bay – Scar Rocks.** Safer water prevails inside St. Bride's Bay east of a line from Caerfai Bay to Martin's Haven. Launching and shelter at Solva harbour, which has a 6 nautical mph restriction, are convenient for this area. In little more than a mile from this harbour, south and west of the prominent Scar Rocks, there are plenty of mackerel for bait to fish the 10 fathoms bottom on a slow drift or at anchor.

continued on next page

Thornback ray to 14–20 lbs abound. There are tope and spur-dog, as well as brill, dabs and plaice for the table. Closer in to the Scar Rocks, small pollack can be taken with jigged red eels, feathers or a well-placed toby spinner.

Bait supply

A coast of scarce bait resources almost always coincides with prolific fish stocks – as here. Visitors will arm themselves beforehand with lures and practise hand netting or drop-netting for prawns and shrimp bait, of which there are plenty. Mackerel arrive in quantity about mid-June or early July and leave in the early part of September.

Crab. Very few, in rocks and weed towards the estuary mouth on Solva Creek's left hand bank and at each side of big bays, (e.g. Newgale) where cliff fall stone is revealed at low springs.

Lug. 75 yards from the car park at Solva on the left of the stream. Not great in numbers because of heavy digging, but of good size.

Tackle shops

Haverfordwest. *County Sports, 3 Old Bridge. Tel.* (0437) 3740. Tackle supply and repair. Flies, advice on where to fish; river authority licences sold for the WWA river area; permits for local rivers and lakes; *Angling Times* weighing station.

Toms Sports, 10 Market Street. Tel. (0437) 3653. Tackle supply; flies,; advice on where to fish; WWA river licences sold.

St. David's. *Chapman's Corner Sea Food & Fishing Tackle Shop, Nun Street. Tel.* (043788) 301. Tackle supply and repair; Brent and frozen baits; advice on where to fish; fishing trips bookable and boat hire (for Solva); *Angling Times* report station.

Boat hire, trips or charter

St. David's. *Mr. Hampson, Chemist and boat chandlers, Cross Square. Tel.* (043 788) 243. Advice on boat hire facilities available in the area and sale of tide tables, charts, etc.

Mr. Eric O'Brien, 29 Goat Street, St. David's. Tel. (043 788) 334.

Porthclais. *Mr. T. H. Beer, Brynawelan, St. David's. Tel.* (043 788) 221. *Fulmar* (M35) 22 ft. Daily pleasure and fishing trips in summer only from landing stage, Porthclais Harbour.

Solva. *Mr. R. G. Sendall, The Smithy. Tel.* (043 785) 337. *Iolanthe*, 27 ft. Angling trips and hire April 1st to September 30th from Solva Quay.

Mr. Idwal J. Chapman, Tackle Shop, 25 Nun Street, St. David's. Tel. (043 788) 301. MFV. *Mizpah*, 28 ft, Licenced for 12 passengers. 1½ hour mackerel trips and 4 hour trips daily. Weekend charter. Tackle supplied.

Boat launching slipways

Abercastle and Abereiddi. Access to beach for launching dinghies.

Newgale. Beach launching for dinghies. Concrete partial run-up over pebbles located at 'Y' road junction 150 yards south of 'Duke of Edinburgh' Inn.

Nolton Haven. Access to beach for launching dinghies.

Porthgain. Slipway. (use free).

St. David's. *Whitesand.* Access to beach for launching dinghies; *Porth Stinian.* Lifeboat slipway only. Not available to public; *Porth Clais.* Limited moorings and launching facilities (small charge) apply to *Mr. David Turner, 13 Pen-y-Garn.*

Solva. Launching facilities available at small charge for boats up to 18 ft.

Fishing advice

Pembrokeshire Anglers' Association, Hon. Sec., Mr. M. Gibby, 22 Greenfield Close, Cardigan Road, Haverfordwest.

Useful telephone numbers

In emergency
Dial 999 and ask for Coastguard.

At other times:
RNLI deep-sea lifeboat. *St. David's, Secretary. Tel.* (043 788) 325. *Coxwain Tel.* 325. **Coastguard.** *St. David's. Tel.* 210. (*not constantly manned*). *Fishguard. Tel.* (0348 3449). **RAF Helicopters.** *Telephone Coastguard who will call on RAF Brawdy.* **Lighthouse.** *South Bishop Rock. Radio contact.* **Weather forecasts.** *Meteorological Office, Gloucester. Tel. Churchdown* (0452) 855566.

Druidston to Linney Head and Milford Haven approaches

This might be the blue riband area of Welsh sea fishing by virtue of the great store of fish to be found around and over reefs and islands west of Milford Haven. The area offers great variety of terrain to the shore and inshore angler: calm but fruitful waters in St. Bride's Bay, pollack and reef bass around Broad Sound, Gateholm Island and Marloes Sands, conger and pollack over the Haven mouth's Chapel Rocks and surf bass along the Freshwater West and Frainslake storm beaches. Little Haven, Dale and Angle are three convenient centres from which to enjoy it.

I. **Broad Haven.** Less exposed than Newgale, it has a good run of surf in a west or north-west wind. Very popular by day in summer, the sand beach can only be fished from late evening. Good bass are caught regularly and there are plenty of mackerel as well as flat fish, whiting and small codling in season. Park at the north end of the beach in a small layby or in the capacious car park 2 minutes away. Cast where the larger of two streams cross the sands. The beach's north end terminates in rock platforms fronting a rocky area with sand between. Approached without too much difficulty from low gorse covered cliffs 150 yards along the Haroldston West road, they form excellent bass stations – though tackle can be temporarily lost – and mackerel regularly chase brit in front of them. Fish the rock stations from 3 hours before high water to an hour or two afterwards. The main beach is fishable at any state of the tide.

II. **Marloes Peninsula – Wooltack Point.** Park 2 miles west of Marloes (car park) at Martin's Haven and walk up over the bank, past the coastguard station, across a sloping heathland to Wooltack Point, with Tusker Rock on your left. In a moderate blow the whole area is covered in what appears to be white cotton wool, and is in fact foam blown off the waves. It is a useful rock mark for pollack, mackerel, wrasse and conger on the flood tide from about 2 hours after low water.

III. **Marloes Sands.** Take a side road south west from the east end of Marloes village to a car park 1 mile down. Walk ¼ mile south to the beach. Popular with holidaymakers, the main beach can be fished only from the evening. Most catches of bass are made on rag or crab from low water up from a position near or on Gateholm Island on the right hand side of the beach. It is a first rate bass mark up to mid-December in a mild winter, despite the depradations of occasional visiting boats. Round the corner, on the Albion Sands, small bass can be taken – and returned – on the early flood.

IV. **The Milford Haven – Sandy Haven.** See 'Bait supply' for how to get there. Recent underwater blasting for pier construction nearby brought up to half a dozen stunned bass of about 4 or 5 lbs to the surface on each occasion. One of the few convenient fishing stations below Hazelbeach on the north bank, it fishes best for about three hours after low water.

V. **Kilpaison Bay.** Very sheltered 'lee' beach, full of marine life, which sometimes yields a good bass early in

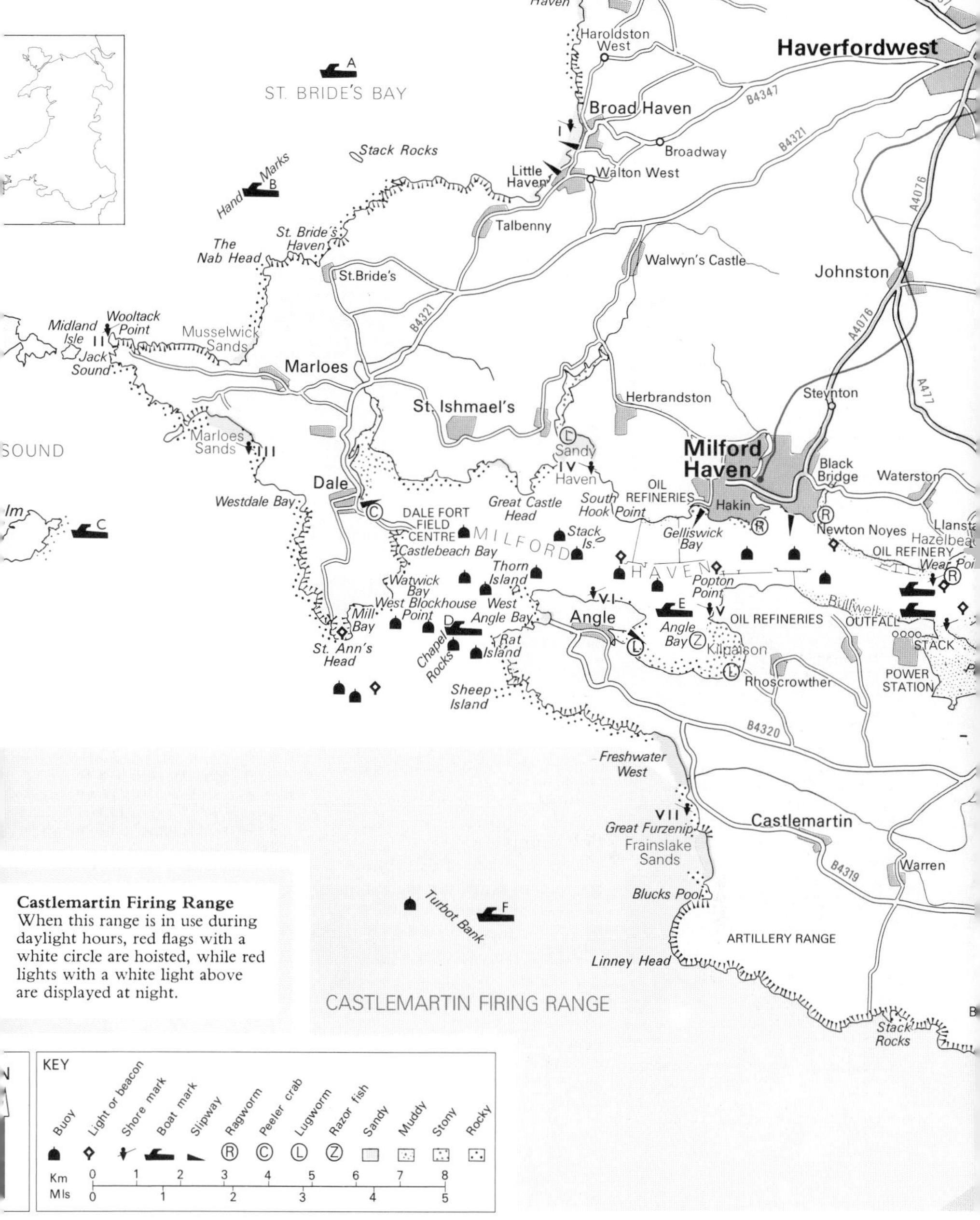

e season, in March/April. Notable
ainly, though, for its very rich bait
ds. (See below under 'Bait supply').

. **Angle – Chapel Bay.** Ap-
oached by a lane north from the
st end of Angle village, or at low
e past the lifeboat station from Angle
y side. Lug, that summer sun has sent
oit high, has accounted for some excellent bass here about a rising mid-tide. Lugworm is plentiful for an angler staying in the vicinity of Angle Bay.

VII. **Freshwater West.** Classic storm beach for bass, low water to high water plus 1 hour. Best results often from fishing between rock outcrops on south end of beach, where dead gunnel and rockling (called locally 'butterfish' and obtainable at low water in tide pools) are often the best bait, though razor, clam and lug will also produce fish. Night fishing best, as on many South Pembrokeshire beaches. Park at a pull in near the junction of Frainslake and Freshwater West beaches. Special attention is drawn to the treacherous

continued on next page

waters here; watch the undertow and occasional huge waves that can sweep away a lone angler.

Boat fishing

Venture outside the comparatively calm and protected waters of St. Bride's Bay or the Milford Haven and you meet fast tide rips, dangerous reefs and rapid changes of wind and tide – Jack Sound funnels water through at 7 knots. Any misjudgment, any failure or neglect of man or equipment, spells immediate danger and many fatalities in small craft take place here every year. Take advice from local boatmen. Better still, hire them for fishing trips and you're sure of enjoying superb fishing in safety. The following advice is for those who are fully equipped in every way:

A. **St. Bride's Bay – Little Haven;**
B. **St. Bride's Bay – Hand Marks.** Little Haven and Broad Haven are neighbours, convenient for dinghy launching, and both marks are in comparatively calm water; mark A is similar to mark C in the previous section. Tope are common and shark are reported – neither are good neighbours in a small dinghy, though it has been done. In Ireland they tail the catch home to shore backwards, thus drowning it but unless you have a distinct use for the meat or the means of releasing the monsters unharmed, leave them alone. Mark B has some good sole and, close in to the reef where the bottom abruptly rises from 17 to 5 fathoms, there are some good sized pollack. Closer in towards St. Bride's Haven large bull huss and lesser spotted dogfish are caught.

C. **Skokholm Island and its vicinity.** Another area of fast tide races and rocky bottoms which demands care in fishing – this is not small boat country – Skokholm Island has a great variety of good fishing. Heavy pollack and big tope may be encountered along the island's north west tip. In foul ground, east of Skokholm, as well as pollack and tope the catch will include coalfish, conger, monkfish, bull huss, angler fish and occasional bass. The south east coast is slack on the ebb and fishable. Skokholm's south west point, off the light, has excellent mackerel. The western side is slack nearly all the time and a broad bay mid way up this coast fishes well in 6–7 fathoms for conger, pollack and heavy wrasse. Back towards the mainland, off West Dale Bay, where it is slack enough most of the time, large bull huss and blonde ray are frequently caught. A little north west, around Gateholm Island, drift lining of mackerel strip, or whiffing a large red gill, frequently gives good sized bass.

D. **Chapel Rocks.** The long reef at the mouth of Milford Haven is full of smallish pollack and can be fished in fine weather from a small boat launched at Angle or Dale. Care should be taken of 300,000 ton tankers and other large craft entering the Haven, but they do not encroach on the Chapel Rocks themselves.

E. **Thorn Island to Popton Point.** This is ideal small boat country with sheltered fishing and bass may be encountered along most of the coast if the angler keeps close in and fishes with lug on to shallow sandy ground. There are no special marks and drifting, so long as the tide is not too fierce, can be a good plan. Launch at Angle, Milford, Dale or Pembroke Dock.

F. **The Turbot Bank.** Of old, a well-known Milford commercial mark where, traditionally, trawlers made their last drag before coming home. Rarely commercially fished now, it holds turbot, ray (including blondes), tope and big whiting, as well as a number of other species. Early summer sees an invasion by spurdog who come to drop their young; these expectant mothers should be put back with as little harm as possible to ensure a continuing supply. Very fast tides make fishing difficult and wire line is useful. Best fished from a large craft out of one of the Haven ports.

Bait supply

The great divide of the Milford Haven puts Kilpaison lug and razor beds out of bounds to boatless fishermen north of the estuary. These are the main bait resources of the area.

Crab. A few in weed towards the Griffin Inn at Dale. Elsewhere rare. Prawns and shrimps can be taken using a hand net or drop net along the tide line at low tide.

Lugworm. Fair lug at Broad Haven, on north side of beach mainly, though not prolific and well dug. Patches at Dale and Sandy Haven, a creek reached by a tortuous, narrow road from Herbrandston. Kilpaison, in Angle Bay (turn to Rhoscrowther off B4320, then sharp left after ¾ mile to an oil tank farm at the head of the bay); lug here are good sized, browns, but strenuous digging is necessary.

Ragworm. Fair rag at Hakin Point on springs. Occasional rag in the Pill, a narrow creek just east of the town of Milford, but it is very muddy.

Shellfish. Clams, good for bass, are found patchily 1 ft down in muddy sand at Dale but you have to be able to spot their new-halfpenny sized blow holes to locate them. Cockles are fairly abundant at Kilpaison (see above for directions) where razor fish are found at spring tides. A few razor fish are also found at Broad Haven in front of the Lion Rock (extreme north end) at low springs. Salt them out of their holes.

Tackle shops

Dale. *Dale Sailing Co. Tel. Dale* (064 65) 349. Tackle supply and artificial baits. Advice given on where to fish. Angling trips can be booked aboard *Dale Queen*, 45 ft.

Milford Haven. *Dudley Marine, inc. Trakka Sports, Charles Street, (opposite Woolworths), Milford Haven. Tel.* (064 62) 2787. Tackle supply; frozen baits and flies; advice on where to fish; WWA river licences sold. *Angling Times* report station.

T. Newing & Sons Ltd, 13 Hamilton Terrace. Tel. (064 62) 3180. Tackle supply, rods, reels, hooks, weights only.

Boat hire, trips or charter

Dale. *Dale Sailing Co. and Chandlers. Tel.* (064 65) 349. *Dale Queen*, 45 ft, toilets. Available at all times for trips and charter by arrangement. Tackle hire.

Dale. *Diver Hire, 30 Nelson Terrace, Llanelli, Dyfed, SA15 2LR. Tel. Llanelli* (05542) 50968. Bookings to above address or to *Burry Port Yacht Chandlers. Tel. Burry Port* (05546) 2740. Day and night charter, summer only (in winter based at Burry Port – see entry) to anglers, up to 12 rods, and divers. Bait and tackle provided by prior arrangement.

Milford Haven. *D. V. Howells & Sons Ltd, The Docks, Hakin Point. Tel.* (06462) 2418. and 2737. 8 launches available all the year round on hire for angling or pleasure trips.

Boat launching slipways

Angle. *West Angle Bay.* Firm launching to water at high water; *Angle Bay.* Firm launching to water at high water.

Broad Haven. Entrance to beach at north and south ends but dinghies have to be carried over 30 yards of sloping soft sand and stones to hard sand.

Dale. Dale Sailing Club slipway. Occasional use with permission, otherwise temporary membership necessary.

Little Haven. Small public slipway from road to hard sand. No charge.

Milford Haven. *Gellyswick Bay.* Public slipway to hard sand. No charge; *Milford foreshore.* 1 slipway at Slip Hill (down hill from Belgian monument, near Town Hall in Hamilton Terrace); *Pill.* Firm launching at high water.

Fishing advice
Pembroke & District Angling Club, Hon. Sec., Mr. T. Caveney, Kiln Back, Angle, Dyfed.

Useful telephone numbers
In emergency
Dial 999 and ask for Coastguard.

At other times:
RNLI lifeboat. *Angle Bay. Tel.* (064 684) 260. **Coastguard.** *St. Ann's Head. Tel. Dale* (064 65) 218. **Trinity House lighthouse.** *St. Ann's Head. Tel. Dale* (064 65) 314. **RAF Helicopters.** *Contact coastguard who will call on RAF Brawdy.* **Weather forecasts.** *Meteorological Office, Gloucester. Tel. Churchdown* (0452) 855566.

Milford Haven (upper reaches) and St. Govan's Head to Giltar Point

Excellent alternatives exist here for good and bad weather: shore and boat angling in the Haven's calm upper reaches when there is a big blow; beach casting outside on the exposed south coast when the wind has died away. Bass are the main quarry, shoaling up the muddy creeks or sporting in the clear waters of sand beaches and reefs. There are good tope, too, as well as prime conger, early spring herring and thornback rays in the most unexpected of places.

I. **Wear Point, Hazelbeach.** Noted not so long ago for easily dug king rag, but is almost dug out now, and king-sized cockles that lie on the sandy mud, the Wear Bank juts out into the Haven opposite Pembroke power station's 700 ft high chimney. Fish it from an hour before low to high water, at any time, for bass, flatfish and plagues of lesser spotted dogfish. Walk along the beach from the convenient Ferry House Inn and hotel at Hazelbeach (Llanstadwell) or take the signposted Coast Path for ½ mile up the lane at the back of the inn. At the mark, stand with your back to the short wall on the beach 10 yards west of the 'No anchoring' sign denoting the under-sea oil pipeline, or further west on one of the two jutting weedy reefs just east of the 'White Lady', a cone-shaped beacon on the shore.

II. **Neyland Pontoon.** The former ferry boat landing stage was dangerous for anglers who floated for small pollack, mullet and bass. The ferry closed with the opening of the new road bridge over the Haven, but there are many alternative marks: the slipway 100 yards west of the ferry point, the hard standing by the side of a rotting brigantine *Sela*, nearby.

III. **Garron Pill.** Typical of upper Haven marks, it yields bass and flounder to bottom fishing techniques but, surprisingly, is one spot where thornback ray may also be taken on fish baits.

IV. **Lawrenny.** School bass often plentiful on both sides of the old ferry landing near the yacht station. Early flood tide best.

V. **The Warrior.** Naval permission must be obtained to fish from the hulk of HMS *Warrior*, the navy's first iron-clad warship, moored nearly under the new Haven Bridge on the south bank near Pembroke Ferry. There are good conger, and bass on bottom baits, also pouting, rockling (large for their species) and small pollack. Occasionally herring plentiful, taken on small feather lures. There's spinning for school bass on ebb tide from rocks near the *Warrior* (no permission needed), occasionally for much bigger bass around mooring chains and ironwork. Cosheston Pill nearby is good, though muddy, fishing for bass, especially early in the season (March can be a good month) with lugworm on the bottom. The first 2 hours of flood are best. Littoral bladderwrack and stones can be a nuisance.

VI. **Pembroke Dock – Hobbs Point.** The slip where a ferry used to depart for Neyland yields little but dogfish (though an occasional bass and mackerel) in summer, but is good for both conger and codling in late autumn, especially on night tides.

VII. **Pembroke Dock – Carr Jetty.** This is the main jetty of the naval dockyard installation; the main gate is approached along Fort Road. Excellent conger fishing at times, especially from anchored naval vessels if prior permission can be obtained from the Queen's harbour-master, Pembroke Dock. Tel. Pembroke 3235.

VIII. **Pennar Gut.** At almost all accessible spots, particularly the small jetty on the eastern shore of Pennar Gut entrance, reached past the conspicuous Pennar oil tank farm, occasional bass are taken on lugworm which can be found in mud on the spot at low water. A new mark for school bass and mullet is the hot water outlet into the Haven from Pembroke power station. Access from Pembroke/Angle road, B4320, through Pwllcrochan. At Bullwell Bay and Martins Haven (not to be confused with beach of same name north of St. Ann's Head), just west of the outlet, there is good bass fishing casting on to mud/sand from rocks on either side. Night tides best.

IX. **St. Govan's Head – New Quay.** Similar rock fishing for tope as at Barafundle Bay (mark XI), but best time is from high water down to low water minus 1 hour. Park at St. Govan's walk east along cliffs to prominent target pole, then descend a grassy slope to fishing ledge. Access is sometimes restricted by military firing. There is excellent bass fishing from nearby Long Matthew Point, but it involves a difficult climb down to tide race at the headland.

Rock fishing in this area can be dangerous and anglers are reminded of a recent tragedy near here in which two very experienced local anglers lost their lives.

X. **Broad Haven Bay.** This south east facing beach fishes best for bass late in the season, with October the peak month and sport sometimes lively well into December. Best results come after a strong south westerly blow. The left hand side of the beach (as you face the sea) fishes best and it is also possible to fish into or behind the surf from rock ledges on that side. Leave your car at cliff top park (small charge) on right hand side of bay.

XI. **Stackpole: Barafundle Bay.** Rock fishing for tope from a prominent ledge on south side of bay is excellent from June to October. Large fish (up to 60 lbs) have been encountered. They come in at anytime but most likely around high water. Monkfish, bull huss, dog and skate are all taken on fish baits. Spinning at high water often produces fresh mackerel bait. Approached from south by the Coast Path from the car park at Broad Haven (mark X) or the shorter ¼ mile walk from Stackpole Quay.

XII. **Pembroke: Freshwater East.** Needs southerly wind to bring up good surf, then beachcasting is sometimes excellent for the first 2 hours of flood and again at high water. This beach fishes very late in the year, December being sometimes a good month. On warm summer days the beach is crowded with holidaymakers. Parking along roadside is limited and well used, even on bright winter weekends.

XIIIa. **Pembroke Mill Pond.** In the middle of Pembroke town, the salt-water lagoon is notable for its very large mullet, catchable on light float tackle and very small red ragworm obtainable at low water below the bridge near Pembroke Castle. Best when fish have been trapped inside mill pond for several days after spring tides.

XIIIb. **Carew Mill.** A creek of the Haven here holds very good mullet and the occasional bass which can be fished on float with ragworm, as at Pembroke.

XIV. **Tenby: Giltar Point.** The extreme right hand (south west) end of Tenby's South Sands break up into very rough ground giving good soft and peeler crab from middle low to very low spring tides in June and

continued on next page

July, and mussels at all times. It's an area that has produced many good bass and mullet shoals feed and play in the sheltered waters over the mussel beds. For a soft bottom, fish straight out on to green weed between two old concrete structures on the beach. The more difficult terrain to the right of them produces the best fish but a good cast is needed and use of a rotten bottom, for snagging is frequent. Active anglers climb a rock right on the point and fish high above the water. Others fish lower down, just on the Tenby side of the headland, from low to high water, for there is no interference from beach visitors.

XV. **Caldy Island.** Access by summer ferry from Tenby. Bottom fishing with peeler and soft crab (available on spot near the sound dividing Caldy Island from St. Margaret's Island, or at Giltar Point on the mainland) and spinning for bass at Eel Point, Sandtap Bay and other rocky points. Best time first two hours of flood. Important: permission in advance to land a boat for the purpose of fishing off the shore must be obtained from the Father Prior, Caldy Island.

Boat fishing

Netting is the problem. One can see three or four men tugging at a loaded net, 150 yards off Pennar Gut, up to their waists at low water, with a boat in attendance; night netters come out from Hazelbeach; Llangwm tars – no longer in their serviceable tarred black bottomed, brown lanteen-sailed boats – turn from late winter herring fishing in Beggars Reach to the rich pickings of bass (and salmon) by the plastic sack full. It's a time honoured way of life along these waters, sailed and settled long ago by Norsemen. There's still grand fishing here and a 10 ft dinghy with the smallest Seagull or Yamaha will do the job at all states of the tide, except in very bad blows. Just watch Pembroke Ferry tide race on the ebb or flood at all times, keep under the main span of the Haven bridge and don't pass between the last Pembroke Ferry side upright and the shore if it can be avoided.

A. **Wear Bank.** Fish in a few feet of water at low tide – and on the rising tide – where 'foreign' yachts constantly run aground as they try to pass between the 24 high Wear Beacon stake and another stake almost in a direct line with, but nearer to, the 'White Lady' conical Wear Point shore beacon. Ragworm drift lined or lightly cast will give pollack up to 2 lbs, bass, mainly school bass, but there are bigger ones, and dogfish. Mackerel ascend the Haven to here regularly. Less frequently they go up to Hazelbeach and odd ones are caught off Hobb's Point, Pembroke Dock.

B. **Pembroke power station outfall.** Conspicuous on the Haven shore just west of the 700 ft high station chimney – you can't miss it! – is the powerful hot water outfall, running east then west as the tide floods and ebbs. It attracts school bass and mullet and not a few boats who find comparatively easy spinning with a white rubber eel. Floating weed can interfere with bottom fishing with rag.

C. **Carr Rocks.** Close to Pembroke Dockyard, these drying rocks yield plentiful pouting and some excellent congers to the night fishermen. Launch at Hobbs Point, Hazelbeach or Neyland.

D. **Pembroke Ferry*: The Conger Holes.*** Found between Pembroke Ferry and HMS *Warrior*, these 60 ft deep holes hold some enormous fish – a 75-pounder has been recorded. However, they are difficult to fish, except at slack water, because of the very fast tides. There are few places, though, in the UK which hold such big congers inshore and it may well be thought that the effort is worthwhile, even for an hour's fishing.

E. **Burton Point Mooring.** This is a little upstream from Burton and gives modest fishing for bass and ray (and many dogfish) in the summer months, but can be quite rewarding for autumn codling on bottom-fished lugworm. Admiralty boom-defence vessels are often moored here. Launch at Pembroke Ferry, Burton, Neyland or Lawrenny.

F. **Beggars Reach and Garron Pill.** From Llangwm to Lawrenny in late winter and early spring, great shoals of herring appear which are promptly netted by Llangwm fishermen. This is a fine bass stretch in summer and autumn and thornback ray – of all things – are taken with fish baits.

G. **St. Govan's Head to Trewent Point.** Heavy tides and overfalls form in rough weather but when accessible has fine fishing for tope, ray, pollack and, closer in, bass. Not recommended for small, beach-launched craft.

Bait supply

Marked and tainted with oil in the early years of the oil refineries, the Haven's beaches have almost regained their pristine sweetness. Animal and vegetable life is nearly back to normal and bait is not too difficult to find, particularly ragworm and shellfish, though the area is normally a little short on lugworm and razor fish. Mackerel are abundant in the Haven below the town of Milford, from June to late August.

Crab. Strangely absent in Milford Haven, particularly in the last 5 years or so; overpicking, not oil, is the probable cause. Any patch of stone and weed near low tide is likely to hold the odd one or two whereas it used to hold dozens. The position is not now much better at Giltar Point, Tenby, and on the reef near Caldy Island (see items XIV and XV above).

Live fish. Small blennies are abundant beneath stones, both at the low water edge and under 'dry' stones at the top of the beach near rocks.

Lugworm. A few are found in Barnlake Pill's mud, in Pennar Gut and under Llanstadwell Church, Neyland, but it's dirty work and largely unrewarding. (See also Kilpaison in previous section).

Ragworm. Milford Pill's king rag were mentioned in the previous coastal section.

There were easily dug large (6 in – 9 in) ragworm at Wear Point, Hazelbeach, available at spring tides but these are now largely dug out. Smaller ragworm can be dug there at most times – and, for some reason, live .303 rifle ammunition – except on bad neaps. Rag but harder digging, is found west of Pembroke Dock, between the Martello Tower (near Carr Jetty) and Llanraeth. Harbour rag is available all along the Milford Haven. A larger species is dug in Barnlake Creek, on the Neyland side, by the first main promontory ¼ mile above the red abandoned ice factory.

Shellfish. *Cockles:* Abundant at Wear Point, at Neyland's promenade beach and in Pwllcrochan mud flats; *Mussels:* Locally abundant all along the Milford Haven shore line as far up as Neyland and Pembroke Dock; *Razor Fish and Clams:* Small pockets at very low springs between Hazelbeach and Wear Point.

Tackle shops

Pembroke. *Mr. H. C. Bagshaw, Sports Gear, 24 Main Street. Tel.* (064 63) 344 *Tackle supply, advice on where to fish. Preserved bait, permits sold for Pembs & District Angling Club.*
Pembroke Dock. *W. T. V. Humber, Newsagents & Fishing Tackle,* 46–48 *Dimond Street. Tel. Pembroke Dock* (064 63) 2132. Tackle supply and WWA river licences for sale.
Pembroke Dock. *Frank Donovan & Co. 61 Bush Street. Tel.* (064 63) 2756. Tackle supply and repair. Frozen bait. Advice on where to fish. River licences sold for WWA.

continued on page 62

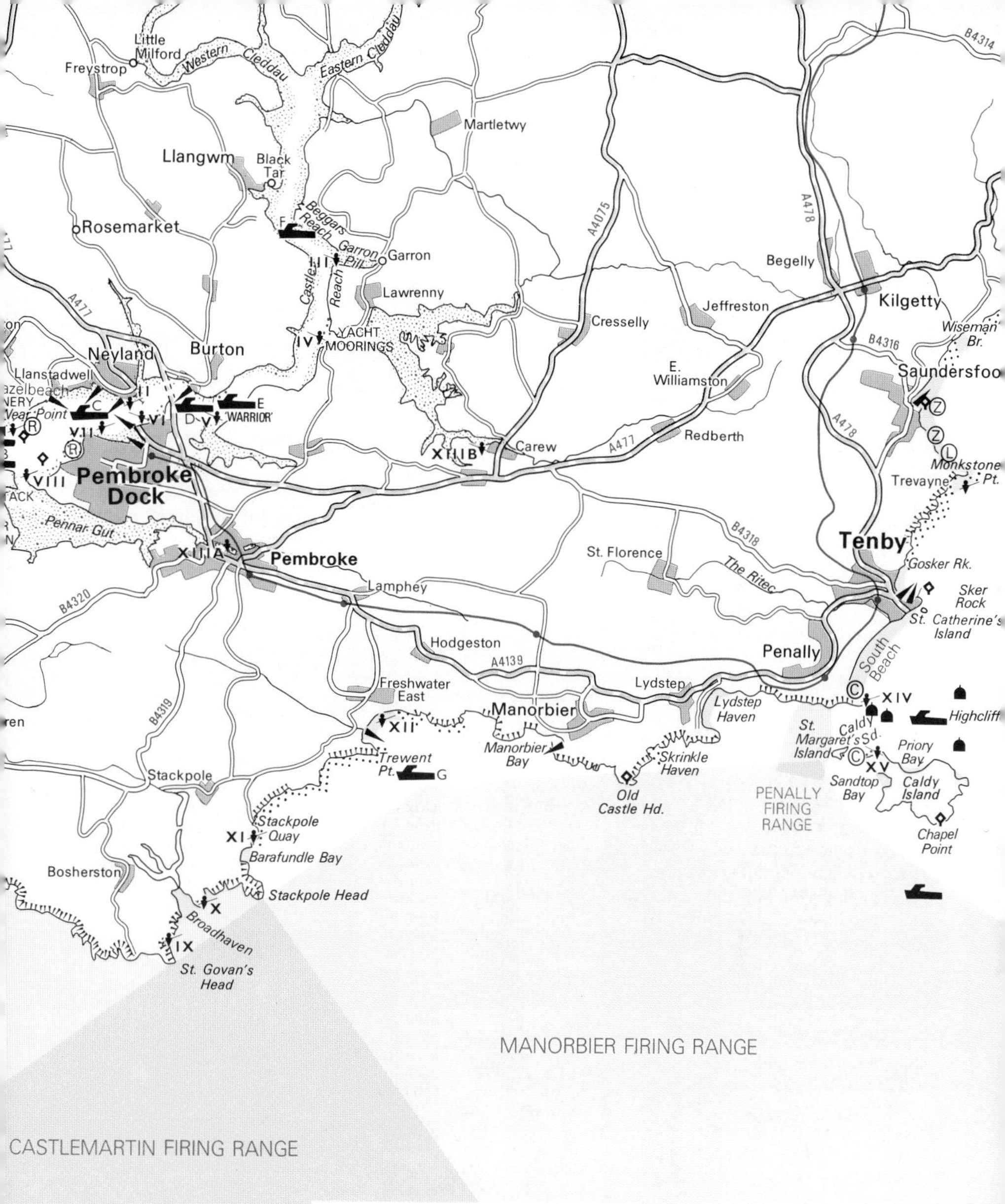

PENALLY FIRING RANGE

MANORBIER FIRING RANGE

CASTLEMARTIN FIRING RANGE

Castlemartin Firing Range.
See notice on page 57

Manorbier Firing Range
When this range is operational red flags are flown by day at the eastern and western side of the range head and a black ball 6 ft in diameter is hoisted on the eastern site. At night red lights are displayed in the flag positions and in addition a flashing red light is visible in a central position between the 2 red lights. The danger area of this range slightly overlaps the danger area for Castlemartin range.

Penally Firing Range
When firing is in progress red flags by day and red lights by night are displayed.

Boat hire, trips or charter

Burton. *Jenkins Boats, Trinity House Yard. Tel. Neyland* (0646) 600234. Boat and outboard motor sales and service only.

Pembroke Dock and Milford Haven. *R. F. Haynes, Dyfed Marine Services, 'The Manse', Crossways, Neyland, Dyfed. Tel. Neyland* (06464) 600717 *after 6 pm.* For hire or charter, the 45 ft MFV *'Pysgotwr Mor'* from April 1st to November 30th. Daily or weekly parties booked, as available. Maximum number of rods per day – 12. Pick-up points Milford Docks or Hobbs Point Pier, Pembroke Dock. Book by telephone at least two days' in advance. Bait provided if ordered in advance. Boat equipped with toilet and full safety equipment.
Daily excursions commence 9 a.m. and return 5 p.m.

Boat launching slipways

Barnlake. (near oil module construction site). Access to the beach (suitable for launching very small craft only at high water).

Burton. Facilities for launching all sizes of craft. Apply. *Jenkins Boats, Trinity House Yard. Tel. Neyland* (0646) 600234.

Freshwater East. Launching for very small dinghies over sand beach but it would be foolish to use such a craft in these waters. A ground swell capsized a cabin cruiser here in 1975 with loss of life.

Hazelbeach. Slipway near the Ferry House Inn from the pier (owned by *Mr. Noel Rees, Mill House, Hazelbeach*) by arrangement with Hazelbeach Boating Club. Suitable for dinghies after half-flood.

Lawrenny. Slipway for all craft by arrangement with the *Lawrenny Yacht Station. Tel. Carew* (064 67) 212.

Manorbier. Launching for small dinghies over sand beach.

Neyland. *Promenade* (west end) Small slipway to the pill available at junction of B4235 with Church Road, Llanstadwell. Really only suitable at full tide. *Yacht Club.* Hard slipway for most pleasure craft through Neyland Yacht Club yard at all states of tide except very low water on spring tides. Permission of Yacht Club to be obtained first. *Sunderland Flying Boat slipway.* Near Neyland old Ferry boat point. A fine slipway – though very slippery from weed growth – suitable at all times except an hour each side of low water on springs when a damaging drop-off at the end causes recovery or launching difficulty. Free use at your own peril.

Pembroke Dock. *Pembroke Ferry.* No slipway. Small dinghies can be hauled on to hard standing. *Hobbs Point.* Suitable for launching craft on all tides except low water springs. Kelpie Boat Services are located here and have first class yacht and boat facilities. *Front Street.* Public slipway in Front Street.

Pennar. Pennar Park Marina. 2 slipways, both available to public at small fee. *Sec. Mr. Dukes. Tel. Pembroke* (06463) 2636. Small fee if slipway used by anyone other than club members.

Fishing advice

See item in previous coast section.

Useful telephone numbers

In emergency
Dial 999 and ask for Coastguard

At other times:
RNLI Lifeboat. *Angle. Tel.* (064 684) 260. **Coastguard.** *St. Ann's. Tel. Dale* (064 65) 218. *Tenby. Tel.* (0834) 2359. (*Not constantly manned*). **Weather forecasts.** *Cardiff (Wales) Airport. Tel.* (0446) 710343 *and Post Office, Swansea. Tel.* (0792) 8011.

Homeward bound to Saundersfoot

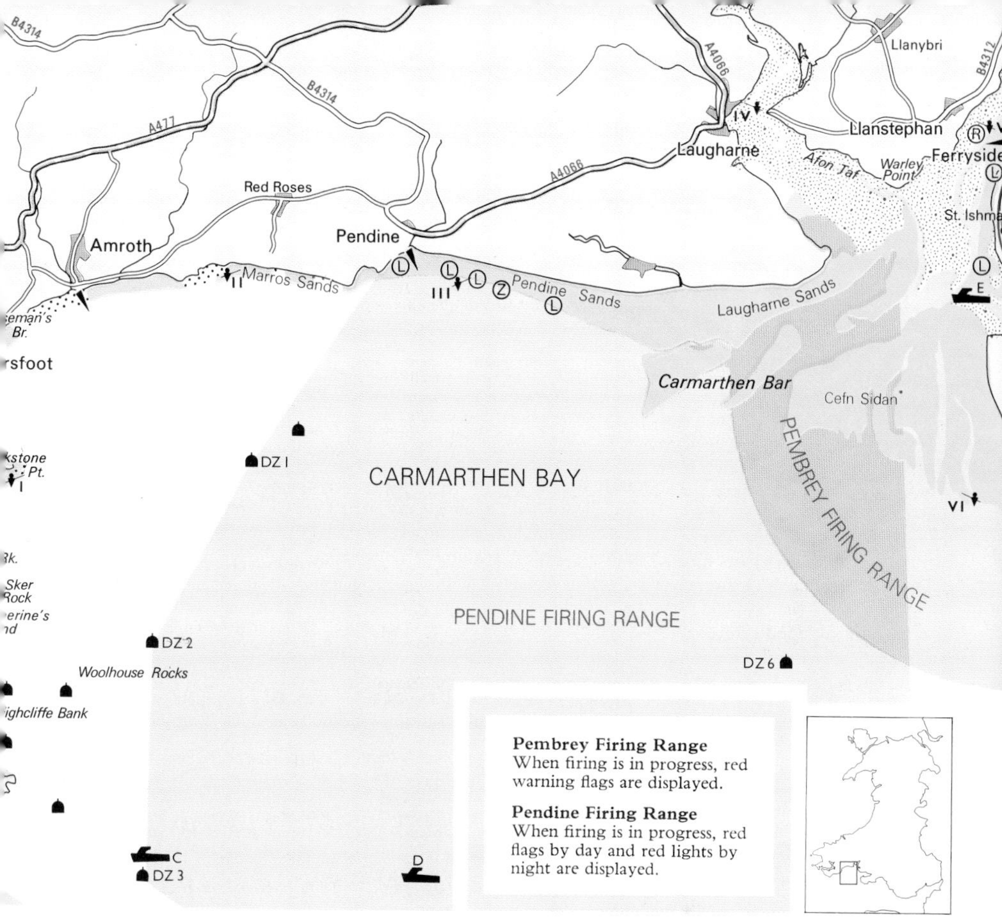

'enby to Kidwelly

armarthen Bay, the sunshine coast ' South Wales, is so popular with olidaymakers that daytime beach shing from late spring to Sept- mber is impossible in the more equented spots. Yet, without oubt, to the shore fisherman and, ore particularly, to the fisherman ho can extend his casting arm into e Bay's tranquil waters by using a owered dinghy or hired motor oat, this is a coast with some of e best holiday fishing Wales has offer.

Monkstone Point. Saundersfoot d Tenby are too popular to fish at, cept from a spot or two off Tenby's astle headland. It's better to turn off e main Tenby to Saundersfoot road st on the Saundersfoot side of the ndowner Motel road junction 478), to Trevayne Farm where you rk for the short walk down a very steep path to Monkstone Beach and Point. Fish the point for bass at low tide with local razor fish or lug, or the open beach later up the tide for dabs and the odd skate. Spring and autumn are best for bass, as on most of the bay's beaches.

II. **Marros Beach.** Splendid bass beach, May to November, but it entails an arduous climb back to Marros village where a car has to be left. It fishes right through flood tide and down to half ebb; best bait razor fish and clam, then rag and lug. The western end is best but be sure to leave this in good time before the tide can cut you off. At high water, a good chance of contacting tope on fish bait. Small turbot (up to 3 or 4 lbs) occasionally met with on small strip of fish (summer).

III. **Pendine.** A little less crowded than other sand beaches only because of its vast extent. You can drive your car right on to the lug beds – if salt water skits and corrosion doesn't worry you – where thick 6 inch brown lug is abundant. So, too, are school bass, plaice and flounders. It is shallow with a good run of surf and anywhere on the beach seems as good as anywhere else though some prefer a position on the extreme west end of the beach – watch that the headland does not cut you off. The first three hours of the flood are a little more lively than the rest of the time, at night if you can arrange it.

IV. **Llanybri.** Good autumn bass and excellent winter flounder fishing. Head for Llanybri village 7 miles south west of Carmarthen. Walk out over mud-flats until you are opposite Laugharne on the far side of Taf estuary. Fish lug or rag from low water to high water.

V. **Ferryside.** Flounder fishing in winter as at mark IV. Easy access from Kidwelly/Carmarthen road. Occasional summer bass but a great roaming weed problem at most times.

VI. **Pembrey-Cefn Sidan.** Excellent bass and flounder fishing the whole length of beach, low water to high water plus 1 hour, from May to

continued on next page

November for bass, until February for flounder. The Pembrey end yields occasional big tope in May and June. Very shallow beach, at least 300, preferably 400 yards of line needed. 'The Target' (conspicuous wooden structure) is a favourite hotspot at the Cefn Sidan end. Access through old ordnance factory, Pembrey (small charge) or (with permission) via forestry road through the old airfield installations. Midweek access sometimes restricted if aircraft firing at targets is taking place on the Ministry of Defence Range.

Boat fishing

There are areas in Wales where fish are more abundant, bigger or more varied, but none such as this where quantity, quality and variety are found together and so near the shore in sheltered waters. The world's record 74 lbs 11 ozs tope – most are females here – came from a spot just 1½ miles E. of Caldy Island. There are good catches of thornback ray and bull huss, pollack, conger and dogfish with large visiting shoals of mackerel (summer) and whiting (winter).

A. **Caldy Sound.** Superbly conditioned bass between 3 lbs and 9 or 10 lbs are caught in the waters off Caldy Island, mainly on a drift in the narrowing strait of Caldy Sound. A red gill fished sink and draw does the trick. Many bass fall to netters and 'professional' fishermen using lures in multiple, but you will still find some if you ledger or drift line soft crab – hard backs at a push – on a rising tide where it swings around headlands or through narrows. Remember, do not land your boat on Caldy for the purpose of fishing from the shore without Father Prior's permission; normally only the licensed Caldy boatmen are granted this right.

B. **The Offing Patches.** On the seaward side of Caldy Island, they can be very productive of shoaling bass on the surface and of good tope fishing on the bottom, though dogfish can be a nuisance at times. Good thornbacks are encountered here, also.

C. **Caldy Island: DZ 3 Buoy.** (The letters stand for Danger Zone since the buoy marks the Pendine military range). This large red and yellow buoy, clearly labelled DZ3, is an historic mark in about 90 ft of water, for it was here that Mr. Albert Harries took the world record tope of 74 lbs 11 ozs. Though tope range the whole of Carmarthen Bay, DZ3 is still a first-class tope mark in warm, calm conditions on the fastest part of a neap tide from May to October and, in some years, even later. Spring tides tend to be a little too fast to keep light tackle on the bottom, where the tope will not be suspicious. Mackerel are abundant to jigged feathers at most times in the vicinity of the mark. On the bottom, one is as likely to take 14 lbs thornback ray, good bull huss or dogfish by the dozen.

D. **Trawler's Dread.** This is an isolated underwater rock, at 7 fathoms in the Bay's overall 12 fathoms around this point, which holds conger and pollack, while there are sometimes good bass in the neighbourhood.

E. **The Paula.** The Paula is a wreck which dries out and can be easily seen in the gullied sandy estuary south of St. Ishmael's near Kidwelly. Its general vicinity is an excellent mark for bass which are usually taken bottom fishing with lugworm in shallow water. This is shallow-draught boat fishing and great care must be taken of sandbanks and overfalls.

Bait supply

Excellent, easily obtained and varied live bait supplies, evenly spread throughout the region.

Cockles. The estuaries of Taf, Towy, Gwendraeth and Loughor sustain cockle picking on a commercial scale.

Crab. *Giltar Point and Caldy Island* (see previous coastal area).

Lug. *Saundersfoot:* The sand beach stretching towards Monkstone Point; Pendine Beach: Excellent brown lug in sand, dug individually to high water –3 hours; *Ferryside:* 150 yards south of the yacht club, big and brown, dug individually from half tide down. See also Pwll in next coastal section.

Razor fish. At Saundersfoot, straight out from the harbour and then all south thereof. Rapidly diminishing supplies for up to one hour each side of low water on spring tides. Don't move about a lot; potter slowly, ejecting ½ spoonful of running table salt from a carton into newly squirted holes, or if your eyesight is good, into smaller clean holes where the razor fish sit just below the surface.

Pendine. Storms here from time-to-time wash up great quantities of razor fish. They are not nearly as abundant now as hitherto.

Tackle shops

Carmarthen. *Coombs and Lawson*, 8 *Lammas Street. Tel.* (0267) 5662. Tackle supply. WWA river licences and permits for sale.

Kidwelly. *Morgan Davies, Newsagents,* 14 *Bridge Street.Tel.* (055 43) 474. Tackle supply only; WWA river licences sold; permits sold for local rivers and lakes. Advice on where to fish.

Pendine. *Ashwell Garage, Pendine. Tel.* (099 45) 232. Tackle supply.

Saundersfoot. *Saundersfoot Marine, The Harbour. Tel.* (0834) 812149. Tackle supply; fresh fish, frozen baits; advice on where to fish; booking of fishing trips; *Angling Times* weighing and report station.

Tenby. *Morris Bros, St. Julian Street. Tel.* (0834) 2105 *and* (0834 2306). Tackle supply; squid, frozen mackerel, herring and razor fish, worms and flies; advice on where to fish; WWA river licences sold, also permits for local waters. *Angling Times* weighing and report station.

Boat hire, trips or charter

Saundersfoot. *Mr. Robert Akers,* 31 *North Close, Ridgeway, Saundersfoot. Tel.* (0834) 812435. *Orion,* 34 ft, toilet. Mackerel trips and charter fishing. Bait provided, 5 hour angling trips, 8 hour charter, tackle available. (Booking on harbour daily).

Mr. G. Baskerville, Rose Cottage, Saundersfoot. Tel. (0834) 812613. *Cherylann,* 32 ft, toilets. Bait and tackle available.

Mr. W. G. Frost, 35 *North Close, Ridgeway, Saundersfoot. Tel.* (0834) 813666. *Shimo-San,* 36 ft, toilets. Radio telephone, echo sounder. Also available for winter charter per day, or two days with hotel accommodation. Tackle and bait provided free.

Mr. C. Morgan, Borrowdale, Ridgeway, Saundersfoot. Tel. (0834) 813314. (*Night Tel.* 813782), and *The Fishmarket, The Harbour, Saundersfoot. Celtic Rose,* 32 ft trawler, toilets, ferrograph. Some tackle available.

Saundersfoot Deep Sea Angling Limited. Contact: Mr. D. H. Fletcher, Mariners, East Williamston, Tenby. Tel. (0834) 812243. *Golden Fish,* 38 ft, toilet, holds Department of Trade Loadline Exempt Certificate i.e. can fish over 3 miles out to sea. Can take 12 people, 3 hour and 5 hour angling trips and 8 hour charter, bait and tackle provided – specialise in deep sea angling. A weekly cash prize is given for the biggest fish caught and at the end of the season a 'Golden Fish' trophy value £250–£300 plus a week's holiday in Saundersfoot is presented to the heaviest catch of the season at an evening function.

Tenby. *Mr. D. Bowler,* 1 *Lexden Terrace, Tenby. Tel.* (0834) 2663. *James Rolfe* 32 ft, and LA7, 36 ft, toilets, echo sounder. Trips in summer, charter in winter. Bait provided.

Boat launching slipways

Amroth. No slipway.

Ferryside. Public access over railway level crossing to hard sand beach.

Laugharne. Firm path launching of dinghies to creek at high water.

Llanstephan. Launching to beach at high water.

Pendine. Two slipways operated by local council. Small charge for cars and trailers driving straight to hard sand.

Saundersfoot. Slipway to harbour. Contact harbourmaster. *Tel.* (0834) 2717.

St. Ishmael's. Launching to sand beach at high water.

Tenby. *South Beach:* Walk down near south beach pavilion. Launching here not encouraged; *Castle Beach:* Walk down to soft sand suitable for dinghies. Launching here not encouraged; *North Beach:* 1 public slipway, The Mayor's slip, through gate near harbour masters office; 2. Yacht club slipway to harbour north side. Approach as item 1.

Sea fishing holidays

Inter Hotels Wales, *Old Market Hall, Tenby, Dyfed (Pembs). Tel. Tenby* (0834) 3214. Inclusive activity holiday – 5 days sea fishing, 7 nights bed and breakfast – at some of Wales' 16 Inter Hotels.

Tenby Travel, *Old Market Hall, Tenby, Dyfed (Pembs). Tel. Tenby* (0834) 3214. 42 hotels in the Tenby and Saundersfoot area have grouped together to offer a holiday which includes 5 days sea fishing for blue and porbeagle shark, tope, ray, etc., plus 7 nights dinner, bed and breakfast at the hotel of your choice. All fishing gear is supplied. The hotels are split into 3 categories – A, B and C according to their degree of luxury – and inclusive rates according to season are quoted on request.

Useful telephone numbers

In emergency
Dial 999 and ask for Coastguard.

At other times:
RNLI deep sea and inshore lifeboat. *Tenby. Boathouse. Tel.* (0834) 2197. **Coastguard.** *Tenby. Tel.* (0834) 2359 (*Not constantly manned*). **The Mumbles Coastguard HQ.** *Tel.* (0792) 66534. **RAF Air/Sea Rescue.** *Tenby. Tel.* (0834) 2124. **Caldy Island Lighthouse.** *Automatic.* **Weather forecasts.** *For Carmarthen Bay and Gower Coast. Tel. Swansea* (0792) 8011 (*summer only.* **Note:** Saundersfoot 2722 referred to in the Meteorological Office publication Met. O. Leaflet No. 3, 1976, is *not* a coastguard station and should *not* be used.

Burry Port to Pwlldu Head

Tope are caught in Carmarthen Bay's low water gullies as early as April. They are closely followed by big bass which frequent the Helwick Shoals, venturing along the rocky headlands and sand shores of Gower well into autumn. Summer sees the tope joining the shark offshore, plus a wide range of bottom feeding species, from rays to dabs. Mackerel are plentiful and bait is varied and locally abundant.

I. **Broughton Bay.** Shore tope in estuary channel, May/June. Leave car near Broughton caravan site, walk in north-north-east direction across the sands to where channel is plainly at its narrowest. Fishing is from low water minus 1 hour to low water plus 2 hours. Bait, ½ frozen herring or mackerel on a wire trace and 15–20 lbs line.

II. **Burry Holms.** An island 1 mile west of Llangennith, reached through the sand dunes from the car park near Broughton caravan site. Spinning and bottom fishing for bass over stony ground. Tidal island – check time with coastguard at Rhosili.

III. **Rhosili Beach.** Surf fishing for bass, flounder, all flood tide and first 2 hours of ebb. This is where George Micklewright's 1972 Welsh record 16 lbs 3 ozs bass came from. Best spots are opposite Old Rectory and where two streams cross beach at Llangennith end. Best baits: lug, rag, razor, clam. Access via Llangennith Caravan Site at Hill End or by unmade road to the point just above the beach at Rhosili end and a scramble down.

IV. a. **Worms Head.** Bass fishing, southern side of the Worm (half-tide island – observe coastguard notices on the Notice Board at Rhosili Coastguard Station in order not to get cut off). July/September tope fishing from ledges on north side, near Kitchen Corner, on

continued on next page

Rhosili village, the ledged National Trust cliffs and Worms Head

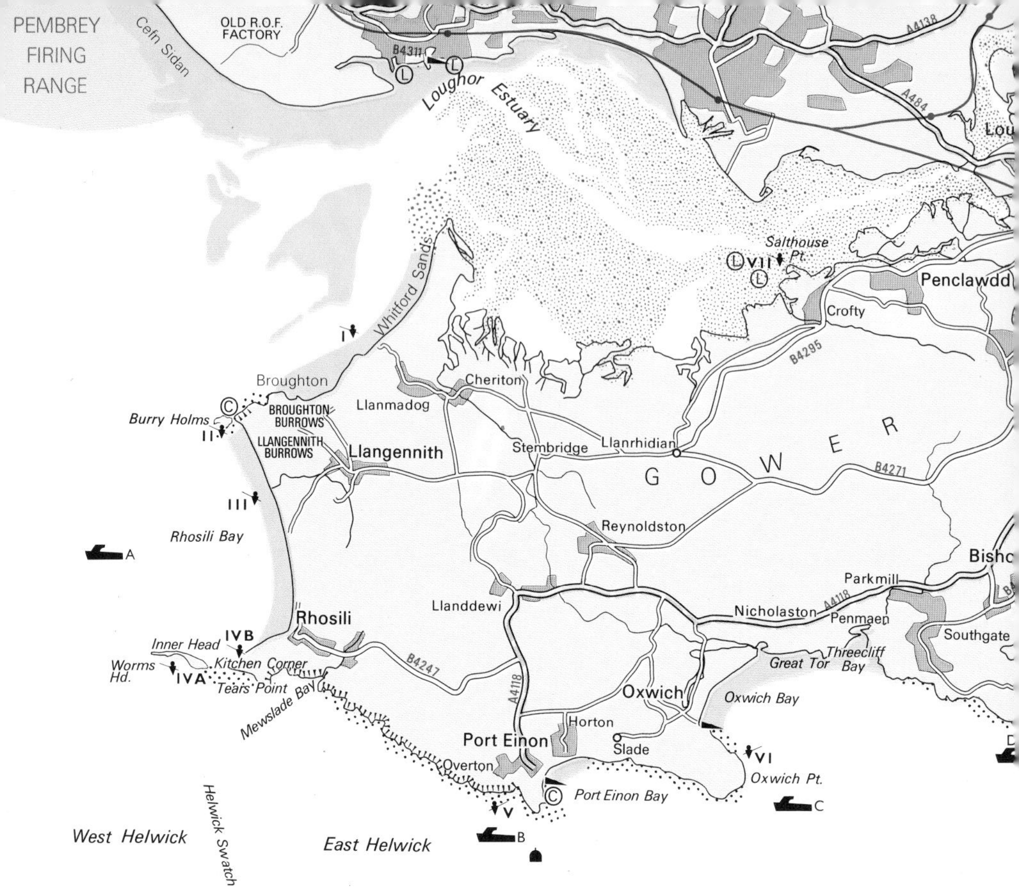

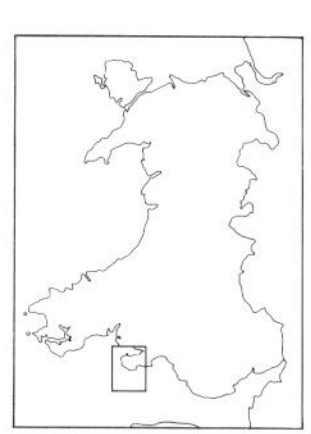

Pembrey Firing Range
When firing is in progress red warning flags are displayed.

Burry Port to Pwlldu Head – continued

to sandy bottom. This mark excellent for whiting in autumn, early winter (see IV b). Soft, peeler crab available in Sound between Worm and mainland or in vicinity of Mumbles Pier, Swansea. Park at Rhosili village for the 1 mile walk to the Inner Head.

IV b. **Rhosili ledges.** Get to the ledges by parking at Rhosili (car park) and walking the coast path towards Worms Head. About 200 yards before the coastguard hut descend on the right a dangerous looking steep footpath – which is quite safe – to comfortable ledges at least 10 ft above the water. You need to winch up your catches. An excellent spot for early winter whiting fishing and in summer tope are taken.

V. **Port Einon – Fall Bay.** Excellent bass fishing, June/September, float or bottom fishing (soft or peeler crab, or with live mackerel) and spinning (large toby or red gill), wherever the angler can reach water-level to rock gullies. Leave car Overton village, follow cliff path to suitable locations. Caution advised. Wear commando boots. Do not fish alone.

VI. **Oxwich Point.** Crowded summer beach with Penrice Estate car park (charge). Right hand side of bay has mussel and winkle beds and weedy rocks with sand between. Fish soft crab in the gullies for bass early morning or late evening low water −1 to low water +2, or float fish high water −2 to high water +2 from higher rock platforms. Shrimp and prawns netted in rock pools.

VII. **Salthouse Point.** Occasional bass, bottom fishing summer, but crabs troublesome. Excellent flounder fishing November/February, rag or lug bait (lug diggable on spot) from low water to high water plus 1 hour. Approach via trading estate at Crofty, on Swansea/Llanridian road. (*Note:* driving on to the commercial cockle beds, possible with a Land-Rover-type vehicle, is forbidden). Similar fishing is found at other points on the estuary's north side up to and including a point between Loughor river and rail bridges, a popular venue for local anglers.

Boat fishing

A major boating centre, The Mumbles, is conveniently near for larger craft and charter trips in this coastal section. Dinghy and power-boat owners can go right to the heart of the area, to Oxwich Bay, before wetting their boat. There is no need to go long distances offshore either, for coastal movement with the tide will take the fast boat to the bass and tope rich Helwick Shoals and into the fish feeding grounds of Carmarthen Bay. Again commercial trolling is likely to interfere with the long term situation; one boat in 5 hours on one tide took 105 4 to 7 lbs. bass.

Swansea from the anchorage at The Mumbles

A. **Rhosili Bay.** Precise marks are difficult to indicate but anchor fishing in the region 1–2 miles due south of the Pendine range's DZ5 buoy and nearby Hall Rock nearly always produces dabs and plaice, dogfish, ray and the occasional tope. Porbeagle of good size have been taken quite consistently by shark anglers inside the 10 fathom line here. No nearer launching facility than Burry Port.

B. **Helwick Shoals – Worms Head.** A first-class area for surface-shoaling bass which usually feed on the morning flood tide, responding best to toby and similar spoons in a variety of sizes. The ¼ mile wide shoals extend from the Helwick Pass buoy at 1–2 fathoms due west for 6 miles. When fish are not showing, trolling with red gill eels often pays off. Unfortunately, launching conditions are difficult, most locals utilising the flat rocks at Fall Bay – and it is a major operation to get a boat down here from the road. However, the owner of a big fast dory could certainly launch further east at Oxwich and be quickly at the fishing.

C. **Oxwich Point.** Fast tides around this headland make it an excellent mark for tope and some big fish, up to 60 lbs plus, have been taken. Mackerel usually plentiful in summer for bait and craft can be launched, on payment of a small fee, from Oxwich beach. Caution should be exercised by owners of small boats, as overfalls can quickly develop in wind-over-tide conditions. Neaps are best: there is a 2½ knot tide on springs.

D. **Pwlldu Head.** As marks B and C, but nearer Swansea Bay, consequently smaller boats can reach it from The Mumbles, 3 miles east. Porbeagle shark, tope, thornback rays, and good winter whiting, are all caught off the south Gower coast.

Bait supply

A good bait area, with variety.

Lugworm. *Pwll, Llanelli:* Leave your car a few hundred yards from the shore and walk south. Excellent quantities of good lug. High water +2 to high water −2. *Crofty, Penclawdd:* Drive a short way on to the beach to a well worn track. A 15 minute walk due west (don't turn north towards some poles) brings you to a stream. Cross it and dig on the other side high water +2 to high water −2 for abundant medium-sized lug. (Do not drive a vehicle on to the cockle beds.) *Port Einon:* Very few and small, where the rocks meet the sand, to low water +2. *Three Cliffs Bay:* A few, beside the old dried-out loop of the stream inside the sand spit.

Crab. Some good peeling crab on the north side of Worms Head causeway, and soft greenback in the weedy rocks towards Port Einon Point.

Shellfish. Clams frequent at the Crofty lug mark (above mentioned) also cockles in commercial quantities. Ample large mussels south of Oxwich Bay car park.

Live fish. Goby, blenny and shrimp about Worms Head causeway.

(For general information see under Swansea and The Mumbles in following coastal section.)

Tackle shops

Burry Port. *Burry Port Yacht Chandlers, Ltd. The Harbour, Dyfed.* Tackle supply.

Llanelli. *Barry Llywellyn Sports, Cowell Precinct, Tel.* (05542) 3720. All types of fishing.

Llanelli. *John James, Anglers Corner,* 65 *Robinson Street. Tel. Llanelli* (05542) 3981. Tackle supply and repair, frozen baits, advice on where to fish. Licences sold for WWA. Permits for Carmarthen and District waters and Lower Lliedi reservoir.

Boat hire, trips and charter

Burry Port. *Carmarthen Bay Yacht Charters, Ltd.* Booking forms etc. from *W. J. Marks,* 31 *West End, Llanelli, Carms. Tel. Llanelli* (05542) 4262 or (05542) 4528. Services provided: (1) *Charter of fishing launches.* Easily arranged. (2) *Dinghy hire.* Triple hulled fibreglass dinghies fully equipped, 4½ hp outboards, long range (2½ gall) fuel tanks. Week or day hire. (24 hours notice). (3) *Yacht charter; Petronella,* 5 tons, *Moyune,* 7 tons. Fully equipped and crewed. Day charter (including meals) or longer periods. Tuition in yacht and boat handling and navigation also provided at reasonable rates.

Burry Port. *Mr. Peter G. Davies, Dwr y felyn, Neath, West Glamorgan. Tel.* (0639) 4976. '*Maxine*', 35 ft, licensed for 8, radio telephone, toilets, bunks. Tackle and bait available if required. Charter for 8 hour or 10 hour trips from Burry Port harbour.

Burry Port. *Mr. George West, Harbour House, The Harbour. Tel. Burry Port* (05546) 2511. *Good Shepherd,* 50 ft, toilets, radio telephone, echo sounder, radar. Trips or charter pick up Burry Port East Dock by arrangement. Max 12 persons. Bait by prior arrangement.

Burry Port. *Burry Port Yacht Chandlers. Tel. Burry Port* (05546) 2740. Bait and tackle provided by prior arrangement.

Burry Port. *Mr. S. N. Ricketts,* 30 *Danlan Park, Pembrey, Llanelli, Dyfed Tel. Burry Port* (05546) 3367 *Rig I Fy* 314, 26 ft, toilets, Ferrograph, radio. Weekends any season. Bait by arrangement. Gear for hire.

Boat launching slipways

Burry Port. 2 public slipways in harbour (small charge for use in and out).

Oxwich Bay. Slipway to hard sand from near Penrice Estate car park. Suitable for all trailed craft. Small charge.

Penclawdd, Crofty. Launching to water covering mud flats at high tide from sandy road.

Port Einon. Small dinghies can be manhandled to beach of hard sand.

Fishing advice

Sweyns'ey Angling Club, Hon. Sec., Mr. R. J. Griffin, 27 *Rodney Street, Swansea.*

Useful telephone numbers

In emergency
Dial 999 and ask for Coastguard.

At other times:
RNLI lifeboat. *Tenby. Boathouse. Tel.* (0834) 2197. *The Mumbles. Hon. Sec. Tel. Swansea* (0792) 68324. *Boathouse. Tel. Swansea* (0792) 66246. **Coastguard.** *Rhosili. Tel. Gower* (044 120) 502 (*Not constantly manned*). **Coastguard HQ.** *The Mumbles. Tel. Swansea* (0792) 66534. **Trinity House lighthouse.** *Mumbles Head. Tel. Swansea* 50626.

Weather forecasts. *For Swansea Bay, Carmarthen Bay and Gower Coast. Tel. Swansea* (0792) 8011 (*summer only*). *Meteorological Office, Glamorgan / Rhoose Airport* (0446) 710343.

Swansea Bay

This is the eastwards limit of the rich, clear and saline waters of South West Wales. Local sea anglers enjoy great variety of boat fishing from Swansea and The Mumbles for summer tope, skate, ray – both thornback and blonde – monkfish, conger and bass, and winter cod and whiting. Bait is fairly abundant and angling services of good standard.

I. **The Mumbles.** II. **Lighthouse Island.** Maroon yourself on the shore steps of the lighthouse island and spin for school bass in the narrows, with a shiny toby lure, as the water rises high enough for them to attempt the run through. They make a similar run back when the tide is dropping towards the same level. The remaining time can be spent on the bottom with local crab, often to very good effect.

III. **Pier.** Capacious pier (small fishing charge) with an upper deck and lower angling end extension. No fishing only on lifeboat extension and access. Beneath is an excellent peeler crab bed. Some quite heavy conger come off the end of the pier in summer and mackerel come in close enough to gather for bait. The odd summer bass is taken as well as a great number of winter whiting, though codling are few. A very long drop involves hauling or use of a drop net if you have one. The bay round to Swansea is a sand/mud mixture and fishes for flatfish high water – 1½ to high water + 1½

IV. **Swansea Bay.** Breakwaters at Swansea Docks, Neath, Briton Ferry and Port Talbot are used by local fishermen for summer bass, flatfish and occasional ray, winter whiting and occasional cod. Access is complicated and these marks are unlikely to be of great appeal to the holidaying angler, though local clubs are always willing to advise the individual visitor on suitable fishing spots.

V. **Porthcawl.** *Sker Rocks, The Breakwater and Newton beach.* Local anglers go afloat to the Tusker Rock and Scarweather sand banks to miss the summer holiday pressure on pier and foreshore anglers. Good casts from the rocks with fishbait give thornback ray, dogfish and flatfish. Some good bass have fallen to local experts who fish the rocky outcrops east of the town, beyond Newton and west to Sker Point. Black rubbery lug is dug on the beach under Trecco Bay Caravan Park. Shrimp are often thrown up on to Rest Bay rocks by spray. (Item 1 of next section).

Boat fishing

The more powerful the craft the more marks there are available. Here are two that can be fished by most craft when weather conditions are suitable.

A. **White Oyster Trench.** This is a distinct deepening in the sea bed which runs roughly from the eastern end of Langland Bay and extends towards Pwlldu Head, parallel with the shore and approximately 1½ miles out. Fast tides between White Oyster Ledge and the mainland have gouged out the sea-bed to a depth of 16 fathoms and this is an excellent mark during the summer for good tope and well into winter for thornback ray. Spring tides, however, should be avoided as it is then extremely difficult to hold ground. It is outside the shelter of Swansea Bay and, therefore, not suitable for dinghies.

B. **Outer Green Grounds.** Perhaps the best known of Swansea Bay marks and one which has been consistently yielding fish to sea anglers since the turn of the century. In summer, tope and ray with small conger are the staple fishing, together with dabs and plaice (the latter very abundant in some years). In winter the grounds have plentiful whiting and occasional cod. Orthodox bottom fishing methods yield results: fish baits in summer-time (when mackerel are occasionally plentiful on the grounds), lug in winter.

Bait supply

Swansea's bigger tackle shops are improving in the supply of live bait. But if you have to grub your own, here is where you can start:

Crab. June and July from The Mumbles pier to Mumbles lighthouse island on low springs, under stones, in weed and buried in sand near rocky outcrops, but very heavily picked.

Lugworm. Small but abundant between Oystermouth and West Cross. Bigger lug close in, where the sand is mixed with stones and grit.

Shellfish and live fish. The island pools and rocks around Mumbles Head, Bracelet Bay and Mewslade Bay hold butterfish, goby, blenny and mussel.

Tackle shops

Port Talbot. *Selwyn Jenkins, 45 Station Road. Tel.* (063 96) 2787. Tackle supply and repairs; flies; advice on where to fish; WWA river licences and permits for local rivers and lakes sold; *Angling Times* weighing station.

Swansea. *Capstan House Limited, Beach Street. Tel.* (0792) 54756. Tackle supply and repair, bait supply, fresh lug, rag, frozen razor fish, cuttle, squid. Boating specialists. Advice on where to fish. *Angling Times* report station. Free tide tables on receipt of stamped addressed envelope.

Swansea. *P. E. Mainwaring, 9 Dillwyn Road, Sketty. Tel. Swansea* (0792) 22245. Tackle and coarse supply and repair. Fresh lug when available, maggots. Advice on where to fish. River licences for WWA.

Boat hire, trips or charter

Swansea South Dock. (rear of Leisure Centre). *Derek Jones, Bank Cottage, Wernffrwd, Llanmorlais, Swansea. Tel. Penclawdd* (044123) 403. *Simon Peter,* 36 ft, Day or evening charter.

Swansea Docks. *Paul Radford, 73 Cherry Grove, Sketty, Swansea. Tel. Swansea* (0792) 23388 for sea angling all year. Individuals and parties welcome. The *Lady Helen* is a fast, purpose-built sea angling boat with toilet, cooking facilities and all safety equipment to local regulations. Brochures available on request. S.A.E. please.

Swansea Docks. *Mr. D. Lawrence, skipper, 10 Gelli, Llanharry, Cowbridge, South Glamorgan. Tel. Tonyrefail* (934) 671351 *or Llantrisant* 222255. M.F.V. *Morning Star,* 52 ft fast ex-RNLI lifeboat, licenced for 12 persons for sea angling and diving. Large, roomy, with twin engines. Ferrograph, 2 RDF sets, available South Dock, Swansea for hire, charter or trips, wreck fishing, shark or general fishing in South Wales or Lundy waters. Bait by arrangement. Some tackle available.

Boat launching slipways

Aberavon. Public slipway on promenade (local council owner). Free use for small craft.

Brynmill (*near Sketty Road junction*). Small craft can be manhandled to hard sand.

Gower. *Caswell Bay.* Access to hard sand but heavily used by holidaymakers.

Swansea. *The Mumbles, Southend.* Two slips opposite Mumbles Yacht Club, useable 3½ hours each side of high water. One slipway opposite village lane used 2 hours each side of high water. All controlled by local council. Free use for small craft, but busy.

Fishing advice and competitions

Mumbles Motor Boat and Fishing Club, Hon. Sec. of Fishing Committee: Mr. Bob Cable, c/o Clubhouse, 642 Mumbles Road, Southend, Swansea. Tel. Swansea 69646. The club is situated in Southend Mumbles and overlooks the moorings, can offer temporary membership and the following facilities to visiting fishermen and boat owners. There is a club room which will accommodate 200, reasonable prices at the bar, social events are held

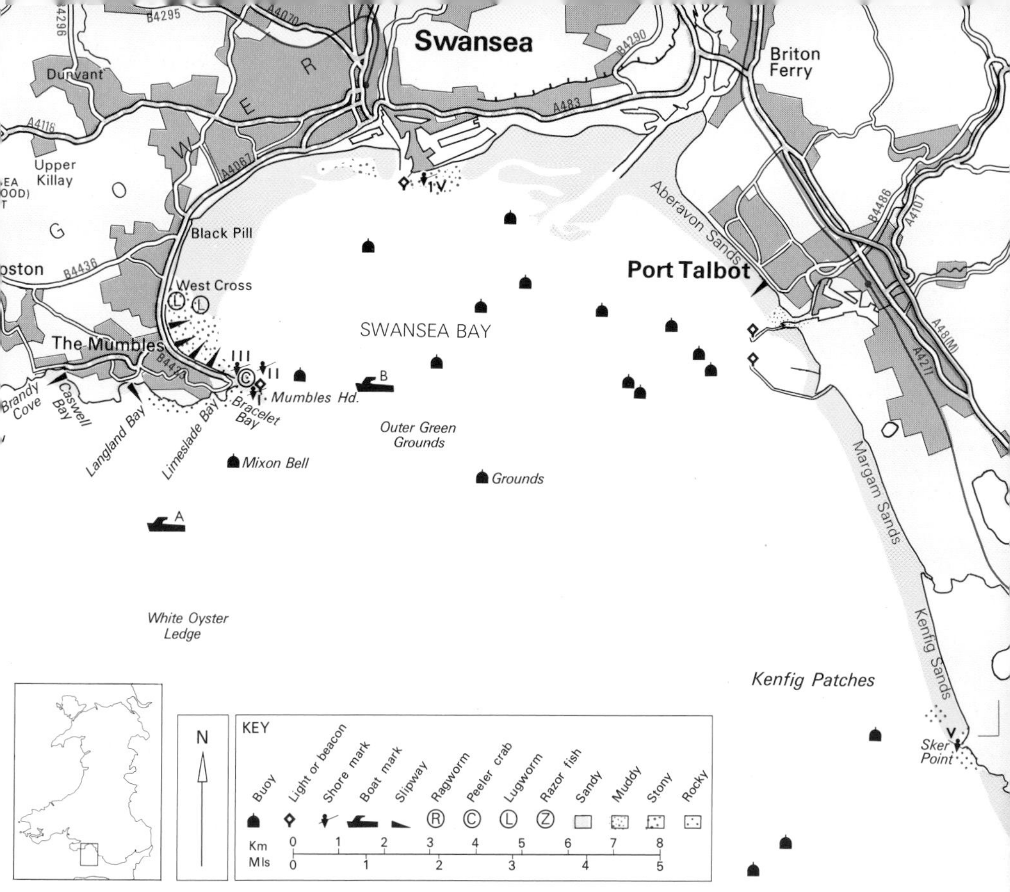

weekly in the club and fishing competitions both on the shore and boats throughout the year. There is also a 2,000 square foot boat building and repair hall, motor room with storage for engines and other gear, also outside accommodation for trailers and small boats. Temporary moorings can be arranged for visitors if required, but please notify the club at least two weeks prior to visit.

Sweyns'ey Angling Club. Hon. Sec., Mr. R. J. Griffin, 27 Rodney Street, Swansea.

Welsh Shark, Tope, Skate, and Conger Club, Hon. Sec., Mr. Eric Woods, 1 Parc Glas, Skewen, Neath.

Useful telephone numbers
In emergency
Dial 999 and ask for Coastguard
At other times:
Coastguard HQ. *The Mumbles. Tel.* (0792) 66534. **Weather forecasts.** *Post Office. Tel. Cardiff* (0222) 8091. *Meteorological Office, Gloucester. Tel. Churchdown* (0452) 855566. *Meteorological Office, Glamorgan/Rhoose Airport* (0446) 710343.

Vary your angling holiday with some trout and coarse fishing with –

Porthcawl Sea Angling Association,
Freshwater Section,
Sportsmen's Club,
The Esplanade, Porthcawl.
Tel. (065671) 3975.
Trout to 2 lbs in The Wilderness Lake, mirror carp to 10½ lbs in the Meadow Lake; both at Newton Nottage road. Day permits and River Authority licences from

Allsports and J. Bridge,
10/12 John Street, Porthcawl.
Tel. (065671) 2873.

Porthcawl to Cardiff

Summer fishing is weak in this area but conditions are just right for winter cod, whiting and flounder. Local anglers find great sport from their arrival in early November right through to early spring. The rise of tide throughout is colossal; 40 feet at Cardiff on a spring tide.

I. See item V in previous section.

II. **Ogmore by Sea.** Like its neighbour, Southerndown, just east, Ogmore is a sand beach backed by convenient rock ledges. It is fished for winter cod and whiting and summer bass. Knowledgeable Porthcawl and Bridgend anglers manage to coax quite a few fish from these waters. A car can be taken near the shoreline between the village and the river estuary.

continued on next page

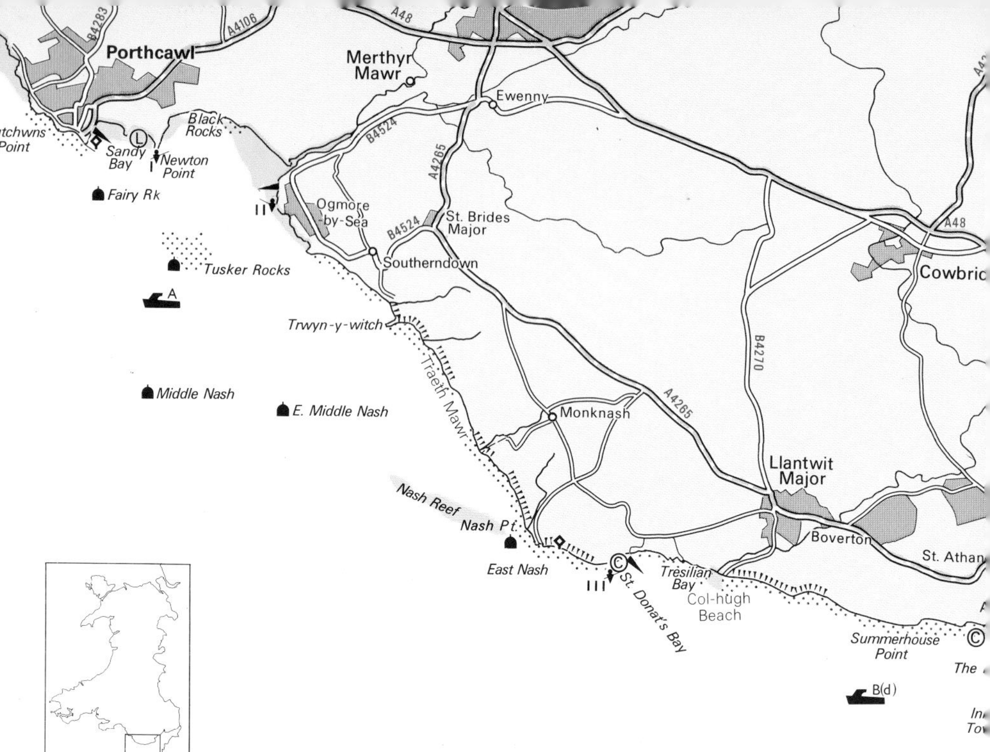

Porthcawl to Cardiff – continued

III. **St. Donat's Castle** (Atlantic College foreshore). Park in a lay-by by a wall just east of the castle grounds gate; enter a wicket gate, follow the west boundary of Atlantic College football field to a stile, then go west to the beach by a steep path. Good soft and peeler crab, found here, ledgered into rough ground has given some excellent bass, wrasse and rockling. This mark is the best of three or four that can be reached by leaving the main coast road A4265 and taking by-roads or footpaths: Col-Hugh beach at Llantwit Major, Tresilian Bay, Nash Point, and Traeth-mawr at Monknash.

IV. **Aberthaw: The Leys.** This, the ecological overlap where cod-land and bass-land mix, is a popular summer and winter mark. A by-road south off the A4265 opposite St. Athan war memorial takes one to a car park on the west side of Aberthaw power stations. To reach the fishing beach, walk east between the sea wall and station perimeter wire for ¼ mile to the second ladder. At low water periods make for the east pair of hot water outfall domes if float fishing for mullet or spinning for bass, and between the east and west pairs of domes if bottom fishing for summer bass or winter cod. Fish high water +4 to low water +2. Small hard-gained beach rag are used to float-fish for mullet close in, in the hot water run, 25–50 yards out in the sea. On times they go wild and give excellent sport. Spin for smaller bass – many too small to take – with a white plastic eel (electric cable) or small red gill, using a quarter of a candle as a weight. It floats high enough to spin in over bad snags. The best bass – early season (4–6 pounders and better) – take ledgered soft crab, a rare bait here. Large fish are also taken in the autumn in the muddy bay below the main car park. Cod from mid-November to early spring take lug and rag or fish at most points along this coast, but not very frequently.

V. **Rhoose: The Lime Kilns.** Walk west a tough ¾ mile along the ebbing beach from Porthkerry Country Park. Fished by knowledgeable locals with fish baits, squid, crab or rag in summer, mainly for conger and bass, in winter for cod. Leave yourself time to get back before water cuts you off, or you have a long walk to the Rhoose road through a caravan park.

VI. **Barry: Cold Knap.** A steep pebble beach on to sand with a rocky headland at the east end. Brandon Jones fishing here about 7 years ago caught the one-time British and now Welsh record cod of 44 lbs 8 ozs. A low water recce and rotten bottoms are necessary to fish off the headland, but the beach is easily fished, both marks giving winter cod, whiting and flounder 2 hours each side of high water.

VII. **Barry: Jackson's Bay.** A popular summer conger and winter cod and whiting venue. The dock's breakwater is easiest to reach – walk out from Barry Yacht Club house from near the old Barry Island pier-head station. Some prefer the point on the south side rocks under Butlin's, though difficult to reach and leave for 3 hours on each side of high water (impossible in the dark).

VIII. **Barry: Bendrick Rock.** Fishes similar to mark IX. Reach it by car to a point near Sully Hospital, then walk across the beach to the dry island. Do not maroon yourself on springs when there is a blow. The beach east to Sully Island gives few but good sized winter cod.

IX. **Sully Island.** Car park opposite the island just off B4267, east of Sully. Causeway dries about 3 hours after high water to 3 hours before high water. It's very dangerous to wade; put up with the wait if caught. *East Point.* From island's highest point follow a path to a pole set in the rock, on extreme point, then climb down to a rock platform, dry between high water +3½ to high water −3½. The deepest point on the coast, with 4 fathoms close in, it fishes well mid-November to early spring for codling (few whiting), summer for small conger averaging

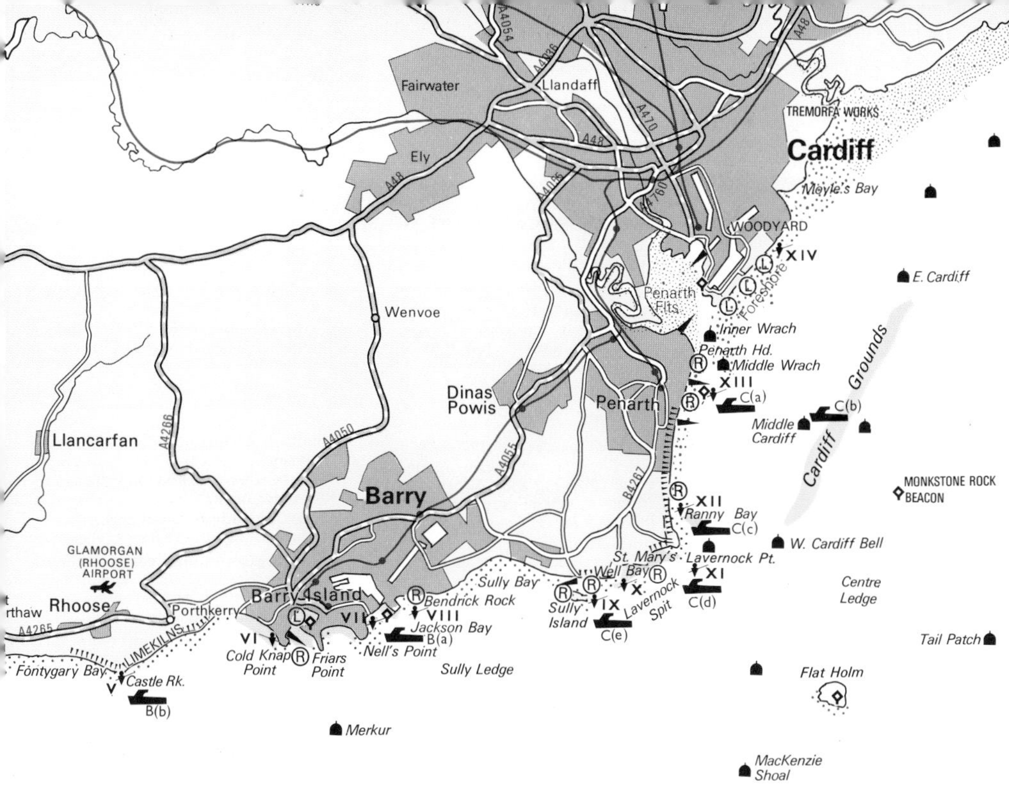

3–4 lbs, dogfish and pouting. *Weed Patch*. In the middle of the Island's south side. Less popular but occasionally good for codling when it dries on spring tides. *West Point*. Poor for winter cod, better for the odd bass and conger in summer.

X. **Lavernock: St. Mary's Well Bay sand spit.** Limited road parking after the summer car park closes. Walk through the wicket gate to beach, heading in the general direction of Flat Holm. The sand spit is revealed on 9.2 metres or more tides (reckoned on Cardiff). Fish low water $-1\frac{1}{2}$ hours to low water + 2 hours, mid-November to early spring. Good cod mainly 3-pounders but some 12 lbs to 15 lbs, and, to a lesser extent, pouting and whiting are taken. The odd small bass is taken in and around the neck of the spit in late summer.

XI. **Lavernock Point.** Fishable only on springs over 12.4 metres (reckoned on Cardiff) and then for only 1 hour before low water to $\frac{1}{4}$ hour after, in winter between mid-November and early spring. A rough swell but little wind is best. Dead on the tide's turn, usually, shrimp-gorging cod up to 5–8 lbs, come around the bend near an outfall pipe, taking a lugworm/squid cocktail cast 70 yards in the general direction midway between Flat Holm and Steep Holme Islands.

XII. **Ranny Bay.** A cliff path, slippery in wet weather, runs north from Lavernock Point church (road parking) skirting a farm, to drop into a shingly bay. Go north for 200–250 yards around a shallow headland to finer gravel. Fish from high water -3 to high water $+2$. The odd whiting and flounder arrive early, but cod, the main quarry, usually arrive about $\frac{1}{2}$ hour after high water.

XIII. **Penarth.** Fishing at Penarth is similar to that at Ranny Bay, but fishing is not allowed directly off the pier at Penarth from 5 pm (6 pm in summer) to 9 am, nor at any time during the month of August. Fishing is not allowed from the promenade between the pier and slipway situated just beyond the multi-storey car park.

XIV. **Cardiff: Foreshore and Moyle's Bay.** (British Docks Board property and can only be fished with their express permission.) This is really the $\frac{1}{2}$ mile long 10 ft high outer wall and bank of Cardiff Docks, facing on to mud and a mixture of sand and stone. Dry at 3 hours before high water, it is fished from $2\frac{1}{2}$ hours before high water to about 2 hours after. Summer's silver eel, tiny flounders and 9 ozs pout give way in the second week in November to the whiting boom with fish of $\frac{3}{4}$ lb to $1\frac{1}{4}$ lb. It fishes better on dark evenings. Whiting are followed in the third week of November by good codling, which stay till early spring. A few fish reach 10–15 lbs. Lug found on the beach is better than rag. Little else attracts them consistently.

Boat fishing

The need for a boat in the eastern half of this coast section is not so pressing. For the boat fishing that exists, fast tide rips and numerous changing shallows demand a solid craft, plenty of power and a knowledgeable skipper. Porthcawl, Barry and Penarth are convenient.

A. **Porthcawl.** Shoal-ridden channels hem in Porthcawl harbour; south east the Tuskar Rock has claimed many lives including a whole Mumbles lifeboat crew. South west lie the Scarweather sands marked by lightship and by buoys at the four corners. It's a popular boat venue and the local angling club's members are among those who make

continued on next page

good catches, starting with mackerel which they freeze down for winter bait. There are good summer thornback ray, plaice and shoaling bass, with flounder, whiting and some sizeable cod at winter marks.

B. **Barry**. Two favourite spots are (a) the mouth of Jackson's Bay, just west of the breakwater, and a point off the lime kilns near Rhoose (b). In summer boats make a trip to The Leys (c), Aberthaw, for bass spinning forays, interspersed with some bottom fishing further out and a mile or two west (d), to catch the ray, conger, skate, bass and dogfish that make the rock/sand bottom in 15–18 fathoms their summer home. Most tide rip headlands or sandbanks (e) from Rhoose to Sully Island and out to the One Fathom Banks hold their attention in winter, for good catches of cod, whiting, pout and flounder are made on lug, rag and squid.

C. **Cardiff/Penarth.** Powered dinghies and larger craft put out from Cardiff Docks' and Penarth Dock's yacht basins, and from the Rivers Ely and Rumney, fishing in summer for odd ray, flatfish, dogfish, silver and conger eels. But from the beginning of winter to early spring, on calm days, the trickle of boats becomes a flood, hunting cod and whiting. Bigger boats try first about ½ mile south east of Penarth pier (a), then, when the ebb has fined down, they move for the flood to the sandbanks 2 miles off Penarth Head or to the cod holes C(b). To find the holes, depressions 2 fathoms deeper than the surrounding seabed, keep Middle Wrack buoy in line with Penarth Head's church until Moyle's Bay comes into view. Smaller boats persist at the first mark, sometimes running down more towards Ranny Pool (c) or taking Lavernock Head well out to come round into Lavernock Bay (d) or close in to Sully Island east point (e).

Bait supply

An area where bait supply can baffle visitors. Cardiff's tackle shops usually have some rag if you are prepared to order in advance. Here are the accessible bait beds:

Lugworm. *Trecco Bay, Porthcawl.* Black lug on spring tides.
The Leys, Aberthaw. Moderate sized lug but very difficult to dig, starting 50 yards from the sea wall, beneath a layer of rounded pebbles itself overlayed by sand. High water +2 to high water −2.
Watchtower Bay, Barry. Moderate lug. Approach from Cold Knap.
Cardiff Foreshore (see directions above). 2½ in to 3 in lug in the flat mud/gravel mixture within 6 ft of the sloping shingle in right hand half of beach. Dig to casts on the edges of small pools and rivulets. A bit overdug for winter cod.

Ragworm *Cold Knap headland (east side) and Bendrick Rock.* Noted as good marks but hard digging.
Sully Island. Large rag beds, not king but some good princes, in very tough digging in stony (not pure mud) ground extending east of the causeway.
Ranny Bay (see above). A few rag where mud, stones and weed join, straight down from the lifebelt post. ½ hour each side of low water on springs.
Penarth Pier. Medium rag mainly alongside gullies, and beach structures.

Tackle shops

Barry. *Barry Chandlers and Marine Services, 20 Plymouth Road. Tel. Barry* 742204.

Astoria Sports, 15 Holton Road, Barry. Tel. Barry 735165.

Clanfield Bros, 21–23 Winston Square. Tel. Barry 741707. Tackle supply and repair, fresh rag and fish baits. Flies. Advice on where to fish. WWA river licences sold.

Bailey Sports, Vere Street, Barry. Tel. Barry 734497. Tackle supply, fresh rag, frozen baits, advice on where to fish. Fishing trips arranged.

B. James, Bev's Tackle Shop, 17 Fontygary Road, Rhoose. Tel. Rhoose 710247. Tackle supply and repair; fresh rag, frozen baits, flies; advice on where to fish; WWA river licences sold. *Angling Times* report station.

Bridgend. *Mr. Brian Rowe, Tackle Shop, 96 Nolton Street. Tel.* (0656) 58254. Tackle supply and repair. Fresh rag, frozen baits, maggots and flies; WWA river licences, permits sold for local rivers and reservoir (Eglwys Nunydd); booking of angling boat trips. *Angling Times* report station.

Cardiff. *Anglers Supplies, 172 Penarth Road. Tel.* 20723. Tackle supply; fresh rag and lug, frozen squid and razor fish. WWA river licences; fishing advice; *Angling Times* weighing station.

Porthcawl. *Mr. G. S. Jackson, 14 Well Street. Tel.* (065 671) 2511. Tackle supply; frozen baits; advice on where to fish. Permits sold for Kenfig Pool and river. *Angling Times* report station.

Boat hire, trips or charter

Barry Docks. *Mr. W. Nemanis, 6 Kingsland Crescent, Barry Island. Tel.* 739754. *Orian* 42 ft, toilets, pick up at pontoon in Barry yacht basin, day rate or charter.

Clanfield Bros., 21–23 Winston Square, Colcott, Barry. Tel. Barry 741707. *Croeso I*, 36 ft, toilets, fish finder, sails daily from Barry Pierhead on 8 hour trips. Bait can be arranged.

Penarth. *Mr. G. Lloyd, 27 Syr David's Avenue, Canton. Tel. Cardiff* 36366. *Michele*, 50 ft. Angling charter from Penarth Dock, daily, trips 10-11 hours duration.

Porthcawl. *Mr. T. Ducker, 3 Pen-y-lan Close, Porthcawl. Tel.* (065 671) 4909. *Dolphin*, P.T.47. Echo sounder, radio telephone, trips or charter

Mr. Ken Parsons, 30 Llangewydd Road, Bridgend. Tel. Bridgend (0656) 56481. *Our Sonia*, 27 ft. licensed for 10 anglers. Echo sounder, radio. Trips or charter.

Boat launching slipways

Aberthaw. *The Leys.* A light dinghy can be manhandled down steep shingle bank to a muddy bay but one should remain close inshore with such a craft.

Barry. *Jackson's Bay.* Yacht Club slipway to harbour. Winch. Club members only. *Old Harbour.* (*Watch Tower Bay*). Council slipway. Only 60 permits issued annually. Charge for key.

Cardiff. *Yacht Club, Cardiff Docks.* Slipway near dry dock. For use of club members only. *Ely River Mouth* (*East bank*). Private yacht club slipway to tidal River Ely.

Llantwit Major. (*Colhugh beach*). Manhandling to beach from adjacent car park (charge). Hard sand channel to low water mark.

Penarth Head. (near old dock office). Private slipway, under development.

Penarth Multi-storey car park. (*north end of promenade*). Council slipway. Free launching with council permit but boats must have insurance cover of £50,000.

Penarth Yacht Club (*south end of promenade*) Council slipway. Free launching with council permit but boats must have insurance cover of £50,000. Yacht club boats have precedence.

Penarth Motor Boat and Sailing Club. Private slipway on north bank of Ely estuary. Club members only.

Porthcawl. *Harbour.* Local authority slipway. Small daily charge or season ticket. Apply to harbour master.

St. Donats. Atlantic College slipway.

Fishing advice

Barry Angling Society, Hon. Sec., I. L. Davies, 16 Herbert Street, Barry.

Cardiff Sea Angling Association, Hon. Sec., Mr. G. E. Jones, 34 Coveny Street, Splott, Cardiff. Tel. (0222) 373730.

Porthcawl Sea Angling Association, Hon. Sec., Mr. W. D. Tucker, 45 Long Acre Drive, Nottage, Porthcawl. Tel. (065671) 4076. (*Headquarters: The Sportsmen's Club, The Esplanade, Porthcawl. Tel.* (065671) 3975).

Useful telephone numbers

In emergency
Dial 999 and ask for Coastguard.

At other times:
RNLI lifeboat. *Barry (Jackson's Bay). Tel.* (91) 4422. **Coastguard H.Q.** *The Mumbles. Tel.* (0792) 66534 *or Barry. Tel.* (91) 5016. **Trinity House lighthouse.** *Nash Point. Tel. Llantwit Major* 3471.

Weather forecasts. *Post Office. Tel. Cardiff* (0222) 8091. *Meteorological Office, Gloucester. Tel. Churchdown* (0452) 855566. *Meteorological Office, Cardiff (Wales) Airport* (0446) 710343.

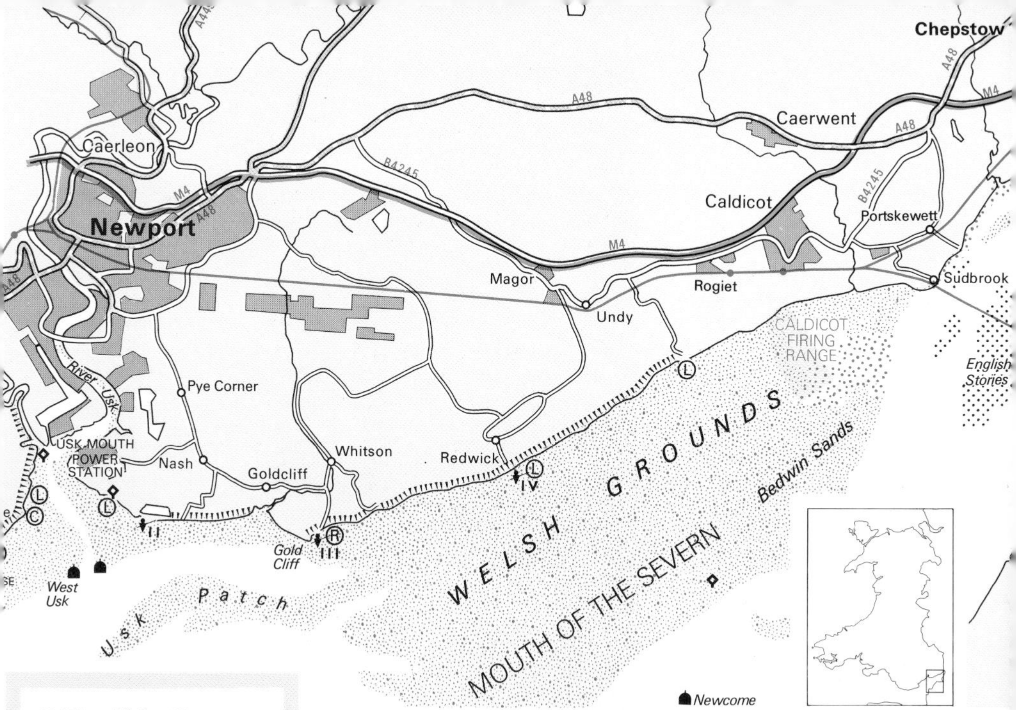

Caldicot Firing Range
Red flags are flown on the sea wall at either end of the range when firing is in progress.

Rumney to the Wye

Gwent anglers would not agree that this part of the coast is the fag end of Welsh fishing. They would agree it takes more skill than most anglers are endowed with to wrest constantly both variety of fish and good weights from these uncompromisingly fast and shallow waters. But it is done, with conger up to 10 lbs, codling in good numbers and whiting as well.

I. **Newport: St. Bride's.** Lying on the west side of the Usk (near the Lighthouse Hotel car park), the foreshore is flat, a mud/sand mixture and suitable for fishing with lug and rag, high water $-1\frac{1}{2}$ to high water $+1\frac{1}{2}$ only. Rough winter conditions are best, on the down tide, and a short cast carries you over the inshore boulders. Summer is silver eel time with occasional sole, plaice, flounder and bass. November brings the pout and whiting glut, which starts to tail off after 3–4 weeks, and the occasional codling.

II. **Nash.** $\frac{1}{2}$ mile along the coast east of the Usk mouth power station. Fishing as at the lighthouse. Access from Newport through Pye Corner.

III. **Goldcliff.** (Hill Farm, Goldcliff Bay, Goldcliff Point). Road approaches sea wall through Goldcliff and Whitson; fish $\frac{3}{4}$ mile each side of the parking space. A weir of large conical basket traps faces upstream from high water mark to low water, indicating this to be a passing place for salmon leaving the Wye and Severn. Fished in front of Hill Farm (to right of sea wall), preferably on an evening tide, high water $-1\frac{1}{4}$ to high water $+1\frac{1}{4}$, for flounder and silver eel, sometimes plaice and sole and occasional bass (summer) and pouting, whiting, cod, (winter) make their way in their seasons into these swift muddy waters where 6 ozs grippers are the order of the day.

IV. **Redwick.** Two miles east of Goldcliff, reached from Newport, west, or Magor, east. Go down the farm lane alongside Redwick Church (through farm), park alongside sea wall. Early morning (summer) and winter nights are favoured when whiting put in an appearance.

Bait supply

Crab. Very few, west of Usk mouth and at Goldcliff beach.

Lug. A few are dug around both sides of the Usk mouth, at St. Bride's (the lighthouse beach) west and Nash east, and along the flats east of Redwick, high water $+2$ to high water -2.

Rag. Just east of Goldcliff Point, a popular local mark, but hard digging among pebbles.

Tackle shops

Chepstow. *Mr. Parfitt, 5 Bank Street. Tel.* (029 12) 2921. Tackle supply and repair. Bait, fresh lug, rag, frozen baits, maggots, worms, flies, advice on where to fish; Permits sold for Wye and Usk. WWA river licences sold.

Newport. *Dave Richards, Angling Supplies, 73 Church Street. Tel.* 54910. Tackle supply and repair; live baits; *Angling Times* weighing station. Angling boat bookings taken.

Boat hire, trips or charter

Anglers usually go west, to Penarth and Barry, for boat angling.

Boat launching slipways

Chepstow and District Yacht Club. Slipway at Mathern Pill for yacht club members. Floating jetty – St. Pierre Pill.

Newport (Uskmouth) Yacht Club. Slipway at Uskmouth power station grounds. Members only.

Fishing advice

Man of Steel Angling Club. Hon. Sec., Mr. W. Roberts, 2 Lyne Road, Newport, Gwent.

Useful telephone numbers

In emergency
Dial 999 and ask for Coastguard.

At other times:
Coastguard. *Barry. Tel.* 5016. **Weather forecasts.** *Post Office. Tel. Cardiff* (0222) 8091. *Meteorological Office, Gloucester. Tel. Churchdown* (0452) 855566.

Game fishing

The right to fish in a river is enjoyed by the owner of the river bank. He may, and often does, lease or sell the right to others who may then keep it to themselves. The Wye, where nearly 8,000 salmon are taken by rod every year, has almost entirely ceased to exist for the occasional angler. Fortunately, however, some hotels own or lease a stretch of their local waters for use by anglers staying at the hotel. Angling Associations, too, usually make a few permits available to *bona fide* visitors. Then there are publicly owned waters, rivers fronting council land, and many well-stocked public water supply reservoirs. This short catalogue of game fishing waters tells the visiting angler where permits are most likely to be obtained. At the same time, it faces up to the problems and gives an honest indication in the maps of where permits will be difficult or impossible to buy.

One pool in 30 miles of well preserved game fishing on Conwy, Llugwy and Lledr rivers owned by the Gwydyr Hotel, Betws-y-Coed.

MAP KEY

The valleys of the Elan and Claerwen in the hills near Rhayader, Mid Wales, shelter a chain of freshwater lakes ideal for trout fishing.

Game Fishing Rivers

The former River Authorities affecting Wales, named on this map (excluding the Severn-Trent Water Authority Area), together form the constituent River Divisions of the Welsh Water Authority

Sewin – a Welsh speciality

Often, it isn't easy to decide where to go if you want a really big fish of a particular species. But no such problem exists when it comes to sea-trout. The rivers of Wales are incomparably the best in the United Kingdom for glass-case specimens. This is no idle surmise. A research paper by Dr. G. S. Harris of Liverpool University, now of the Welsh Water Authority, published late in 1972 in the journal of the Salmon and Trout Association, showed that one Welsh river alone – the Towy, which flows through Carmarthen – yielded more sea-trout of over 10 lbs than *every river in England and Scotland put together.* Its nearest rival, the Dovey, itself within one fish of equalling the English/Scottish total, produced the biggest post-war fish recorded – a 24½ pounder. The Towy, Teifi and Taf in South West Wales, the Dovey, Dysynni and Conwy in North Wales, are all classic rivers for sewin, as you had better get used to calling sea-trout when you come fishing in Wales. Early on, often in April, there's a sparse run of very big fish, though most Welsh anglers start their serious fishing in May and June when very large numbers indeed of fish in the 3 to 7 lbs range run the major rivers. In late July or August, the school sewin turn up – bright little fellows of 1 lb or so which give fine sport on the fly. Then, in September, there's a final run of big 'uns. Though these are the rivers (together with the Rheidol, the Mawddach, the Glaslyn and the Clwyd) which give you the best chance of a specimen fish, almost every stream in Wales has a sewin run when a summer flood colours the water.

Trout of the tranquil waters of Lake Vyrnwy in the hills of Powys can be fished by guests staying at the Lake Vyrnwy Hotel.

Welsh Water Authority

Every river and stream, lake, reservoir and canal in Wales falls within the territory of one of two new water development authorities. As the map on page 75 shows, the river systems of the former authorities for Dee and Clwyd, Gwynedd, South West Wales, Glamorgan, Usk and Wye, fall in the Welsh Water Authority's Area, whilst the Severn's upper waters belong to the Severn/Trent Water Authority. But, for all practical purposes, the former river authorities offices continue to function as before and you must obtain their licence before you begin fishing. A permit to fish, verbally, but preferably written, must also be obtained from the owner of the fishing rights – this might be a local farmer, local angling club, sometimes a syndicate or club from many miles away. Fortunately, as you will see in the information that follows, in many places the local tackle shop or local post office sell both permit and licence. Many hotels, too, provide both for their guests.

Licences and permits are not needed to fish with rod and line in the sea, except for the three species of game fish likely to be found in salty water (but permission is needed to fish in the sea from private land; from dock and harbour walls, for example). Excellent little booklets available on fishing in their areas are issued by the River Divisions and can be obtained by sending a large stamped and addressed envelope to the area offices named.

Useful addresses:

Welsh Water Authority, Cambrian Way, Brecon, Powys. Tel. Brecon (0874) 3181.

Area offices:

- *Gwynedd River Division, Highfield, Caernarfon, Gwynedd. Tel.* (0286) 2247.
- *Dee and Clwyd River Division, Shire Hall, Mold. CH7 6NG. Tel.* (0352) 2121.
- *Wye River Division, 4 St. John Street, Hereford. Tel.* (0432) 6313.
- *Usk River Division, The Croft, Goldcroft Common, Caerleon, Newport, Gwent. Tel.* (90) 420399.
- *Glamorgan River Division, Tremains House, Coychurch Road, Bridgend, Mid Glamorgan. Tel.* (0656) 2217.
- *South West Wales River Division, Penyfai House, Penyfai Lane, Llanelli, Dyfed. Tel.* (05542) 57031.

Severn/Trent Water Authority, Abelson House, Coventry Road, Sheldon, Birmingham, B26 3PU.

Area office for Wales:

- *Upper Severn Division, Shelton, Shrewsbury, ST3 8BJ. Tel.* (0743) 63141.

Though one of the richest rivers in salmon, the Wye is a difficult river for the holidaying angler to find a stretch where he will be permitted to fish. The best introduction to angling waters is obtained through local tackle shops like that of the late Lionel Sweet at Usk – pictured here. A master angler, his wealth of knowledge of the river's beats, flies and tackle needed to catch salmon, is continued in his successors.

Your licence . . .

The Welsh Water Authority (WWA) has obtained full approval to introduce a new fishing licences structure and new fishing licence duties. This system and the new charges to be applied are outlined below.

Salmon and Sea Trout

Each river has been placed into one of five different classes – A, B, C, D or E – on the basis of the potential and general quality of the fishing (some rivers have been placed into two classes). The best waters are those of class A.

A licence for a particular class of water entitles the angler – if he has permission to do so – to fish in all waters of the same or lower class but not waters of a higher class. For instance, a class C licence covers all waters of classes C, D and E but not waters of classes A or B. Categories of licence will be season, week or day. There will be concessions for juveniles and Old-Age Pensioners (OAP's) for the season category only of all five licences. Weekly licences will cover a period of 168 hours.

The charges are:

	A £	B £	C £	D £	E £
Season					
adult	21.60	18.00	10.80	7.20	4.80
juv/ oap	10.80	9.00	5.40	3.60	2.40
Week	10.80	9.00	5.40	3.60	2.40
Day	3.60	3.00	1.80	1.20	0.90

Trout

Similarly, trout fishing licences will cover the entire WWA area and all waters in that area, that is, rivers, lakes, ponds, etc. There will be three categories – season, week and day – but juvenile and OAP concessions will be allowed only on season categories.

The charges are:

Season	**adult**	£3.00
	juv/oap	£1.50
Week	**adult**	£1.80
Day	**adult**	£0.60

Freshwater fish and eels

A licence to fish eels and coarse fish is now required throughout the WWA area though it will be universal, covering this class of fishing on all waters. There will be two categories of licence – season and day – though juvenile and OAP concessions will apply only to the season category.

The charges are:

Season	**adult**	£1.80
	juv/oap	£0.90
Day	**adult**	£0.60

In all cases a juvenile is defined as someone under 16 years of age at the time of the issue of the licence.

Note: A permit or permission to fish is not to be confused with the WWA licence; both must in all cases be obtained before starting to fish. On the following waters only, the WWA licence includes the permit to fish:

Llandegfedd Reservoir, near Pontypool
Upper Lliedi Reservoir, near Llanelli
Usk Reservoir, near Trecastle, Brecon.

Classification of salmon and sea trout waters

Class		
A	WYE	main river below Llanwrthwl Bridge (see also class C waters)
B	USK	main river below Talybont Bridge (see also class C waters)
C	CONWY	main river below Conwy Falls (see also class D waters)
	DEE	main river below R Alwen junction (see also class D waters)
	DYFI	entire main river (see also class D waters)
	TEIFI	main river below Lampeter Bridge
	TYWI	main river below Brianne Dam
	—(Cothi)	main river below Aberbranddu Falls
	USK	main river above Talybont Bridge (see also class B waters)
	WYE	main river above Llanwrthwl Bridge (see also class A waters)
D	AERON	entire main river
	ALWEN	entire main river
	EAST CLEDDAU	entire main river
	WEST CLEDDAU	entire main river
	CLWYD	entire main river
	—(Elwy)	entire main river
	CONWY	(see also class C waters)
	—(Lledr)	entire main river
	—(Llugwy)	main river below Swallow Falls
	DEE	(see also class C waters)
	—(Dee)	between Bala sluices and Alwen confluence
	—(Alwen)	entire main river
	DWYFAWR	entire main river
	DWYRYD	main river below Rhydysarn
	DYFI	(see also class C waters)
	—(Twymyn)	entire main river
	—(Dulas North)	entire main river
	—(Dulas South)	entire main river
	—(Cleifion)	entire main river
	DYSYNNI	entire main river (including Llyn Tal-y-Llyn)
	EDEN	main river below Bont Dolgefeiliau
	ELWY	entire main river
	GLASLYN	entire main river (including Llynnoedd Dinas and Gwynant)
	GWYRFAI	entire main river
	LLYFNI	entire main river
	LOUGHOR	entire main river
	MAWDDACH	entire main river
	—(Eden)	main river below Bont Dolgefeiliau
	NEATH	main river below confluence with R. Mellte
	NEVERN	entire main river
	OGMORE	main river below confluence of main Ogwr Fawr and Ogwr Fach
	OGWEN	entire main river
	RHEIDOL	main river below Cyfarllwyd Falls
	SEIONT	entire main river (including Llynnoedd Padarn and Peris)
	TAF	entire main river
	TYWI	(see also class C waters)
	—GWILI	entire main river
	YSTWYTH	main river below Llanafan Bridge
E	OTHERS	ALL RIVERS, TRIBUTARIES AND STREAMS NOT SPECIFICALLY INCLUDED BY NAME AS CLASS A, B, C, OR D WATERS ABOVE ARE CLASSIFIED AS CLASS E

For details of fishing available on all the Welsh Water Authority's rivers and lakes in Wales buy the WWA Guide to Freshwater Fishing in Wales, £1.99 from: Welsh Water Authority, Cambrian Way, Brecon, Powys. Tel. (0874) 3181.

Catch returns

Anglers fishing for salmon, sea-trout and trout are reminded that they must submit a true and accurate return of catch (including a 'Nil' return) immediately their licence expires. This information is vital to the Authority so that it can properly manage your fisheries. Help the WWA to help you.

Byelaws

Fisheries byelaws are currently under review and may be substantially modified for future seasons. Copies of byelaws currently in force may be obtained from the Authority's River Division offices.

Severn-Trent Water Authority Licence Duties

Note: *Concessionary Licences are granted to juveniles* (12–15) *years, OAP's and the registered disabled.*

1. Trout and freshwater fish (rod and line)

	£
(i) Severn catchment, season	1.50
(ii) Severn and Trent, 28 day	0.75
(iii) Severn and Trent, season	2.25
(iv) Severn and Trent, season, concessionary	0.30

2. Salmon licences

Season. Rod and line, Severn Catchment	15.00
Season. Rod, Restricted. Severn Catchment	11.25
Day. Rod. Severn Catchment	2.25

Reduction to 1/5 of these charges for those qualifying for concessionary licences.

Close seasons

Divisional Area	*Salmon*	*Trout (non migratory and char)*	*Freshwater Fish*
Dee and Clwyd	R. Dee between Suspension Bridge and Grosvenor Bridge 15 Oct-15 June* R Dee elsewhere 15 Oct- 1 Mar R Clwyd 15 Oct-15 Mar	Non migratory—Bala Lake 14 Aug-15 Jan Elsewhere 30 Sept-1 Mar*°	14 Mar-16 Jun *(no close season for eels)*
Gwynedd	All Waters 17 Oct-1 April*	Trawsfynydd Lake 31 Aug-1 Feb Trawsfynydd (Rainbow) 30 Sept-1 Feb Tanygrisiau (Rainbow) 31 Oct-3 Mar Elsewhere 30 Sept-3 Mar°	None
SW Wales	All Waters 7 Oct-10 Mar*	All Waters 30 Sept-10 Mar° *(but see by-laws)*	14 Mar-16 June
Glamorgan	All Waters 31 Oct-2 Mar	Migratory 16 Oct-1 Apr Non Migratory 30 Sept-1 Mar°	14 Mar-16 June
Usk	Above Talybont 15 Oct-15 Feb Elsewhere 30 Sept-15 Feb	Lakes and ponds° 31 Oct-4 Apr Lower Usk *(see By-law)* 30 Sept-1 May* Elsewhere 30 Sept-15 Mar*	Lower Usk *(see By-law)* 14 Jan-16 June Elsewhere 14 Mar-16 June
Wye	Below Llanwrthwl Bridge 30 Sept-26 Jan All other waters and tributaries 25 Oct-26 Jan	All Waters 30 Sept-1 Mar*°	14 Mar-16 June *(no close season for eels)*

*Including Migratory Trout

°Including Rainbows

DURATION OF THE SEASON

Only the River Divisions' own guides and bye laws can give the exact position for any particular stretch. (See table on this page)

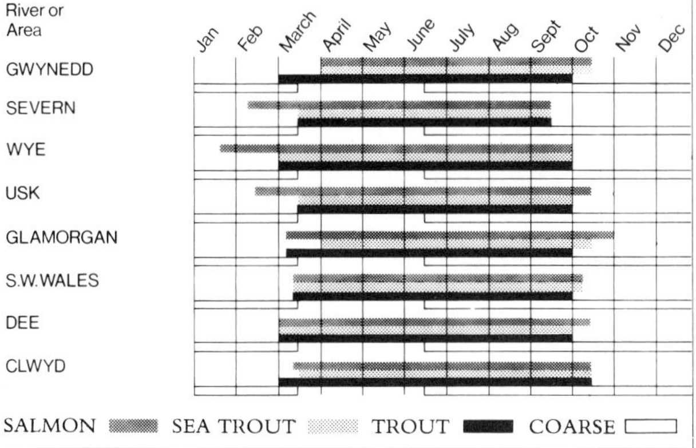

River or Area: GWYNEDD, SEVERN, WYE, USK, GLAMORGAN, S.W.WALES, DEE, CLWYD

Jan, Feb, March, April, May, June, July, Aug, Sept, Oct, Nov, Dec

SALMON — SEA TROUT — TROUT — COARSE

Welsh record game fish list

	lbs	ozs	drs
Trout, Brown	9	4	8
Eglwys Nunnydd, Margam			
Trout, Rainbow	13	1	0
Llwyn Onn Resr., Merthyr Tydfil			
Trout, Sea	21	8	0
R. Conwy			
Salmon	35	0	0
Vacant *(Qualifying Weight)*			

Game Fish Rivers

Important
Stand with your back to the source to determine the left and right hand banks of rivers listed here.

Birmingham Anglers' Association

40 Thorp Street, Birmingham B5 4AU
Tel. 021-622 2904 & 021-622 1025

The Association controls about 400 miles of fishing rights on twenty seven rivers in England and Wales, ranging from the Vyrnwy in Montgomery, southwards to the Thames in Berkshire, and from the Trent in the east, to the Teme, Lugg and Wye in the west; many of which contain trout and grayling, as well as coarse fish. In addition the BAA has fishing rights on five canals, several pools and hundreds of acres of gravel pits. Entries for waters in Wales are included under the following rivers: Banwy, Ithon, Monnow, Severn, Vyrnwy, Wye.

Associate membership is available to any angler and covers the right to fish all BAA waters, provided they are not booked for contests. A list of waters so booked appears in the local and National Angling Press every week. Categories of annual membership are:

Associate Coarse Membership covering coarse fishing in all BAA waters and trout fishing in waters not designated as 'fly only'.

Associate Coarse and Trout Membership covering coarse and trout fishing in all waters, including 'fly only'.
(Note: The above two types of Associate Membership *does not include the right to fish for salmon*).

Associate Junior Membership (age limits 6 to 16) covering the right to fish for coarse fish, trout and salmon.

The fees include free insurance (adults only) against the loss of tackle, personal accident etc., as well as the right to enter all BAA contests.
Membership runs from 1 January to 31 December each year. Apply to the General Secretary at the above address.

Eastern and Western Cleddau

Cleddau – Welsh for swords – scythes the western country of Wales with its twin blades. Sea trout far outnumber salmon, but they are small fish, rarely reaching the classic proportions of their Teifi and Towy brethren. Llys-y-frân, a new reservoir, is well stocked with trout and is giving good results. 10,000 smolts annually are released into the Eastern Cleddau to compensate for loss of Llys-y-frân rearing ground.

Nevern

The tiny Nevern rises in the Preseli Mountains and reaches the sea at Newport. Most stretches are owned or leased by clubs but several stretches in the lower river are available. Trout and sea trout predominate though there is a fairly substantial salmon run as well.

Welsh Water Authority, West Wales Water Division, Pembrokeshire Unit, Meyler House, St. Thomas Green, Haverfordwest, Dyfed. Tel. (0437) 3881.

1. Prescelly Reservoir: 39 acres of brown trout fishing. Fly fishing only. Boats available. *Day permits from Water Bailiff, Blaenpant, Nr. New Inn, Rosebush, Maenclochog. Season £10.00, Day £1, (OAP's and juniors half price).*

2. Llys-y-frân Reservoir: 3 miles of bank fishing for brown and rainbow trout. Boats available for hire. Fishing allowed from 1 April to 30 September one hour before sunrise to one hour after sunset, from banks and boats only. No fishing is permitted from the dam. Natural or artificial fly or worms only allowed. Maximum catch 6 fish not less than 9 ins long. *Permits from the reservoir office or address: Season £20, Day £2.00 (OAP's and juniors half price). Boats for hire.*

Pembrokeshire Anglers' Association. Hon. Sec: Mr. Summers, 72 City Road, Haverfordwest.

3. Western Cleddau: 7 miles. Various short stretches from Welsh Hook bridge, 1¾ miles SW of Letterston, to Trefgarn bridge. Then most stretches from a point above Trefgarn bridge to St. Catherine's bridge, ½ mile east of Camrose, on left bank from here to lower boundary of Prendergast Place excluding small field at lower end of Mile Field. Salmon, sea trout and brown trout.
Permits from County Sports, 3 Old Bridge Street, Haverfordwest. Tel. (0437) 3740, where maps of the water and its immediate area are available.

Mr. W. I. Griffiths, Hunters Lodge, Robeston Wathen, Nr. Narberth, Dyfed. Tel. Narberth (0834) 860270.

4. Eastern Cleddau: 1 mile on left bank from a point below St. Kenox to the marker 200 yards above Canaston Bridge. Salmon up to 22 lbs, sea trout and brown trout. September 1973: 20 lbs salmon taken, 11 salmon taken one day in 1975. *Day, weekly and season permits from Mr. Griffiths or enquire at the Bush Inn, Robeston Wathen.*

Nevern Angling Syndicate, Sec. H. Betty, 56 High Street, Fishguard, Dyfed. Tel. (0348) 873215.

5. Nevern: 1 mile on banks starting about ¼ mile upstream of Trewern Arms. Salmon, sea trout and trout. *Day permits from Secretary.*

Newport (Pembs.) and District Angling Association, Secretary: Mr. Wyn Tucker, Parrog Road, Newport, Dyfed.

6. Nevern. From Pwll Cornel to cottage above Pont Newydd on right bank; from Pont Newydd on left bank to Nevern bridge near Trewern Arms; right bank from Nevern Bridge for about ¼ mile upstream; left bank for ¼ mile in vicinity of Pwll Jack. Trout, sea trout and salmon. *Day, week and fortnight permits available from Beynon's Fishing Tackle, (W. Beynon Williams), Temple House, Newport. Tel.* (0239) 820265.

Tackle shops

Crymych. *Barclay Edwards, The Garage. Tel.* (023973) 204.

Haverfordwest. *Tom's Sports, 10 Market Street. Tel.* (0437) 3653.
County Sports, 3 Old Bridge Street. Tel. (0437) 3740.

Narberth. *Salmon & Sons, (Narberth) Ltd, High Street. Tel.* (0834) 333.

Newport (Dyfed). *Beynon's Fishing Tackle (W. Beynon Williams), Temple House. Tel.* (0239) 820265.

St. David's. *Chapman's Corner, Sea Food & Fishing Tackle Shop, Nun Street. Tel.* (043 788) 301.

---

continued on next page

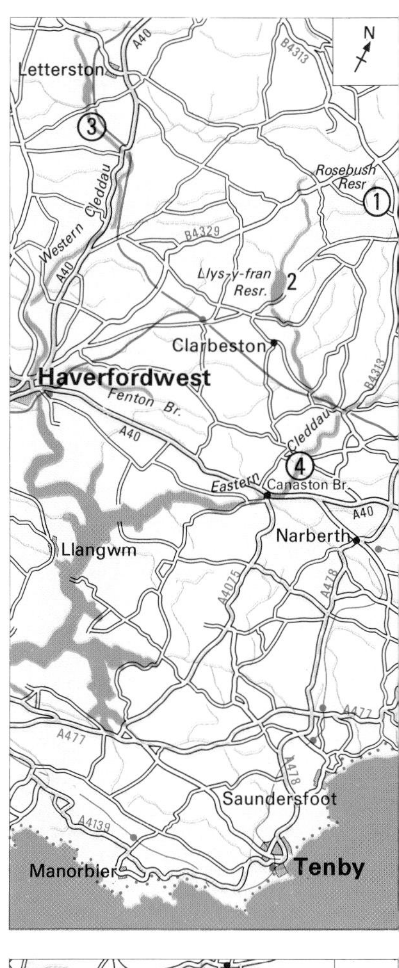

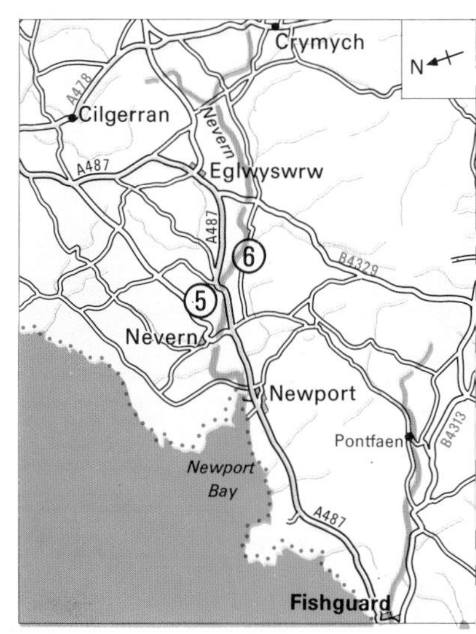

Tenby. *Morris Bros., St. Julian Street. Tel.* (0834) 2105/2306.

Other accommodation offering angling

Clarbeston Road. *T. C. Arthur, Ivy House, Llysyfran. Tel. Maenclochog* (09913) 473.
Newport. *Llwyngwair Manor, Newport, Dyfed. Tel.* (0239) 820498.
Narberth. *Robeston House Hotel, Robeston Wathen, Narberth, Dyfed. Tel. Narberth* (0834) 860392.

Tâf

Pronounced Tav. Several useful stretches between Whitland and St. Clears should appeal to the angler holidaying at Tenby, Saundersfoot or Pendine. Brown trout are plentiful and there is a strong run of June sea trout to 17 lbs. Coracles float on the river around St. Clears netting sea trout and salmon – an age-old form of fishing in the rivers of Dyfed.

Gwili

Rising in the woollen mill country north of Cynwyl Elfed, the Gwili flows through wooded ravines to its confluence with the Towy just east of the important market town of Carmarthen. It has some fine stretches of sea trout fishing, as well as salmon.

Whitland Anglers Association.
1. Taf: 2 miles on both banks from the road bridge below Pengawse, 1 mile west of Whitland on A40 to Haverfordwest, to a point below railway bridge at Pontyfenni, 2 miles east of the town. Salmon, sea trout and brown trout. *Day permits from Rees Garages, Ltd., Station Garage, Whitland. Tel.* (09944) 304.

Carmarthen and District Angling Club, Sec. D. T. Lewis, 25 Park Hall, Carmarthen, Dyfed.
2. Taf: 1 mile on right bank from Venture Life Bridge below Woolstone Farm, ¾ mile from milestone at the junction with A477, approx. 1 mile SW of St. Clears to a point 1 mile upstream. Good early salmon, sea trout and brown trout.
3. Dewi Fawr: 600 yards on right bank at Pentowin Estate on B4299 St. Clears to Meidrim road. Mainly trout.
4. Gwili: ¼ mile on right bank from Abergwili bridge to the confluence of the Gwili with the Towy. Sea trout and trout. Weekly tickets only: Covers all club waters. *Permits from J. M. Dark, Tackle Shop, 16 Chapel Street, Carmarthen. F. M. & H. E. Davies, Newsagents, Bridge Street, Kidwelly.*

5. Towy: 2½ miles on right bank from Cwmoernant marshland near the old tinplate works at Carmarthen to Bwlch land at Abergwili, excluding two fields on Cystanog land. 3 miles of fishing on left bank from a point below Danyrallt Farm to a point beyond the confluence on Church Farm land, then most stretches from Penlan Cystanog to Penddaulwyn Farm. Generally salmon up to 20 lbs. Sea trout up to 5 lbs taken. Weekly permits only; covers all club waters. *Permits from J. M. Dark, Tackle Dealer, Chapel Street, Carmarthen.*

R. Alison, Home Farm, Llanllawddog. Tel. Llanpumsaint (026 784) 436.
6. Llanllawddog Lake: Fly fishing for rainbow trout. Rods limited. *Day permits issued.* Book in advance.

Tackle shops

Carmarthen. *Coombs & Lawson, 8 Lammas Street, Carmarthen. Tel.* (0267) 5662.

Messrs. Davies & Jones, Lyric Sports Centre, King Street, Tel. (0267) 7166.
J. M. Dark, Tackle Shop, 16 Chapel Street.
Crymych, *Barclay Edwards, Tackle & Bait, The Square. Tel.* (023973) 204.
Laugharne. *Clarke's Gift Shop. (Bait).*
St. Clears. *Mrs. Griffiths, Post Office, Pentre Road. Tel.* (0994) 230432.
Whitland. *Rees Garages Ltd, Station Garage. Tel.* (09944) 304.

Teifi

One of the Big Three salmon and sea trout rivers of Wales, the Teifi from the Teifi Pools to the sea is a much sought after angling river. Once heavily fished by coracles, the netting licence now dies with the holder.

continued on next page

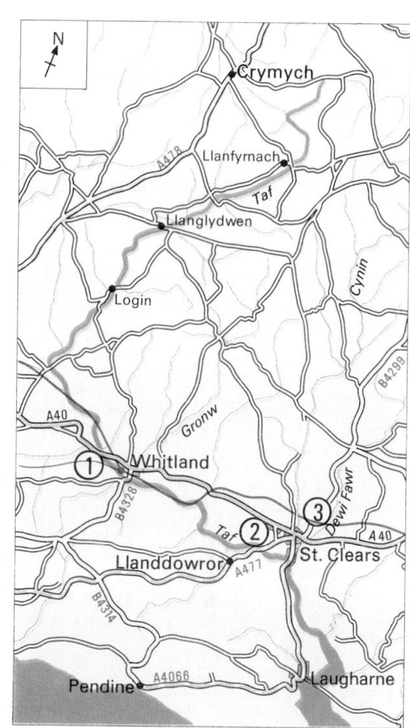

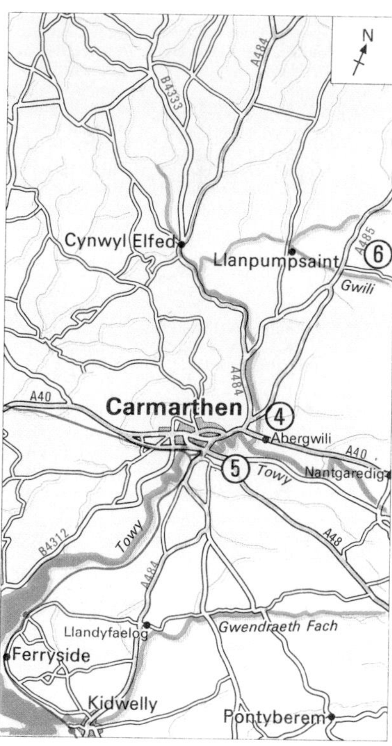

continued from previous page

Llyn Egnant and Teifi Pools.
See page 90.

Tregaron Angling Association, Tregaron, Dyfed.

1. Teifi: Approx 12 miles mostly on both banks from confluence with River Camddwr to bridge below Llanio Mill on A485 and small stretch above Gogoyan Bridge. Afon Pysgotwr from Llanddewi Bridge to confluence. About 3 miles above Lampeter and also 3/4 mile near Llanfair Clydogau. Good salmon pools and trout abound. Maps available. *Season, monthly, weekly and day permits available from Peter Morgan, Caron Stores, Tregaron. Post Office & London House, Llanddewi Brefi, Megicks Stores, Lampeter and Financial Secretary, Barclays Bank, Tregaron, Tel. Tregaron* (09744) 207.

Sunny Hill Hotel, Tregaron, Dyfed. Tel. (09744) 303.

2. Teifi: 800 yards left bank, 1600 right bank, between Llanddewi Brefi and Lampeter. Salmon and brown trout. 1978: 14 lb salmon. *Permits available at the hotel. Day £2, week (including Sunday £6, Season £8.*

County Gate Hotel, Llanfihangel-ar-arth, Pencader, Nr. Llandysul, Dyfed. Tel. Maesycrugiau (055 935) 285.

3. Teifi: 660 yards on left bank, 400 yards above Llanfihangel-ar-arth Bridge. Salmon up to 20 lbs, sea trout ¾ lbs to 1½ lbs. *Permits exclusively to hotel guests.*

Llandysul Angling Association, Secretary, A. Jones, Siop-y-Jones, Llandysul. Tel. (055932) 2317.

4. Teifi:
Beat No. 1 – Penddol (Llangybi) 1¼ miles of good salmon and trout fishery. Cardiganshire Bank.

Beat No. 2 – Llety Twppa right hand bank (Cardiganshire side) 700 yards in length. Five salmon pools, good trout water. Access from farm yard.

Beat No. 3 – Brongest Waters

Beat No. 4 – Lampeter Waters left bank from Lampeter Bridge to Dolau Gwyrddion Waters. Also right bank to beat No. 5, Cefnbryn.

Beat No. 5 – Cefnbryn Waters Carmarthenshire bank – continuation from beat 4 for 880 yards.

Beat No. 6 – Dolgwm Mill Waters
1,800 yards good salmon fishery, Carms. bank. Entry to railway embankment.

Beat No. 7 – Maesisaf Waters
From adjoining Railway Embankment at Napier pool – upstream. 1 mile, Carms. side.

Beat No. 8 – Brynhawc Waters
1½ miles of good all round fishery. Entry from Maesycrugiau Bridge, sign-posted. Cardiganshire bank.

Beat No. 9 – Church Farm Fishery left hand bank (except first meadow) from Llanfihangel Bridge.

Beat No. 10 – Mackwith Castle Waters
1½ miles left bank following from beat No. 9. Entry from Llandysul to Llanfihangel Road.

Beat No. 11 – Porth Hotel Waters 1½ miles continuation of beat No. 10 to 1st Suspension Bridge. (See map for access).

Beat No. 12 – Tydref Waters right bank only. Comprising 2 meadows immediately below Llandysul Park Boundary.

Beat No. 13 – Cilgwyn Estate Waters
On the right bank below Llandysul Bridge Fishing from Oak Tree to boundary of Gilfachwen Isaf Farm and on the left bank from the confluence of the River Twelly to Rhydygalfe Farm.

Beat No. 14 – Penbeili Fishing, N. C. Emlyn
850 yards near Llandyfriog (Newcastle Emlyn to Lampeter Road) sign-posted and 720 yards behind filling station at Pentrecagal on the Henllan Newcastle Emlyn Road.

Salmon, sea trout and trout. *Season, weekly and day permits from Megicks, Corner Shop, Harford Square, Lampeter. Tel.* (0570) 422 226, *also from Hon. Sec. A. Jones, see above.*

Teifi Trout Association, Sec. C. Jones, Emlyn House, Newcastle Emlyn. Tel. (0239) 710405.

5. Teifi: 10 miles. On left bank from old railway bridge opposite Llandyfriog to junction with Afon Cych including Cenarth Falls. Right bank from a point 1 mile west of Cenarth on A484 to a point ¼ mile east of Cenarth Falls and from a point ¼ mile east of Cwmcoy on B4333 to a point ¾ mile east of Newcastle Emlyn.

Cych: Right bank from junction with Teifi to Penrhiw bridge. Salmon, sea trout and trout.
No day tickets: season and weekly available from local tackle shops.

continued on next page

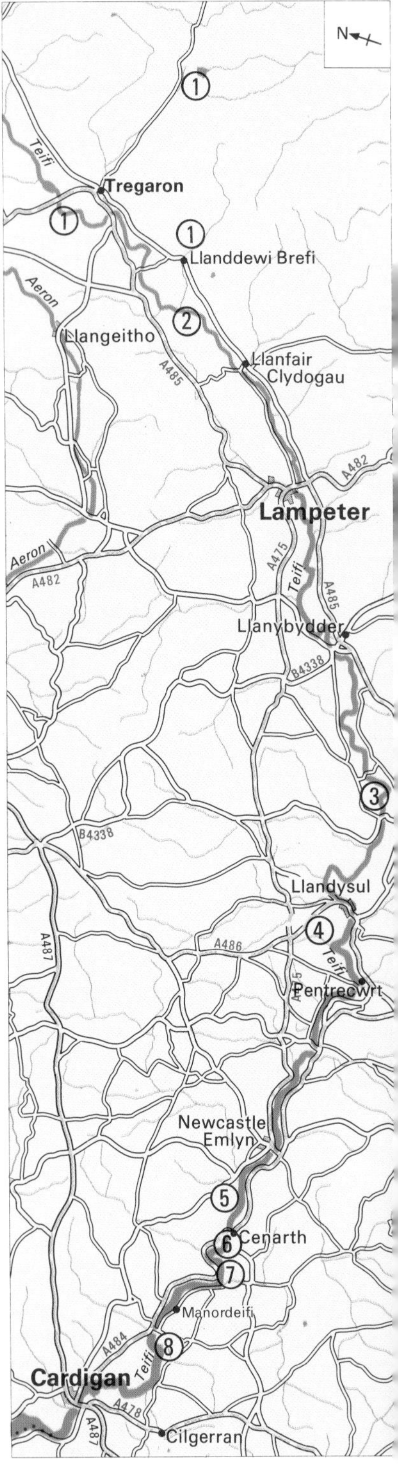

continued from previous page

Mrs. Davies, Stradmore Gardens, Cenarth, Nr. Cardigan, Dyfed.

6. Teifi: 660 yards downstream on right bank from Stradmore Gardens Cottage to marker post. Salmon, sea trout and trout. Salmon up to 18 lbs. 3 salmon caught on 3 casts by J. Smith, Cardigan. *Season ticket only, from Mrs. Davies, see above.*

Emlyn Arms Hotel, Newcastle Emlyn, Dyfed. Tel. Newcastle Emlyn (0239) 710317.

7. Teifi: 9 miles on left bank from Pentrecagal to Abercych. Salmon, sea trout and brown trout. *Special rates for hotel guests.*

Gwesty Castell Malgwyn Hotel, Llechryd, near Cardigan, Dyfed. Tel. Llechryd (023987) 382.

8. Teifi: 1 mile left bank between Llechryd and Cilgerran. Salmon, sea trout and brown trout.
Available to guests of hotel only, Day: £1.80, *week:* £5.40, *season:* £10.80.

Tackle shops

Cardigan. *M. & A. Williams, 10a Pendre, Cardigan. Tel.* (0239) 2038.
Cilgerran. *Mr. E. Brown, Post Office. Tel. Llechryd* (023987) 322.
Newcastle Emlyn. *Mr. Cliff Jones, Emlyn Boot Stores, Newcastle Emlyn. Tel.* (0239) 710405.
Tregaron. *Arthur Morgan, Caron Stores.*

Tywi (Towy)

The Tywi with its tributaries – Cothi, Gwydderig and Bran – competes with the Dyfi and Conwy as the most prolific river in Wales for specimen sea trout, a great number of the fish being in the 10 lbs to 20 lbs category. Brown trout are pretty well universal and, as the river has a substantial run of salmon as well, its beats are much sought after by wealthy clubs and groups. The angler's choice of a place to stay falls between the main market town of the area, Carmarthen, the more rural towns of Llandeilo and Llandovery, or a completely pastoral hotel.

Cothi

The sylvan beauty of Afon Cothi above Pumsaint, scene of Roman gold mining activity, and the meandering lower vale, are the centre of intense angling activity when salmon invade the river from June to September.

Mrs. E. Thomas, Tonn Farm, Rhandirmwyn Road, Llandovery, Dyfed. Tel. 20276.

1. Towy: 800 yards on both banks from upper limit at the boundary fence downstream past Tonn Island to the Chain Bridge on A40 above Llandovery. Salmon, sea trout, brown and rainbow trout. *Day permits from Tonn Farmhouse.*

Llandovery Angling Association. Sole permit distributors: W. Aldred Thomas, 6 King's Road, Llandovery. Tel Llandovery (0550) 20267.

2. Towy: Three stretches about half of it on both banks. Top stretch about 1 mile length from a point near Divlyn to a point near Glanrhyderryd. Middle stretch of about ½ mile, from a point near Towy Cottage to junction with a brook near Dolauhirion. Lower stretch of about 1¼ miles from a point near main A40 bridge to junction with Afon Gwydderig. Salmon, sea trout and brown trout. *Permits available for season, 2 weeks, 8 days and 1 day. Reductions for juniors.*

3. Bran: One stretch, both banks, from a point near junction with Afon Gwydderig to a point near Pen-y-bont on A483, 2 miles north of Llandovery.

4. Gwydderig. Two stretches both banks, in the vicinity of Glangwydderig at Velindre 1 mile east of Llandovery on A40. One stretch from town bridge over Afon Gwydderig to Pont Rhyd y Ceir, 1 mile south, mainly one bank only.

Millbank Dyfed Estate, W. H. Cooke & Arkwright, Estate Office, Llangathen, Carmarthen. SA32 8QF. Tel. Dryslwyn (055-84) 494.

Towy:

5. Upper Water: Llandeilo Bridge to Myddfi Brook, Cilsane, 1 mile single bank: 1½ miles double bank. Fly only. *Season tickets only. No daily or weekly tickets.*

6. Middle Water: Old footbridge at Glantowy to the Rofawr boundary post,

continued on next page

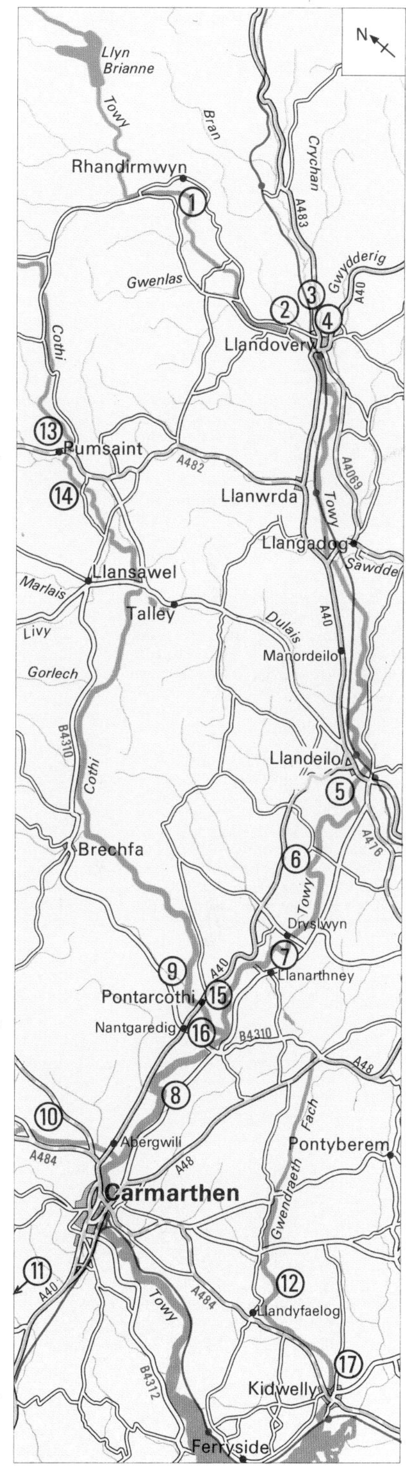

continued from previous page

approximately 4¼ miles of double bank fishing. Fly only but minnow when fly impossible. *Season tickets and a minimum of 10 weekly and daily tickets.*

7. Lower Water: Bremenda Isaf boundary to old footbridge at Glantowy approximately 1½ miles of single bank fishing. Any legal means allowed. *Season tickets only: no day or weekly tickets.* Salmon, sea trout and trout. *Permits from the Estate Office at above address and from Gamekeeper J. S. Bellamy, Ty Castell, Dryslwyn, Llandeilo, Dyfed. Tel. Dryslwyn 433.*

Carmarthen Amateur Angling Association. Secretary: Mr. Gwilym James, 50 St. David's Street, Carmarthen. Tel. (0267) 7997.

8. Towy
Capel Isaf, Glantowylan and Llwyndewi Waters: Left bank upstream from Wern Farm, Capel Dewi to start of Danyrallt Water.

Tyllwyd Water: Right bank from Brynmyrddin Water to junction of Anell Brook with River Towy. Access to this fishing through Tyllwyd Farm yard which is situated off the A40 road between Abergwili and Whitemill villages.

Cwm and Palace Farms: Right bank upstream from boundary with Bwlch Farm for approx. 880 yards. The Palace water also includes the left bank at the top of the stretch, that is, both banks of the pool known as the Bishop's Pool or Island Pool. Access to this water is obtained from Abergwili village.

Ty-Castell, Glanyrynys, Plasnewydd and Rwyth Farms: Below Nantgaredig Bridge, right bank for approx. 1,000 yards, but missing out first field immediately below above bridge. (Right of way through this field to start of water.)

9a. Cothi
Perllwyne, Nantsaer and Mynachdu Waters: Right bank upstream from in front of council houses, Cothi Bridge up to small wood where Cloidach stream joins the Cothi.

Graig and Penygraig Waters: Right bank from the first Association sign above the old swing bridge (approx. 200 yards above Alltyferin Church) upstream for approx. 900 yards.

Upton Hall Water: Left bank from first meadow above Pontynyswen Bridge upstream for approx. ¾ mile to boundary with Dyffryn Isaf Farm.

Waungranod Water. From Pontynyswen Bridge, right bank above bridge to boundary with Penrhiw-Meredith water, and right bank below stream from approximately 150 yards to marker boundary post.

Penrhiwmeredith Water: Right bank upstream from boundary with Waungranod to boundary with Tycrug.

Tycrug Water: Right bank from small stream at top end of Penrhiwmeredith Farm, upstream for approx. 800 yards.
(See end of section on page 85).

10. Gwili
Derwydd Water: From Glangwili Bridge on Carmarthen–Lampeter road right bank upstream for approx. 400 yards.

Cwmgwili Water: From end of Derwydd Water right bank upstream to Tew's Pool, then miss one meadow, then both banks up to Bronwydd Arms Bridge.

Trefynys Water: From one field above Bronwydd Arms Bridge, left bank upstream to Barnsfield Bridge.

Glangwili Water: From Gwili Lan on Bronwydd–Llanpumsaint road, right bank upstream to Barnsfield Bridge.

Glynderi Water: Right bank upstream from Barnsfield Bridge, Bronwydd Arms for about ¾ mile.

Troedyrhiw, Troedyrhiw Woods, British Railways, Dyffryn Gwili, Forge Farm Waters: Left bank upstream from just above Bronwydd Village Hall to Quarry No. 1, left bank up to railway bridge below Carmarthen Road petrol station on Carmarthen–Conwil road and right bank to corner, 100 yards below above bridge.

Gwili Vale Water: Left bank upstream from Pontarsais Bridge for approx. 800 yards.

11. Cynin
Panthowell, Fron Isaf, Pantymaen and Lindre Waters: From Aberdauddwr Bridge on Gellywen–Velindre road, upstream both banks for approx. 1 mile, to end of meadow immediately below Lindre Farm.

12. Gwendraeth
Gelli Farm Water: From

Kidwelly Castle stands beside Afon Gwendraeth Fach a few miles west of Llanelli in Dyfed.

Llandyfaelog Bridge left bank upstream for five meadows and downstream for two meadows. *Permits can be purchased at Messrs. Davies & Jones, Lyric Sports Centre, King Street, Carmarthen. Tel.* (0267) 7166.

Dolaucothi Arms Hotel, Pumsaint, Llanwrda, Dyfed. Tel. Pumsaint (05585) 204.

13. Cothi: 4 miles on both banks from Cwrt-y-Cadno to a point below Pumsaint road bridge. Also ¾ mile stretch on the Twrch from the pipe bridge to the confluence with River Cothi. Salmon in late season, sea trout up to 5 lbs and brown trout. *Free to residents, who have priority. Day permits from hotel for non-residents.*

Glanrannel Park Hotel (David and Bronwen Davies), Crugybar, Llanwrda. Tel. Talley (05583) 230.

14. Cothi: 5,000 yards on Island Farm, Upper Joynson and Glanrannell waters lying 1 mile south and west of the village of Crugybar, near Pumsaint. Salmon, sea trout and brown trout.

Recent catches:

Sewin (Sea Trout) 6 lbs 9 ozs, Salmon 11 lbs 14 ozs. *Day and weekly permits available to residents at hotel.*

Cothi Bridge Hotel, Pont-ar-Gothi, Nantgaredig, Dyfed. Tel. Nantgaredig (026 788) 251.

15. Cothi: 40 yards from Pont-ar-Gothi road bridge on A40 to end of hotel garden. Trout, sea trout and salmon. *Residents at hotel – free: non-residents can purchase day, weekly, and season permits at the hotel. Also local private fishing arranged for residents elsewhere on Cothi and on Towy.*

Carmarthen and District Angling Club. Secretary D. T. Lewis, 25 Park Hall, Carmarthen, Dyfed.

16. Cothi. 1 mile on both banks for ½ mile from a point 25 yards below road bridge at Pontargothi, then ½ mile on right bank for one large field and on left bank alongside lane. Salmon, sea trout and trout.

17. Gwendraeth Fach. 3 miles on both banks from Mill-lands Farm, ½ mile from Kidwelly to a point near the old tinplate works on Broadford Farm. Then from the 'Weir' on Peny-back land to Maesgwenllian Farm, excluding stretches on Forge Farm and Danyrallt Farm. Also small stretch for two fields on Plas-y-wenallt land. On left bank from Kidwelly on the main Carmarthen/Kidwelly road to two fields below Glanmorlais Bridge. Mainly trout with small sea trout in the lower reaches. *Weekly tickets only. Permits from J. M. Dark, Tackle Shop, 16 Chapel Street, Carmarthen: Nantgaredig Post Office. Tel.* (0267) 201.

9b. *Ty Mawr Country Hotel and Restaurant, Brechfa, Dyfed. Tel.* (026789) 330332. Upton Hall Water: Pontynyswen to Brechfa-Llanfynydd road junction. Salmon. Free to guests of the hotel.

Tackle shops

Carmarthen. *Coombs & Lawson, 8 Lammas Street. Tel.* (0267) 5662. *J. M. Dark, Tackle Shop, 16 Chapel Street. Tel.* (0267) 201. *Messrs. Davies & Jones, Lyric Sports Centre, King Street, Tel.* (0267) 7166.

Kidwelly. *F. M. & H. E. Davies. Newsagents, 14 Bridge Street, Kidwelly. Tel.* (05543) 474.

Llandeilo. *Mr. Roberts, Iron-monger & Hardware Stores, Rhosmaen Street. Tel.* (05582) 2663.

Llandovery. *W. Aldred Thomas, 6 King's Road. Tel.* (0550) 20267.

Tawe

The Tawe illustrates the remarkable recovery possible when a river is cleaned up. Always beautiful in its upper stretches where it flows from the limestone caverns of the Brecon Beacons National Park, sea trout and salmon are recovering lost ground to join the plump trout which have long thrived in this surprisingly pleasant spot.

Taff and reservoirs

Popularly known as the Taff (distinct from the West Wales river, the Taf – with a 'v' that is) this is another river of South Wales that has a surprise in store in its upper reaches for the trout angler. The staggeringly beautiful reservoirs of Llwyn-onn and Taf-fechan are folded into the mountains of Brecon Beacons National Park.

Brecon Beacons National Park, Craig-y-Nos Country Park, Abercraf, Swansea Valley. Tel. (063 977) 395.

---

continued on next page

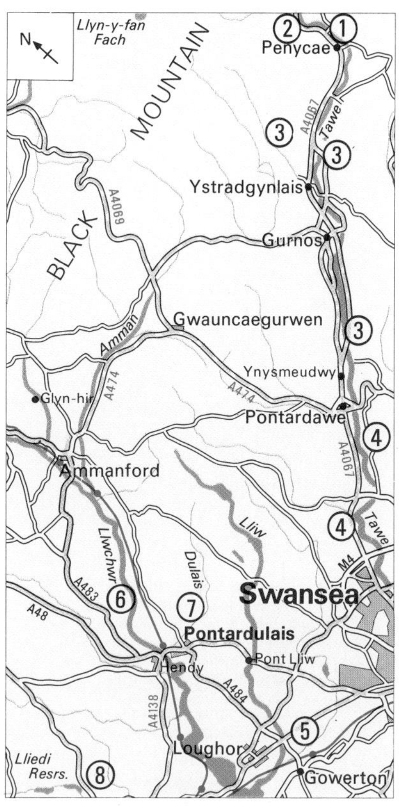

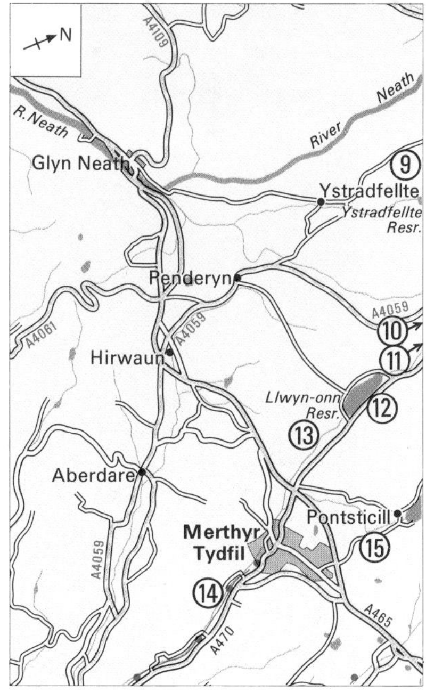

continued from previous page

1. Tawe and Llynfell. Most waters within the Craig-y-Nos Park. Managed on behalf of the Park by Tawe and Tributaries Angling Association. *Day permits available at the Country Park Office.*

Dan-yr-Ogof Caves Ltd., Penycae, Swansea Valley. Tel. Abercrave (063977) 284.

2. Tawe: Adjacent to caves. 1,014 yards from Glan Haffes house to the mill. Mainly brown trout. *Day permits from Dan-yr-Ogof Caves Office.*

Tawe and Tributaries Angling Association, Hon. Secretary, Ken Jones, 21 St. David's Road, Ystalyfera, Swansea, West Glamorgan SA9 2JQ.

3. Tawe and Twrch: 20 miles. Most stretches on both banks from the mountain source to a point above Ynysmeudwy Arms. Mainly brown trout. *Adult Season, Junior* (*under* 16) *weekly and Day Permits from Secretary or D. Watkins, Tawe Sports, Commercial Street, Ystradgynlais. Tel. Glantawe* (0639) 2166. *J. G. Davies, The Pharmacy, Brecon Road, Abercraf. Mr. Hoare, General Stores, Penycae. Linnards Sports Shop, High Street, Swansea. D. C. Rowlands, Sports Shop, Gurnos Road, Ystalyfera and Colin Jones, Sports Shop, Pontardawe.*

Pontardawe and District Angling Association.

4. Tawe: 7 miles. Most stretches on both banks from Cwmdu Brook above Ynysmeudwy to Beaufort Weir at Morriston Cross. *Weekly Tickets only. Permits from Clive Rowlands' Sports Shop, Woodfield Street, Morriston, Swansea. Tel.* (0792) 75993.

Llangyfelach and District Angling Association, Hon. Secretary, M. L. Griffiths, 3 Aldwyn Road, Cockett, Swansea. Tel. 581711.

5. Llan: 6 miles between Llangyfelach and Gowerton. Brown trout to 2¼ lbs. *Week and season permits from: John Harrison, 110 Clase Road, Morriston, Swansea. Tel.* (0792) 71052. *Tom Day, 27 Vicarage Road, Morriston, Swansea. Tel.* (0792) 72065. *Mathew Haeney, 75 Tan-y-lan Road, Morriston, Swansea. Tel.* (0792) 794228.

Pontarddulais Angling Association.

6. Llwchwr (Loughor): 3 miles on right bank from Erw Fach Farm downstream to bridge and on left bank from Hendrewen Farm to the bridge excluding Ynys Farm waters.

7. Dulais: 1 mile on both banks from source to confluence. Average year's catch 40 salmon, 400 sea trout and 1,200 brown trout. *Day permits from Secretary or W. A. & A. J. Williams, Ironmonger, 16 St. Teilo Street, Pontarddulais. Tel.* (0792) 882321.

Welsh Water Authority, South West Wales River Division, 19 Pen-y-fai Lane, Llanelli. Tel. 57031.

8. Upper Lliedi. Reservoir 3 miles north of Llanelli on A476. Brown Trout. *Permits available at the reservoir office on site. Adult, Day £2, OAP's and juniors £1.33. Boat: all day £2.00. Evenings (from 4 p.m.) £1.50. No separate River Division Licence needed on this water.*

Welsh Water Authority, Glamorgan River Division, Tremains House, Coychurch Road, Bridgend. Tel. (0656) 2217.

9. Ystradfellte Reservoir: 3 miles north of Ystradfellte village in Brecon Beacons National Park, 59 acres moorland reservoir containing brown trout.

Taf-fechan, one of the many pleasant reservoirs to be fished in the Brecon Beacons National Park.

Permits: Adult Season (available on Beacons, Cantref and Llwyn Onn reservoir also) £7.50. Day 50p. from Llwyn Onn reservoir filter house.

Welsh Water Authority, Taff Water Division, Cardiff Unit, Crwys House, Crwys Road, Cardiff. Tel. (0222) 395704.

10. Beacons Reservoir: 52 acres of brown and rainbow trout fishing 9 miles north of Merthyr Tydfil on A470. Average size 12 ins, best 2 lb. No boats. Fly only. Stocked at intervals throughout season. *Open March 21st–September 30th. Permits available from Filter House, Llwyn-Onn Reservoir, Cwm Taff. Adults £15 per season, £1 per day. Under 16s and OAP's 50%.*

11. Cantref Reservoir: 42 acres of brown and rainbow trout fishing, 9 miles north of Merthyr Tydfil on A470. Average size 12 ins, best 2 lbs. No boats, fly only. *Permits from Filter House, Llwyn-Onn Reservoir, Cwm Taff.* Stocked at intervals throughout season. *Adults £23 per season, £1.50 per day. Under 16s and OAP's 50%.*

12. Llwyn-Onn Reservoir: 150 acres of brown and rainbow trout in landscaped reservoir, 3 miles north of Merthyr Tydfil on A470. Average 12 ins, best brown 4 lb, rainbow 2 lb. Fly only, no boats. Stocked at intervals throughout season. *Permits from the Filter House at the Llwyn-Onn reservoir. Adults £30 per season, £2 per day. Under 16s and OAP's 50%.*

Merthyr Tydfil Angling Association, Secretary, T. R. Norman, 2 Wesley Close, Dowlais, Merthyr Tydfil, Mid Glamorgan.

13. Taf-fechan: 2½ miles on both banks from outlet of Taf-fechan reservoir to the confluence at Cefn Coed.

14. Taff: 7 miles on both banks from this confluence of Taf-fechan and Taf Fawr to Pontygwaith downstream of Aberfan. All waters well stocked with brown trout and rainbow trout up to 2 lbs. *Season and day tickets only*

15. Coarse fishing: Two lakes in the Merthyr area, namely Bryn Cae-Owen, holding carp to 20 lbs, tench, roach, bream and perch and trout. *Day tickets available from Secretary, A. Rees, 13 Alexandra Avenue, Merthyr Tydfil or from E. Thompson, 1 Rowan Way, Gurnos Estate, Merthyr Tydfil.*

Tackle shops

Ammanford. *Don Chiswell Amman Sports, 25 Wind Street, Ammanford. Tel.* (0269) 2394.

Morriston. *Clive Rowlands' Sports Shop, Woodfield Street. Tel.* (0792) 75993.

Swansea. *Linnards Sports Shop, High Street, Swansea.*

Ystradgynlais. *D. Watkins, Tawe Sports, Commercial Street, Tel. Glantawe* (0639) 842166.

Usk

The Usk flows from the 2,500 ft Carmarthen Fan through the pleasant market towns of Brecon and Abergavenny, passing many a beauty spot on the way. The middle and upper stretches are situated almost wholly in the Brecon Beacons National Park, and they attract great attention for the quality of the trout and salmon fishing. The reported rod-caught salmon catch exceeds 800 fish a year, many running 10 lbs to 12 lbs, though fish to 20 lbs are not uncommon and the odd one of over 30 lbs continues to be reported.

Welsh Water Authority, Cambrian Way, Brecon. Tel. 3181. Reservoir Superintendent, Usk Reservoir, near Trecastle, Powys.

1. Usk Reservoir: Brown and rainbow trout fishing on 290 acres of landscaped reservoir at 1,000 ft altitude. Best brown 5 lb 6 ozs, average 10–14 ins; best rainbow 2 lb 8 ozs (1975), average 9–12 ins. *Permits: Season £50, day £2.00 (Under 16s and OAP's 50%. Boats available for hire. Permit entitles holder to fish 14 reservoirs in all.*

Brecon Angling Society, Brecon, Powys. Secretary: L. Peters, 53 Ffynnon Dewi, Llanfaes, Brecon.

2. Usk: 2 miles on right bank from Llanspyddid to Llanfaes Bridge. Salmon and brown trout. Limited to four rods per day. Monday to Friday each week. Also ¼ mile on left bank from boathouse to Llanfaes Bridge. *Day Permits from R. & C. Denman, 11 Watergate, Brecon. Tel.* (0874) 2071.

Brecon Fishery Association, c/o The Town Clerk, The Guildhall, Brecon, Powys.

3. Usk: 1½ miles on right bank from Llanfaes Bridge to top of

continued on next page

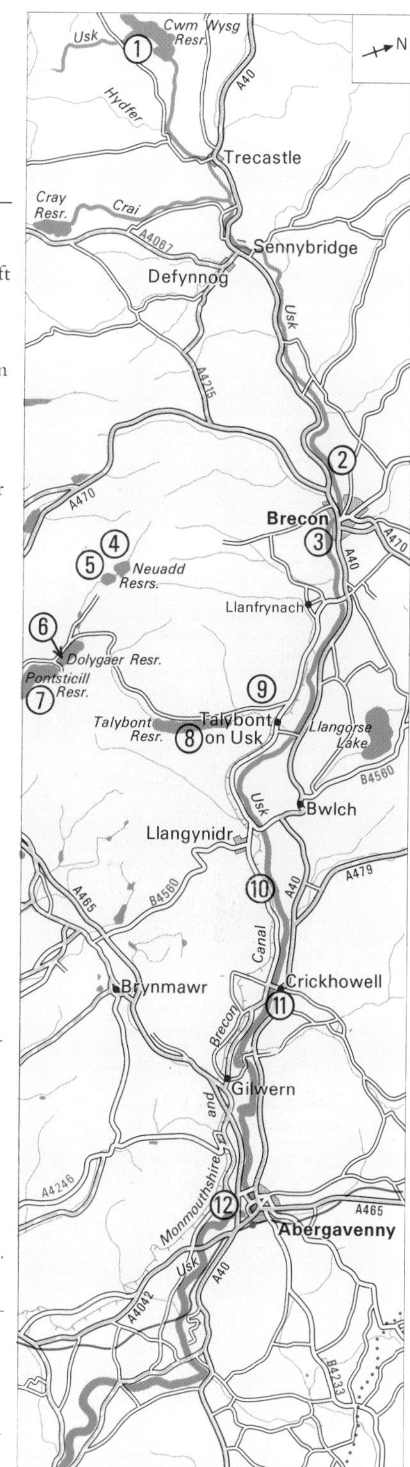

River Usk – continued from previous page

Little Wood below Dinas House and on left bank from the bridge to Kennel Lane. Salmon and trout. *Day permits from R. & C. Denman, 11 Watergate, Brecon. Tel.* (0874) 2071.

Welsh Water Authority, Glamorgan River Division, Tremains House, Bridgend. Tel. (0656) 2217.

4. Upper Neuadd: 57 acres landscaped reservoir 8 miles north of Merthyr Tydfil in Brecon Beacons National Park. Brown trout to 2½ lb; rainbow trout to 2 lb. No boats, fly only, restocked at intervals.
(American Brook Trout have been introduced here. If you catch any please report them specially to the Water Authority on forms available where you buy your licence).

5. Lower Neuadd: 12 acres landscaped reservoir, 7½ miles north of Merthyr Tydfil in Brecon Beacons National Park. Brown trout to 4 lb (average 12 ins); rainbows to 2 lb. No boats, fly and spinning. Restocked at intervals.

6. Dolygaer: 96 acres shallow landscaped reservoir, 7 miles north of Merthyr Tydfil in Brecon Beacons National Park. Brown trout to 7 lb (average 12 ins); rainbow trout to 3 lb. No boats, fly only. Restocked at intervals.

7. Ponsticill: 253 acres landscaped reservoir. 5 miles north of Merthyr Tydfil in Brecon Beacons National Park. Brown trout to 14 lb (average 12 ins); rainbow trout to 2½ lb. No boats. Fly and spinning only. Restocked at intervals. *Permits available at Filter House, Pontsticill Reservoir,*

Llanishen: (not on adjacent map). 20 acres concrete bowl reservoir at Llanishen in Cardiff 's north-east suburbs. Brown trout to 4 lb (average 12 ins); rainbow trout to 3½ lb. No boats, fly only. *Permits from reservoir keeper.*

Lisvane: (not on adjacent map). 19 acres concrete bowl reservoir at Lisvane in Cardiff 's north-east suburbs. Brown trout to 4 lbs and rainbows to 3 lbs (average 12 ins). No boats, fly only. *Permits from reservoir keeper.*
Permits entitle holders to fish at reservoirs of Upper & Lower Neuadd, Dolygaer, Pontsticill, Beacons, Cantref, Llwyn Onn, Ystradfellte, Llanishen, Lisvane, Pantygroes and Talybont. Day £2, Season £30. Under 16s and OAP's 50%.

Welsh Water Authority, Gwent Water Division, Station Buildings, Station Approach, Newport, Gwent, NPT 1RT. Tel. (0633) 67147.

8. Talybont Reservoir: 318 acres brown and rainbow trout fishing on landscaped reservoir. Best brown 2 lbs 8 ozs, average 10–14 ins; best rainbow 2 lbs 12 ozs, average 10–14 ins. *Permit rates: Adult: season £30.00, day £1.50. Juniors and OAP's half price from the Reservoir Superintendent, Talybont Reservoir, Talybont-on-Usk. Tel.* 237. Boat available. Mainly fly but spinning allowed in certain areas. Restocked regularly.

Usk Hotel, Talybont-on-Usk, Powys. Tel. Talybont (087487) 251.

9. Caerfanell: ½ mile of fishing on both banks of Caerfanell from Talybont bridge of confluence with Usk on Maesmawr Farm. Trout only. *Day permits from Maesmawr Farm and Usk Hotel, Talybont.*

Gliffaes Hotel, Crickhowell, Powys. Tel. Bwlch (0874) 730371 and 730372.

10. Usk: 1 mile at Gliffaes on left bank below the hotel. Red Barn water 1¼ miles on left bank upstream from Llanfoist Bridge, Abergavenny. Salmon and trout. *Day permits from hotel. Permits for lower water (Red Barn stretch) also available from P.M. Fishing Tackle, 12 Monk Street, Abergavenny. Tel.* (0873) 3175.

Crickhowell and District Angling Club, Hon. Secretary, J. Stenner Evans, Heddfan, Ffawyddog, Llangattock, Crickhowell, Powys. Tel. (0873) 810563.

11. Usk: 400 yards on left bank above and 800 yards on right bank and 400 yards on left bank below Crickhowell Bridge. Salmon average 12 lbs, brown trout up to 1½ lbs. Limited to four rods (two salmon). *Permits from the Vine Tree Inn, Llangattock. Tel. Crickhowell* (0873) 810514.

Monmouth District Council, Council Offices, Whitecross Street, Monmouth, Gwent. Tel. (0600) 2122.

12. Usk: Both banks, approximately 1,900 yards each bank, from Llanfoist Bridge downstream to below sewer bridge – trout, salmon and coarse. Permits and licences available from: *P. M. Fishing Tackle, 12 Monk Street; Abergavenny. Tel.* 3175; *Fussell's Sports Ltd, 53 Cross Street, Abergavenny. Tel.* 3333; *Bridge Inn, Llanfoist. Tel. Abergavenny* 3045; *Permits only – Area Chief Clerk, Town Hall, Abergavenny. Tel.* 2721.
Coarse fishing by season ticket only or Angling Club daily competitions. Children using any legal bait to fish on restricted water.

Tackle shops

Abergavenny. *Fussell's Sports Ltd., 53 Cross Street, Abergavenny. Tel.* (0873) 3333.

P.M. Fishing Tackle, 12 Monk Street, (opposite St. Mary's Church). Tel. (0873) 3175.

Brecon. *R. & C. Denman, 11 Watergate. Tel.* (0874) 2071. *Gibb Sports, 43 High Street, Brecon. Tel.* (0874) 2949.

Crickhowell. *Kirkland and Co. (Crickhowell) Ltd., 2 High Street. Tel.* (0873) 810268.

Usk – lower river

Lionel Sweet, the well-known casting champion and angler, reigned as king of the Gwent rivers from his tackle shop in Usk. From Usk to the sea the river becomes increasingly plump and bloated and below the Usk Town Fishery it has little to offer the occasional visitor. Trout up to 4½ lbs are taken in the 435 acres Llandegfedd Reservoir situated a few miles south west of the town of Usk.

Monnow and Trothy

For much of its short life the Monnow forms the boundary between England and Wales, looping lazily by the castles of Grosmont and Skenfrith and under the fortified Norman watergate of Monmouth town.

Birmingham Anglers' Association, 40 Thorp Street, Birmingham B5 4AU. Tel. 021-622 2904 *and* 021-622 1025.

1. Monnow: At Skenfrith, ½ mile of both banks below Garway Mill, and a further ¾ mile of left bank down to weir above bridge (excluding Priory water). See page 89.

Monmouth and District Angling Society, Secretary F. Hughes, Brook Cottage, Rockfield, Monmouth, Gwent, NP5 4ER. Tel. (0600) 3793.

2. Monnow. 1 mile on right bank from a point 30 yards above Monnow Mill weir to the fence opposite bus station. Mainly brown trout. Limited to 12 rods.

3. Trothy: 2 miles on right bank from Jingle Street bridge, Wonastow to Dingestow Bridge. Also 2½ miles on left bank upstream from a point two fields above Dingestow Church to

Monnow Bridge, Monmouth, with its mediaeval gateway.

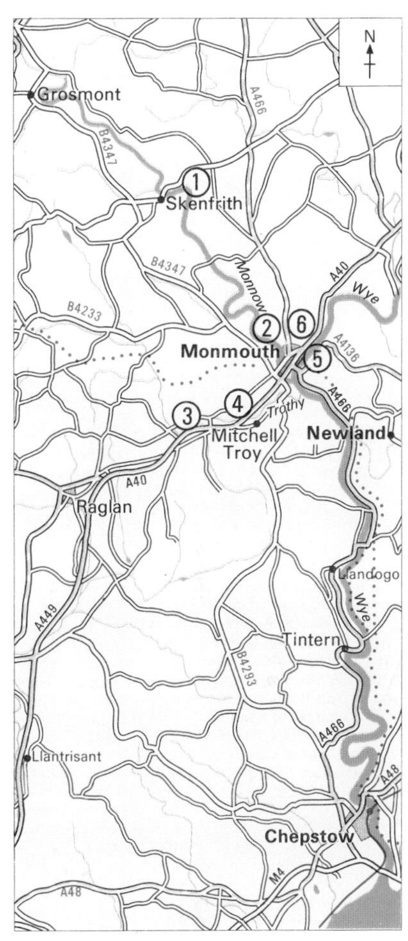

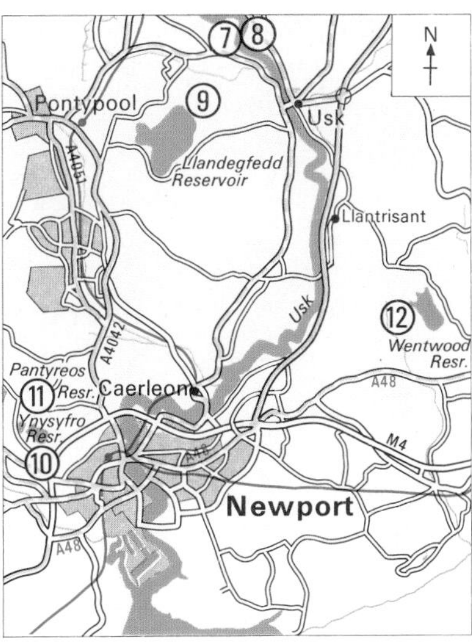

brook above Upper Llantrothy Farm. Brown trout up to 1 lb. 4 ozs. *Approved temporary membership only.*

Glen Trothy Caravan and Camping Park, Mitchel Troy, Monmouth, Gwent Tel. (0600) 2295.

4. Trothy: 760 yards on right bank from a point directly behind Glen Trothy Hotel downstream for two meadows. Mainly brown trout. *Restricted to campers and caravanners. Permits available at the site.*

Birmingham Anglers' Association, 40 Thorp Street, Birmingham B5 4AU. Tel. 021–622 2904 *and* 021–622 1025.

5. Wye: At Monmouth, both banks below Mally Brook to the site of the Old Town Ditch, Monmouth – individual fishing on the left bank – right bank holds 30 pegs.

Monmouth District Council, Council Offices, Whitecross Street, Monmouth. Tel. (0600) 2122.

6. Wye: 300 yards on both banks from Wye Bridge upstream to just above Rowing Clubhouse. Salmon, trout and coarse fish. *Daily, weekly, monthly and season permits from Monmouth District Council Offices.*

Usk Town Water Fishery Association, Secretary, Mr. Chris Brain, 56 St. Julian's Road, Newport, Gwent. Tel. Newport (Gwent) 55587.

7. Usk: 2 miles. Most stretches on both banks from Gargoed Pool, 1½ miles above the town to Llanbadoc Church on Usk-Caerleon road. *Only trout permits issued. Available from Sweet's Tackle Shop, Porthycarne Street, Usk. Tel.* (029 13) 2552.

Bridge Inn, Chain Bridge, near Usk, Gwent. Tel. Nantyderry (0873) 880243.

8. Usk: 400 yards left bank from bridge downstream. Brown trout and coarse fish. (**Note.** Permission to take Salmon has to be obtained separately). *For residents at hotel and day visitors permits available from hotel.* £1.50.

Welsh Water Authority, Cardiff Water Unit, Crwys House, Crwys Road, Cardiff. Tel. (0222) 395704

9. Llandegfedd Reservoir: 435 acres of brown and rainbow trout fishing. Situated between Pontypool and Usk, 2 miles east of A4042, Newport to Pontypool road. Approaching from Usk turn left at Llanbadoc. Trout up to 5½ lbs are taken. *Permits: Adult: season* £62.50, *day* £2.50. *Under 16s and OAPs* 50%. Self service ticket machine also operated at the reservoir and at Water Treatment Works. Boats available. *Book at Sluvad Treatment Works, Pontypool. Tel.* (97) 55333/4/5.

continued on next page

continued from previous page

Welsh Water Authority, Cambrian Way, Brecon, Powys. Tel. (0874) 3181.
Three reservoirs near Newport (Gwent) with brown trout to 3-3½ lbs, and rainbow trout to 2½-3 lbs.

10. Ynysyfro Reservoir: Two reservoirs of 16 and 10 acres, 2 miles north-west of Newport (Gwent) off M4 motorway. No boats, fly with spinning in certain areas. Restocked regularly. *Permits from Reservoir superintendent at the reservoir. Permits: season £50.00, day £2.00.*

11. Pantyreos Reservoir: Landscaped reservoir of 16 acres, 4 miles north-west of Newport (Gwent) off main Newport to Abertillery road. No boats; fly, with spinning in certain areas. Regularly restocked. *Permits from Reservoir Superintendent at the reservoir. Permits: season £30.00, day £1.50.*

12. Wentwood Reservoir: 41 acres of landscaped reservoir 7 miles north-east of Newport (Gwent) off M4 or A48 Newport-Chepstow road, in delightful surroundings with nature trails in vicinity for rest of the family. Boats available, fly with spinning in certain areas. Regularly restocked. *Permits from Reservoir Superintendent at the reservoir. Permits: season £50.00, day £2.00.*

Tackle shops

Chepstow. *Mr. Parfitt, Fishing Tackle Shop, Bank Street. Tel.* (02912) 2921.

Monmouth. *H. H. Keeling & Sons,* 48 *Monnow Street. Tel.* (0600 2010.

Newport. *Dave Richards, Angling Supplies,* 73 *Church Street. Tel.* 54910.

Usk. *Mr. L. Sweet, Tackle Shop, Porthycarne Street. Tel.* (02913) 2552.

Wye

If you can get hold of Les Baverstock's book, *The Wye* (an *Angling Times* book in the Fishing Famous Rivers series), study it well before you fish the river.

Several hotels in and around the attractive little town of Rhayader own useful stretches on these upper reaches towards Llangurig. Kelts, salmon that have spawned, must be returned to the river. So, too, must salmon parr (small immature salmon) which will be found in most of the Wye above Monmouth. The Welsh Water Authority's excellent guide to angling facilities explains how to tell them from the similar trout.

Elan and Claerwen Lakes

Constructed to supply the City of Birmingham with water, this system consists of five main reservoirs on the two water catchment rivers of the Elan and the Claerwen.

Black Lion Hotel, Llangurig, Nr. Llanidloes, Powys. Tel. (05515) 223.

1a. Wye: Approx. 2 miles of fishing south-east of hotel between Clochfaen Farm and Sain-y-Coed, excluding Pant-y-drain Farm (approx. ¾ mile). *Free to residents at the hotel. Non-residents can buy day and week permits from the hotel.*

1b. *Glansevern Arms Hotel, Pantmawr, Llangurig, Powys. Tel.* (05515) 240. Wye: 1 mile single bank at Glansevern, 2 miles both banks at Ty mawr (1½ miles east of hotel). Brown trout. *Permits available at hotel.*

Welsh Water Authority, South West Wales River Division, 19 *Penyfai Lane, Llanelli. Tel.* (055 42) 57031.

2. Llyn Egnant and Teifi Pools (O.S. 1:50,000 map No. 147, ref. 793674): 9 miles north-east of Tregaron at headwaters of River Teifi reached by side road east from Ffair Rhos near Pontrhydfendigaid. Reservoir formed by enhancing natural lake. Good fishing for brown trout to 3 lbs (average ½ lb), rainbow trout to 4 lbs (average ½ lb) and American Brook Trout. No boats, 6 fish limit, size lower limit 9 ins, fly only. Stocking throughout season. *Permits from above address or from licence distributors in Tregaron and Pontrhydfendigaid.*
Charges: Adult season £15.00, day £1.50. OAP's and juniors 50% of above rates.
American Brook Trout have been introduced into Llyn Egnant and the Teifi Pools. Report their catch specially on forms provided with your licence.

Welsh Water Authority, Cambrian Way, Brecon, Powys. Tel. (0874) 3181.

3. Elan and Claerwen lakes: 1,600 acres of brown trout fishing on the following landscaped

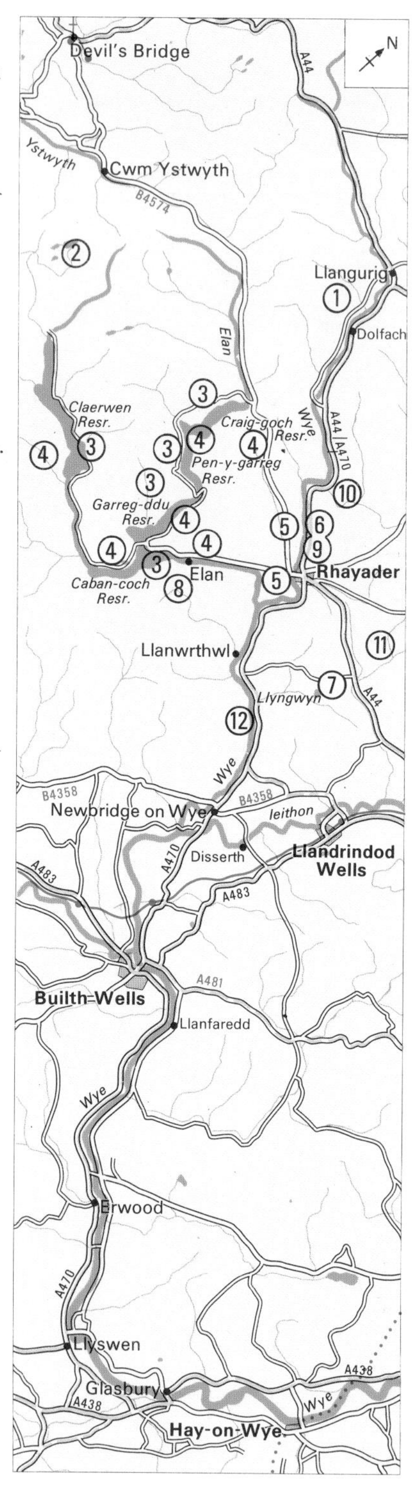

reservoirs in beautiful mountain scenery:
Claerwen: no restocking;
Caban coch: regularly restocked;
Craig-goch: regularly restocked; (American Brook Trout have been introduced here and anglers are requested to make a special report to the Water authority on forms available where they buy their licence should any be caught.)
Pan-y-garreg: regularly restocked;
Garreg-ddu: no restocking.
Permits available from the Estate Office, Elan Village, near the bottom end of Caban coch reservoir. (Tel. Rhayader (059782) 449: All waters: Adult season £20.00, week £6.60, day £1.80: 90p per day, £4.40 per week to cover Claerwen and Craig Goch only. OAP's and juniors 50% of above rates. Boat hire: row £1.00, outboard £2.50.

Elan Valley Hotel, Elan Village, Nr. Rhayader, Powys. Tel. Rhayader (059782) 448.

4. **Elan Valley Lakes:** 1,600 acres of brown and rainbow trout. Claerwen and Craig-goch lakes, River Claerwen to Dol-y-Mynach lake and River Elan behind hotel. Fishing also available on Pen-y-garreg, Carreg-ddu and Caban-coch lakes.

5. **Wye:** 4 miles mostly both banks, 3 miles above Rhayader and 1 mile below Rhayader.

6. **Marteg:** 2½ miles on both banks from confluence with Wye to St. Harmon. Brown trout.

7. **Llyngwyn Lake:** 16 acres. Rainbow trout. *Permits for day or week available at the hotel.*

Glanrhydwen Guest House, Elan Valley, Nr. Rhayader, Powys. Tel. Rhayader (059782) 427.

8. **Elan:** 200 yards on left bank directly in front of guest house. Rainbow trout. *Free to residents.*

Rhayader Angling Association, Rhayader.

9. **Wye:** Total of approximately 6 miles on either bank from 1 mile south of Rhayader up to Marteg Bridge. Salmon and trout.

10. **Marteg:** Approximately 4 miles of river, both banks from junction with River Wye. Trout.

11. **Llyngwyn:** Fly fishing only for trout.

Tickets from Vulcan Motel, Doldowlod, near Llandrindod Wells, Powys. Tel. (059782) 438.

Birmingham Anglers' Association, 40 Thorp Street, Birmingham B5 4AU. Tel. 021-622 2904 and 021-622 1025.

12. **Wye:** At Doldowlod, left bank from behind the Vulcan Arms upstream to the culvert. From below the old railway bridge for four meadows downstream. Also a short length on the right bank upstream of the old railway bridge for approx. 300 yards. Fly only during the trout season. See page 79.

Tackle shops

Builth Wells. *Mrs. Asbrey, 17 High Street.*

Llandrindod Wells. *C. Selwyn & Sons, 4 Park Crescent. Tel. (0597) 2397.*

Hay on Wye. *H. R. Grant & Sons, Newsagents, 6 Castle Street. Tel. (04972) 309.*

Rhayader. *P. G. Pugh, Drug Store and Fishing Tackle, West Street. Tel. (059782) 342.*
R. M. Powell, Garth House. Tel. (059782) 451.

Other accommodation offering angling

Rhayader. *Lion Royal Hotel, Rhayader, Powys. Tel. (059782) 202.*

Irfon, Ithon (Ieithon) and Cammarch

The Wye between Builth Wells and Newbridge is noted for its big salmon, yet the two main tributaries that join the main river here see only the odd salmon, the Irfon doing slightly better in October. The strength of the tributaries lies in their trout stocks which can be effectively fished through some excellent little specialist fishing hotels with which this beautiful area is endowed. The Ithon follows the north-south main road A483 for much of its life, skirting the inland resort of Llandrindod Wells, famous for its healing springs. It joins the Wye below the fisherman's retreat of Newbridge-on-Wye. The Irfon, and its tributary the Cammarch, approaches Builth Wells from another famous spa region, that of Llanwrtyd Wells and Llangammarch Wells.

---

continued on next page

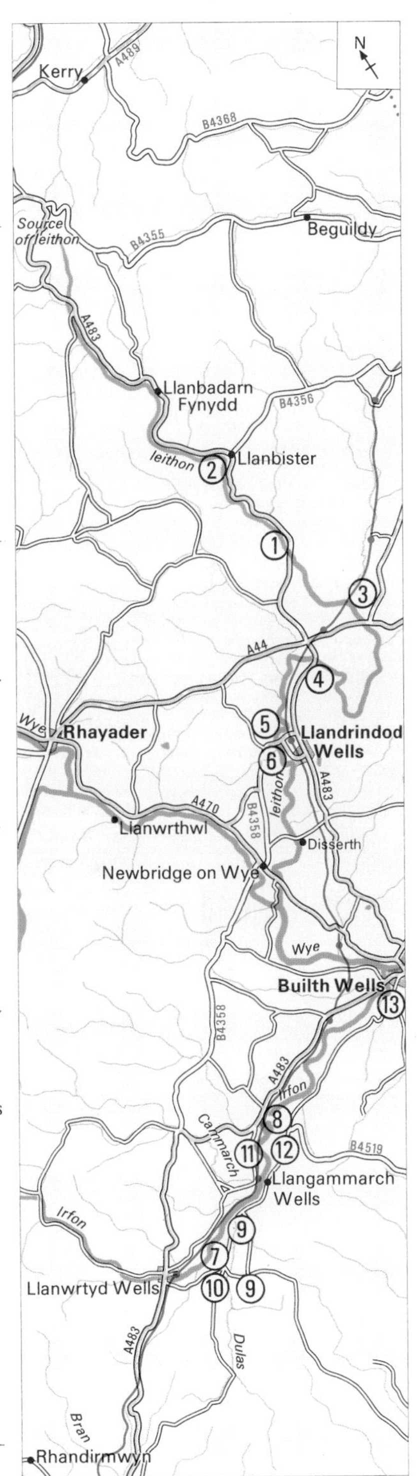

Ithon – continued from previous page

Severn Arms Hotel (Mr. Davies), Penybont, Powys. Tel. Penybont (059787) 224.

1. Ithon: 1½ miles, mainly both banks, between Llanddewi village and Rabber Bridge; 1½ miles both banks from Penybont bridge to Bryn Thomas bridge; 1 mile, one section left bank but mainly both banks between Llanbister and Llanddewi village. Mainly brown trout ¾ lb to 1 lb. *Permits for day and week and Wye River Division licences available at the Severn Arms, Penybont, Powys.*

Birmingham Anglers' Association, 40 Thorp Street, Birmingham B5 4AU. Tel. 021–622 2904 and 021–622 1025.

2. Ithon: At Llanbister, ¾ mile mainly double bank fishing. Access near where the river runs close to the road in the village of Llanbister. See page 79.

3. Ithon: At Penybont, both banks for a short distance above and a short distance of the right bank below the road bridge by Rabber Farm. A further ¾ mile of the double bank starting a short distance below the railway bridge. Also from the road bridge at Penybont for ½ mile downstream on the left bank. Fly only water. See page 79.

4. Ithon: At Llanbadarn, approx. ¾ mile on both banks. Rights on the right bank start ¼ mile below Alpine Bridge and extend upstream for ½ mile. On the left bank the rights start a short distance above Alpine Bridge and extend upstream. Below Llanbadarn Road bridge there is a further ½ mile of the right bank, starting below the road bridge and 700 yards of the left bank which starts one meadow below the road bridge. Fly only water. See page 79.

5. Ithon: At Llanyre, about a mile of right bank at Lower Dol-llwynhir Farm, near Llandrindod Wells. See page 79.

Llandrindod Wells Angling Association, Secretary A. H. Selwyn, Sports Shop, Park Crescent, Llandrindod Wells. Tel. (0597) 2397.

6. Ithon: 4 miles mostly on both banks from Llanyre Bridge to Disserth Bridge. Mainly trout. *Day permits from Secretary.*

Abernant Lake Hotel, Llanwrtyd Wells, Powys. Tel. (05913) 250.

7. Irfon: ¾ mile of left bank from a point below railway station to the boundary of Glan Irfon Farm. Few late salmon, but mainly brown trout. *Day permits from hotel – residents only.*

The Lake Hotel, Llangammarch Wells, Powys.

8. Irfon. Left bank between Llangammarch Village and Garth and left bank at Llanfechan for ¾ mile downstream.
Salmon, brown and rainbow trout. 1978 April salmon caught by G. V. Richards, 23 lbs. *For guests of the hotel only.*

Neuadd Arms Hotel, Llanwrtyd Wells, Powys. Tel. (05913) 236.

9. Dulas: 300 yards on both banks from a point ¾ mile upstream of the confluence with River Irfon to a point 100 yards above the bridge between Cefn-gorwydd and Cynala. Salmon in late summer and brown trout. *Permits from hotel.*

Cammarch Hotel, Llangammarch Wells, Powys. Tel. (05912) 205.

10. Dulas: ⅔ mile on both banks, 1 mile below Pont-ar-Dulas at confluence with River Irfon. Limited to 2 rods.

11. Cammarch: 2½ miles. 3 stretches upstream of the Cammarch Bridge. Limited to 3 rods. Salmon, and brown trout.

12. Irfon: 3½ miles. Various stretches above and below Llangammarch Wells, mostly on left bank. Limited rods.

13. Wye: 2 miles on left bank from confluence with River Irfon at Builth Wells downstream to Cnitho Brook.
Available to hotel residents only, on written application.

Eagle Hotel, New Radnor, Powys. Tel. New Radnor (054421) 208.

14. Lugg: ¾ mile both banks from Yew Tree Farm, Maestrala to a point ¾ mile downstream. Mainly brown trout. *Free to residents at the Eagle Hotel, New Radnor.*
Not featured on maps.

Tackle shops

Builth Wells. *Mrs. Asbery, 17 High Street.*

Llandrindod Wells. *C. Selwyn & Sons, 4 Park Crescent. Tel. (0597) 2397.*

Other accommodation offering angling

Llandrindod Wells, Powys.
Metropole Hotel. Tel. (0597) 2881.
Glen Usk Hotel. Tel. (0597) 2085.

Llanwrtyd Wells, Powys.
Dol-y-Coed Hotel, Tel. (05913) 215.

Cardigan Coast

Dyfi, king of the sea trout rivers gives a number of massive fish. Dysynni flows through beautiful scenery with good trout in the upper reaches and strong sea trout and salmon runs. Rheidol forms a hydro-electric complex. Ystwyth falls from Plynlimon to join the Rheidol at Aberystwyth.

Brigands Inn, Mallwyd, Machynlleth, Powys, SY20 9HJ. Tel. Dinas Mawddwy (06504) 208.

1. Dyfi and Cleifion: 5 miles at Mallwyd. *Inn guests only.* Catch in recent years: 110 sea trout, 27 salmon to 20½ lbs. *Day permit from Inn.*

New Dovey Fishery Association, (1929) Ltd., Hon. Secretary Mr. D. M. Jones, B.A., Plas, Machynlleth. Tel. (0654) 2721.

2. River Dovey: 15 miles on Llyfnant Stream (Glandyfi) to Cwm Llinau and left bank from Cwm Llinau to Nant Llywelyn (Aberangell). *Visitors permits available to persons staying in hotels or rooms in district on application to Hon. Secretary. Permits on Monday, Tuesday, Thursday and Saturday – £22.68 for 4 days. Permits for any weekday on a section of the upper reaches also available from:*
Mr. D. G. Evans, Garage, Cemmaes Road. Mr. E. Jones, Post Office, Cemmaes. Mr. E. Francis, Nant y Nest Stores, Dinas Mawddwy.
The Dyfi has produced the largest rod caught sewin (20¾ lb) and the largest net caught sewin (24½ lb) in Wales.

Tynycornel Hotel, Tal-y-Llyn, Nr. Tywyn. Tel. Abergynolwyn (065477) 282.

3. Tal-y-Llyn Lake: Brown trout. Few salmon caught late season. Approx. 2,000 trout caught annually. *For hotel residents mainly. Permit from hotel.*

Estimaner Angling Association.

4. Dysynni: 6–7 miles from marker below Pont-y-Garth to a point north-east of Abergynolwyn, with minor exceptions. Also stretch on Afon Gadair. *Permits from E. H. & M. A. Rowlands, Post Office, Abergynolwyn.*

Col. J. F. Williams-Wynne, Peniarth Estate, Tywyn, Gwynedd.

5. Dysynni: 5 miles near Bryn Crug. *Day, fortnight and season permits from J. J. Roberts, Trefellyn, High Street, Tywyn. Tel. (0654) 710697, or The Sports Shop, College Green, Tywyn, Gwynedd.*

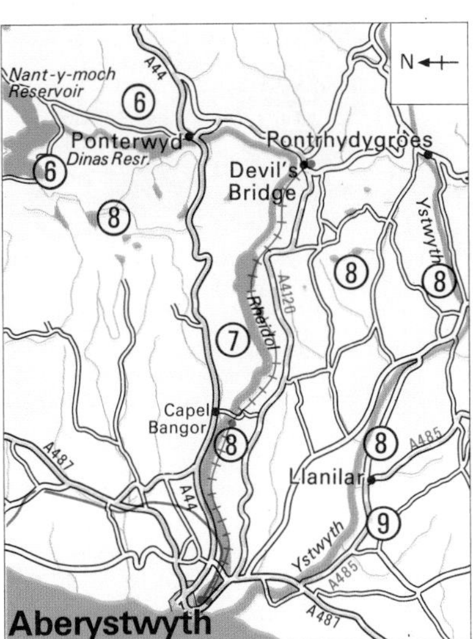

CEGB Rheidol Power Station, Capel Bangor, Nr. Aberystwyth, Dyfed. Tel. Capel Bangor (097 084) 465.

6. Dinas Reservoir. 60 Acres reservoir of the Rheidol hydro-electric scheme maintained on a put-and-take basis. Brown and rainbow trout. (Season 1 April–30 September). *Licences and permits available from Evans Garage, Ponterwyd and by post from CEGB, Bron Heulog, Conway Road, Llandudno Junction.*

Endeavour Deep Sea Group, Schooners Landing, Aberystwyth. Tel. Aberystwyth (0970) 612818. Personal members of the club can obtain 33⅓% reduction for fishing on (6) Dinas and Nant-y-Moch reservoirs. Sea (boat and beach) game and spinning tackle available for hire.

J. E. Rosser, Fishing Tackle Shop, Maesyplwm, 3 Queen Street, Aberystwyth. Tel. (0970) 617451.

7. Rheidol: Private fishing on ¾ mile of best beats. *Day ticket only available from this tackle shop.*

8. *Aberystwyth Angling Association Ltd., Box 15, G.P.O. Aberystwyth, Dyfed SY23 1AA. Hon Secretary, AAA Ltd, P.O. Box 15, Abertsytwyth.*

General

Many of these safe wading lakes lying at about 900 ft, were formed by damming during the last century to provide water power for lead mines in the valleys below. They contain good populations of wild brown trout, chiefly in the 6–12 oz range, and usually pink fleshed for excellent eating. Many of these lakes are stocked annually with hatchery brown and rainbow trout. Others are kept stocked by the addition of wild trout captured from local mountain streams.

Map references O.S. Sheet 135 1:50,000 *series.*

Penrhyncoch Lakes

Five lakes 10 miles east-north-east of Aberystwyth.

Llyn Craig y Pistyll (*O.S.* 7285) is a public water supply source and the largest of the five lakes. Sound bank fishing all round. Trout average 6–8 ozs and some of a pound are recorded.

Llyn Syfydrin (*O.S.* 7284) has an island inhabited by black-headed gulls. Some of the banks are boggy but are not dangerous. Trout are of superb quality, averaging about 12 ozs, but ones of 1½ to 2 lbs, are often brought to net. A boat is available and, in season, the sedges hatch out in goodly numbers.

Llyn Blaenmelindwr (*O.S.* 7183) is set in a conifer forest, and its waters are very clear. Good baskets of 8–16 oz fish have been taken from this lake, especially in the evenings, and some very large trout are known to be present.

Llyn Rhosgoch (*O.S.* 7183) lies above the road from Blaenmelindwr and within a short walk. Trout are second to none in quality. The sedge hatches out here and this fly accounted for the 2½ lbs record fish for the lake.

Llyn Pendam (*O.S.* 7083) set amongst trees. This lake has a large population of small trout, but trout of one and two pounds are occasionally caught.

Ponterwyd Lakes

Llyn yr Oerfa (*O.S.* 7279) about 2 miles south of the Aberystwyth road (A44). Black-headed gulls rest on one shore area. Trout breeding is subdued but re-stocking has given a good head of handsome fish of up to a pound or more, with a shy reputation, calling for a cautious approach. Oerfa has a good hatch of sedge.

Bray's Pool (*O.S.* 7281) otherwise known as Lake Llywernog, lying alongside the A44, 2 miles from Ponterwyd. The eastern half of the lake is private. Trout tend to be small (6–8 ozs) but numerous, to give good bags.

Trisant Lakes

These three lakes are south of the Aberystwyth–Devil's Bridge road (via Capel Seion), where one can often see red kites and ravens.

Llyn Frongoch (*O.S.* 7275) alongside the road, often yields more fish in the pound and two pound range than other lakes. Lake birds include grebes. There are two 6-berth caravans on the shore, with electricity and flush toilets for hire (apply P.R.O.) and the fishing, with two boats provided, is reserved to the caravan occupiers, except for Wednesdays, Saturdays and Sundays when the permit holders may fish and also reserve the boats.

Llyn Rhosrhydd (*O.S.* 7075) is reached over a farm road on which the gates should be kept closed. The lake does not allow for breeding and consequently the size of the fish is above the usual – from one to two pounds. They are not easy to deceive. A boat is available.

continued on next page

Guests at the Tynycornel Hotel can fish for brown trout on Talyllyn Lake. Non-residents may also purchase permits, subject to availability.

Llyn Glandwgan (*O.S.* 7075) visible $\frac{1}{4}$ mile from Rhosrhydd dam, the lake is secluded and has a good waterfowl population. It may be fished all round except for the marked sector towards the dam end, which is private. Trout are plentiful and $\frac{1}{2}$ lb fish common. Larger fish include the Association's record fish of 5 lbs. Boat available.

Streams and Rivers
Rheidol
The Association holds rights on several mountain streams, most of River Rheidol and on parts of the upper and lower River Ystwyth. Anglers to whom small remote streams appeal may sample the Llechwedd Mawr which flows from Angler's Retreat (Talybont) to Llyn Nant-y-Moch, or the Rheidol sources above Llyn Nant-y-Moch. Salmon and sewin migrate up both rivers, but the River Rheidol only to the high falls at Devil's Bridge. From the gorge below this point the river emerges to run down to the fish-laddered Rheidol Falls. This lies at the head of the Cwmrheidol reservoir whose dam contains a fish-lift. The river then twists, ribbon-like, in its flat bottomed valley before partnering the River Ystwyth in Aberystwyth harbour. The hydroelectric requirements

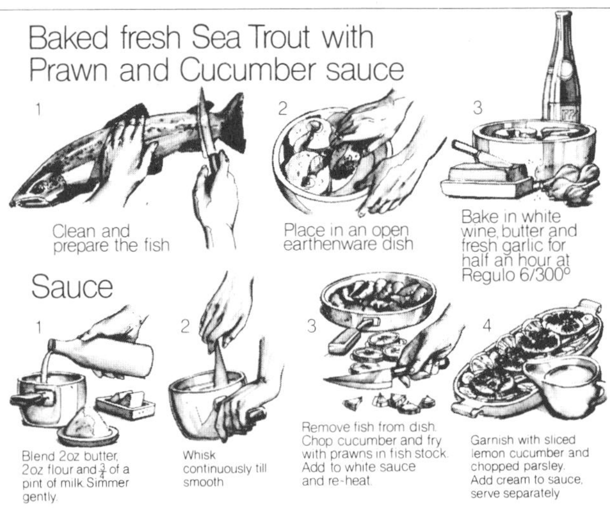

Are you staying in a caravan or flat? Perhaps you are one of the lucky ones with a holiday cottage alongside the Artro, the Dysynni, Dovey, Ystwyth or Rheidol! Whatsoever, remember this area of Mid Wales is the richest in Britain for sea trout. If you have no inclination for the chase – nor the skill – enquire of the local fresh fish shop in the towns, or of a local angler in the village; he will put you onto the trail of a plump fish of about 3 or 4 lbs, which is enough for a small family. The recipe given in the above picture strip has been kindly provided by the chef at the George III Hotel, Penmaenpool, Dolgellau, whose restaurant has excellent sea and river foods in season.

Vale of Rheidol narrow gauge railway is a convenient way of reaching the angling beats on Afon Rheidol from Aberystwyth. There is a station at Capel Bangor, another at Aberffrwd, convenient for the waters of the Aberystwyth Angling Association (see item 8).

control flow so that the main river is rarely really low or very high, giving good fishing water much of the time, whatever the weather. In recent seasons there has been a marked improvement in the Spring salmon runs. The main run starts in late May-June when large sewin also enter. The main run of sewin and salmon follows from July.

Ystwyth
The River Ystwyth, in contrast, is still a spate river, very clean and rocky as well as gravelly. Its run of salmon may be smaller but its sewin are numerous and may be easier to catch in daylight, given the right water!

Angling permits: These are available from J. Rosser, Tackle Shop, Queen Street; Aber Gun Supplies, Terrace Road, Aberystwyth. Boat Hire by arrangement with Mr. J. Rosser, Tackle Shop, Queen Street, Aberystwyth. Tel. (0970) 617451. Caravan Hire by arrangement with the P.R.O., Aberystwyth Angling Association, P.O. Box 15, Aberystwyth, Dyfed, SY23 1AA. Fees for daily, weekly and season permits are given in the Association's Rules.

Llanilar Angling Association, Secretary Dr. P. Callaghan, Tanycastell, Llanilar, Aberystwyth. Tel. Llanilar (09747) 213.

9. Ystwyth: 5 miles excluding private stretches from Grogwynion Bridge to Llanfairian Bridge. *Day permits from J. E. Rosser, 3 Queen Street, Aberystwyth. Post Offices at Llanilar and Crosswood, Oak Inn, Llanfarian. Morfa Bychan Caravan Park, Llanfarian. Shop., Rhydfelin.*

Aberdovey is a good centre for sea angling in the estuary and game fishing on the River Dovey.

The upper reaches of the Dysynni river have excellent salmon pools and fast flowing stretches. Both the waters of the Estimaner Angling Association and those of Colonel J. F. Williams-Wynne can be fished on permit. (see items on page 92).

At Felin Newydd, Capel Bangor, the CEGB's viewing terrace overlooking the lower reservoir, of the Cwm Rheidol Power Scheme.

Tackle shops

Aberdovey. *W. D. Evans & Son, London House, 4/5 Sea View Terrace, Tel. (065472) 353.*

Aberystwyth. *J. E. Rosser, Tackle Shop, 3 Queen Street. Tel. (0970) 617451.*

Tywyn. *F. R. Porter, The Sports Shop, 6 College Green. Tel. 710772.*

Other accommodation offering angling

Aberystwyth, Dyfed. *Castle Hotel, South Road. Tel. (0970) 7392.*
Crystal Palace Hotel, Queens Road, Tel. (0970) 7167.
Seabank Hotel, Promenade. Tel. (0970) 617617.
Glanaber Hotel, Union Street. Tel. (0970) 617610.

Dinas Mawddwy, Gwynedd. *Buckley Arms. Tel. (065 04) 261.*

Eglwysfach, Dyfed. *Ynyshir Hall, Eglwysfach, Machynlleth. Tel. Glandyfi (065 474) 209.*

Mallwyd, Powys, *Brigands Inn. Tel. Dinas Mawddwy (065 04) 208.*

Pennal, Gwynedd. *Riverside Hotel, Pennal, Nr. Machynlleth. Tel. (065475) 285.*

Tywyn, Gwynedd. *Corbett Arms. Tel. (0654) 710264.*
Gorlan Hotel, 6 Marine Parade. Tel. (0654) 710404.

Clywedog

This sizeable tributary of the Severn, and the town of Llanidloes at their confluence, have gained in angling importance in recent years with the construction on the river and stocking of the giant Clywedog regulating dam and reservoir. Its 615 available acres of brown trout fishing are an idyllic setting for an angling holiday.

Severn

The Severn's river basin is the only one in Wales not covered by the Welsh Water Authority. It stays part of the England-based Severn-Trent Water Authority. Llyn Clywedog's regulating role has meant more stable water conditions in the Severn. The upper river sees the occasional salmon but it is the area's trout and coarse fish waters – listed below – which continue to attract a regular flow of anglers, mainly from the Midlands of England.

Montgomeryshire Angling Association

1. Afon Carno: 1 mile on right from Pontdolgoch Bridge to Wig Bridge and left bank from point below Inn to ford. Trout. *Day permits available from H. L. Bebb, Home Handicrafts, Short Bridge Street, Newtown. Tel.* (0686) 26917.

2. Llyn Tarw: 14 acres 2½ miles north of Pontdolgoch on A489. American brook trout. 400–500 trout per annum, best 1 lb 4½ ozs. *Day permits from H. L. Bebb (see above).*

3. Afon Rhiew. 2½ miles on right bank downstream from ford above Hirrhyd to two meadows below Felindre Bridge on Berriew-Manafon road. Brown trout in flood. *Day permits from H. L. Bebb (see above) and Bond's, Hall Street, Welshpool. Tel.* (0938) 3327.

Llanidloes and District Angling Association, Secretary J. Dallas Davies, Dresden House, Great Oak Street, Llanidloes, Powys. Tel. (05512) 2644.

4. Llyn Clywedog: 615 acres of brown and rainbow trout

fishing. Trout averaging 1 lb 5 ozs. *Permits from Travellers Rest Cafe, Longbridge Street, Llanidloes. Tel.* (05512) 2329. *Boats available from Mrs. J. Evans, Dyffryn, Llanidloes. Tel.* (05512) 2129.

5. Clywedog: 3 miles mostly on both banks from a point below dam to confluence with Severn. Mostly brown trout although some salmon are taken towards the end of season. *Day permits.*

6. Severn: 1 mile stretches upstream and downstream of Longbridge, Llanidloes. Also 1¼ miles on both banks upstream from Glanhafren Bridge.

Birmingham Anglers' Association, 40 Thorp Street, Birmingham B5 4AU. Tel. 021–622 2904 *and* 021–622 1025.

7. Severn: At Llanidloes, more that a mile of the left bank, about a mile upstream from Llanidloes. Fly only during trout season. See page 79.

Dinam Estate Fishery, Severn-Trent Water Authority, Upper Severn Division, Shelton, Shrewsbury, ST3 8BJ. Tel. (0743) 63141.

8. Severn:
Game beats
(*i*) The Upper (or Llandinam) Beat, extending from the top limit on the Severn down to Llandinam Hall, on both banks. (Excluding the length between the two bridges at Llandinam).

(*ii*) The Lower (or Caersws) Beat, extending from Llandinam Hall down to the Trannon confluence on both banks.

Coarse beat
(*i*) The Caersws Bridge Beat, extending from the Trannon confluence down to the upper boundary of the Caersws Recreation Ground, on both banks, and from Caersws road bridge down to the lower limit of the water, *on the right bank only.*

(*ii*) **Trannon**
The Carnedd Beat, which is wholly on the River Trannon, extending from the first road bridge on the minor road past Carnedd Farm down to the Trannon's confluence with the Severn, on both banks. Salmon and trout. Fly-fishing only during game fishing season. Coarse fishing (any bait) at other times. *Day permits from E. Evans Jones, 2 Broneirion Cottages, Llandinam.*

Maesmawr Hall Hotel, Caersws, Powys. SY17 5SF. Tel. (068684) 255.

9. Severn: 3½ miles on both banks from stream confluence opposite Llys Maldwyn Hospital downstream to marker post; also salmon pools at Cilgwrgan. Salmon and trout. *Day permits from hotel.*

Birmingham Anglers' Association, 40 Thorp Street, Birmingham B5 4AU. Tel. 021–622 2904 and 021–622 1025.

10. Severn: At Caersws, left bank from one field below bridge to hospital, and right bank from ½ mile below bridge to opposite hospital. No contests.
See page 79.

11. Severn: At Caersws (Red House), ¾ mile of both banks. Access to the right bank opposite Red House Farm. The water starts just upstream of the car park and goes downstream to within a short distance of Victoria Bridge. There is a small meadow on the left bank that is not available. *Members crossing from the main road to the Red House Farm car park must at all times beware of aircraft that may be landing, as this meadow is used as a landing strip.* Parking is also available at Trecastell Farm for access to the left bank.
See page 79.

12. Severn: At Newtown, two meadows on left bank at Bryn Hyfryd Farm, also ½ mile of right bank at Glan Hafren Farm.
See page 79.

13. Severn: At Aberbechan a length of about ½ mile in all, above and below the bridge (20 pegs).
See page 79.

14. Severn: At Forden, rights start 250 yards below the level crossing and extend upstream for about 2 miles.
See page 79.

15. Severn: At Buttington Bridge, number 1 section starts below the Crewe Pioneers' Water on the left bank above Buttington Bridge and goes upstream to Hazeldine Waters (20 pegs). Number 2 section extends from two meadows above the access opposite the Powis Arms down to Maginnis Bridge (30 pegs). Number 3 section from Maginnis Bridge to below the broken railway bridge (40 pegs).
See page 79.

16. Severn: At Pool Quay (Maesydd), three sections on left bank (A, B and C), including 'The Roundabout' (90 pegs). Car park at riverside.
See page 79.

17. Severn: At Pool Quay (Lower Water), about ½ mile of same bank further down river, above and below feeder stream (40 pegs).
See page 79.

18. Severn: At Criggion, approx. 6 miles of almost continuous fishing on the right bank upstream and downstream of Llandrinio Bridge. There is a further ¾ mile below the Crewe Anglers' Water.
See page 79.

19. Severn: At Crewe Green, ½ mile of right bank at Bellan House Farm.
See page 79.

Newtown and District Fishing Club, Newtown, Powys.

20. Fachwen Pool: 10 acre lake, 2 miles north-west of Newtown. Brown and rainbow trout, re-stocked at intervals throughout the year. Best rainbow trout 2 lbs 4 ozs. *Day and season permits available from: H. L. Bebb, Home Handicrafts, Short Bridge Street, Newtown. Tel. (0792) 26917. The Bear Hotel, Newtown (to residents). The Grapes Hotel, Newtown (to residents).*

Tackle shops

Llanidloes. *The Grapple Tackle Box, China Street. (Open evenings and weekends).*

Tackle hire also available from *J. Dallas Davies, Dresden House, Great Oak Street, Llanidloes. Tel. (05512) 2644.*

Newtown. *H. L. Bebb, Home Handicrafts, Short Bridge Street. Tel. (0686) 26917.*

Welshpool. *Bond's, Hall Street. Tel. (0938) 3327.*

Other accommodation offering angling.

Welshpool, Powys. *Lion Hotel, Berriew, Nr. Welshpool.*

Vyrnwy

The fishing rights in the lake are administered by the attractive Lake Vyrnwy Hotel. The lake is stocked with brown trout averaging ¾ lb and fish are taken up to 1½ lb in weight.
The trout waters immediately below the dam, and on the tributary Cownwy, are also vested in the Hotel.

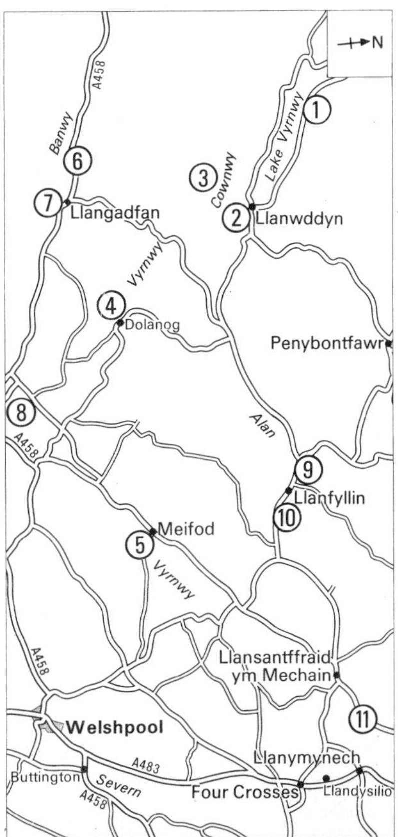

Pistyll Rhaeadr, a spectacular 250 ft high fall on Afon Disgynfa, upper tributary of the Tanat in Powys.

continued from previous page

Tanat

Small, shallow, yet surprisingly good for trout and the occasional salmon, the Tanat flows through beautiful hill country.

Lake Vyrnwy Hotel, Llanwddyn, Via Oswestry, Salop. SY10 0LY. Tel. Llanwddyr (069173) 244.

1. Lake Vyrnwy: 1,100 acres of brown and rainbow trout fishing. 1977: 1,859 trout caught averaging 14 ozs. Best rainbow 3½ lbs. Best brown trout 2¾ lbs. The hotel reserve the right to retain all fish caught over a total of four per rod per day. Bank fishing is for hotel residents only. Boat fishing available to resident and non-resident permit holders.

2. River Vyrnwy: 3 miles on right bank downstream of the weir below Dam Pool to a point beyond the confluence of the Rover Cownwy.

3. Cownwy: 1 mile on left bank upstream of the confluence. Brown trout only, though very few now. *Permits from the hotel.*

Birmingham Anglers' Association, 40 Thorp Street, Birmingham B5 4AU. Tel. 021-622 2904 and 021-622 1025.

4. Vyrnwy: At Dolanog, 3 miles of left bank below bridge towards Pont Robert and two small lengths of right bank. Fly only during trout season.
See page 79.

5. Vyrnwy: At Meifod, about 3 miles of river, mainly both banks, situated above and below Cil Mawr Farm, 2 miles down stream of Meifod. Fly only below Broken Bridge.
See page 79.

6. Banwy: At Foel, 1,600 yards on the right bank at Foel. Fly only in the trout season.
See page 79.

Cann Office Hotel, Llangadfan, Nr. Welshpool, Powys. Tel. Llangadfan (093 888) 202.

7. Banwy: ¼ mile stretch immediately above hotel and ½ mile stretch 2 miles down river. Trout and grayling, also salmon in the lower stretch. *Permits available from the hotel.*

Birmingham Anglers' Association, 40 Thorp Street, Birmingham B5 4AU. Tel. 021-622 2904 and 021-622 1025.

8. Banwy: At Llanfair Caereinion, about ½ mile of left bank above bridge at Dolgead Hall. Fly only during trout season.
See page 79.

Bodfach Hall Hotel, Llanfyllin, Powys. Tel. Llanfyllin (069184) 272.

9. Cain: 300 yards on both banks in the hotel grounds. Mainly trout. *Free to hotel residents. Arrangements can also be made for residents to fish on Lake Vyrnwy.*

Cain Valley Hotel, Llanfyllin, Powys. Tel. Llanfyllin (069184) 366.
Fishing on grounds of Mr. Trevor Lewis, Greenhall Farm, Llanfyllin. Tel. Llanfyllin 364.

10. Cain: 1 mile of fishing on both banks, some 2 miles south-east of Llanfyllin. Three fields (both banks) downstream from Pentre Farm bridge and one field downstream from Greenhall Farm bridge. Trout to 1 lb and grayling. *Day permits from either of above addresses.*

Bryn Tanat Hotel, Llansantffraid, Nr. Oswestry, Powys. Tel. Llansantffraid (069181) 259.

11. Tanat : ¾ mile on both banks within hotel boundaries. Trout and grayling. Priority given to hotel residents. *Permits from hotel.*

Tackle shops

Welshpool. *Bond's, Hall Street. Tel. (0938) 3327.*

Other accommodation offering angling

Llanymynech. *Cross Keys Hotel, Llanymynech, Nr. Oswestry, Powys. Tel. (0691) 830233.*

Mawddach

Mawddach, Eden and Wnion can scarcely be beaten for splendid river scenery. Salmon and sea trout make their way upstream from May as far as the falls of Pistyll Mawddach.

Llyfni

Dyffryn Nantlle is drained by the Llyfni, which meets the sea between the bass angling beaches of Dinas Dinlle and Aberdesach.

Dolmelynllyn Hall Hotel, Ganllwyd. Dolgellau, Gwynedd. Tel. Ganllwyd (034 140) 273.

1. Mawddach: 1¼ miles on left bank from footbridge by village cemetery to Ty'n-y-Groes Hotel. Good quality salmon and sea trout. *Permits from hotel.*

Bontddu Hall Hotel, Bontddu, Nr. Dolgellau, Gwynedd. Tel. Bontddu (034 149) 661.

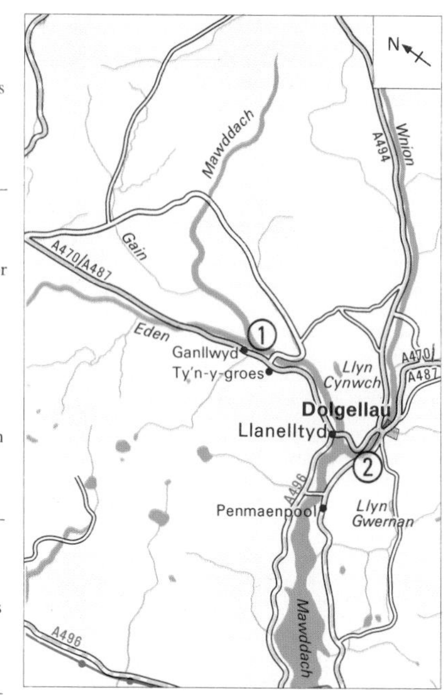

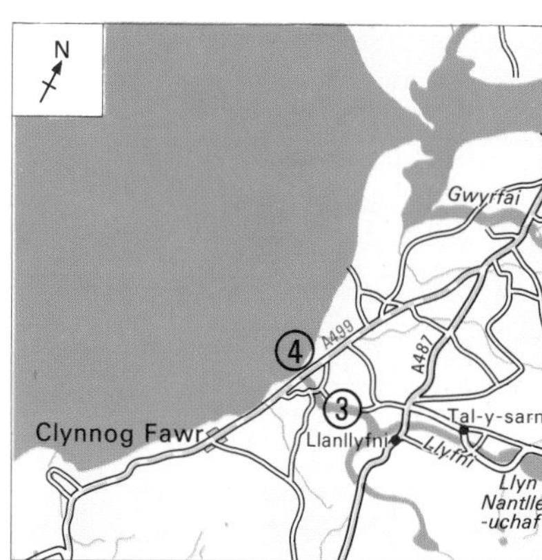

2. Wnion: 5 miles. ½ mile on right bank upstream from Bont-y-Wernddu bridge (railway embankment) to Dolgellau and ½ mile on left bank from school house boundary to Llwyn Farm. Then various stretches on alternate banks. *Free to hotel residents. Limited number of permits.*

Seiont, Gwyrfai and Llyfni Anglers' Society, Secretary Mr. Adrian Roberts, 17 Castle Street, Caernarfon, Gwynedd.

3. Llyfni: 4 miles, most stretches on right bank from Caerengan Bridge near Talysarn to Pont-y-Cim and on left bank from Pont-y-Cim to Glandwr Guest House at Pontllyfni. Also small stretch on right and left banks from the bridge on A499 to the sea. Salmon and sea trout. *Permits from Mr. Roberts, Newsagent, Snowdon Street, Penygroes. Huxley-Jones, Tackle Shop, Bangor Street, Caernarfon. Tel.* (0286) 3186.

Glandwr Guest House, Pontllyfni, Nr. Caernarfon, Gwynedd. Tel. Clynnog Fawr (028 686) 432.

4. Llyfni: 280 yards on left bank in the grounds of the guest house off the A499 Caernarfon-Pwllheli road. Salmon, sea trout and brown trout. *Free to guests.*

Cymdeithas Enweiriol Pwllheli a'r Cylch, (Pwllheli and District Angling Association), Secretary Mr. G. W. Pritchard, Edwyfed, 30 Lôn Ceredigion, Pwllheli, Gwynedd. Tel. Pwllheli (0758) 3531.

5. Rhyd-hir: Most of the river bank between the bridge at Efail Newydd and Pwllheli harbour.

6. Erch: 4 miles on both banks from Rhyd-y-gwystl bridge near Fourcrosses to outflow at Pwllheli harbour. Salmon, sea trout and brown trout. *Weekly and day permits from D. & E. Hughes, 24 Penlan Street, Pwllheli.*

Tackle shops

Caernarfon. *Howards, Ironmongers, 72 Pool Street. Tel.* (0286) 2671. *Huxley Jones, Tackle Shop, Bangor Street. Tel.* (0286) 3186.
Criccieth. *D. A. C. Morgan, Newsagents, 1 High Street. Tel.* (076 671) 2557. *R. T. Pritchard & Son, Sheffield House, High Street. Tel.* 2116.

Penrhyndeuthdraeth. *S. Pierce & Son, Ironmongers, Bank Buildings, The Square. Tel.* (076 674) 236.

Pwllheli: *D. & E. Hughes 24 Penlan Street. Tel.* (0758) 3291.

Porthmadog. *J. & R. T. Davies, Angling Centre, 11–13 High Street. Tel. Porthmadog* (0766) 2464.

Trawsfynydd. *H. K. Lewis, Newsagents, Trawsfynydd. Tel.* (076687) 234.

Other accommodation offering angling

Ganllwyd. *Ty'n-y-groes Hotel, Ganllwyd, Nr. Dolgellau. Tel. Ganllwyd* (0341) 40275.

Llanfrothen. *Brynllydan Hotel and Licensed Restaurant, Llanfrothen. Tel. Penrhyndeudraeth* (076 674) 442 *(advice on fishing only).*

Talsarnau, Gwynedd. *Maes-y-neuadd Hotel. Tel. Harlech* (076673) 200. *Ship Aground Hotel. Tel. Penrhyndeudraeth* (076 674) 240.

Dee

The Dee offers variety though the salmon fishing has suffered much in late years from the effects and after-effects of disease. Its lower reaches are well stocked with coarse fish – these are mainly confined to the Cheshire Plain in England.

Ceiriog

Though the Ceiriog offers limited waters, its salmon and trout fishing is highly respected as are the excellent little hotels through which the visiting angler can buy a permit.

Owain Glyndwr Hotel, Corwen, Clwyd. Tel. (0490) 2115.

1. Alwen: 1 mile. ¾ mile on both banks upstream of bridge at Cefn Ceirch, Nr. Betws Gwerfil Goch, ¼ mile downstream on right bank. Mainly trout fishing. *Day permits from hotel.*

Bala and District Angling Association.

2. Cwm Prysor Lake (above Llyn Celyn on River Tryweryn). Trout only.

3. Dee: 600 yards on both banks from outlet of Bala Lake. Trout only.

4. Hirnant: 4 miles on both banks from source to the old vicarage. Trout only. *Permits from W. E. Pugh, 74 High Street, Bala. Tel.* (06782) 248. *E. Evans, Bradford House, Bala.*

---

continued on next page

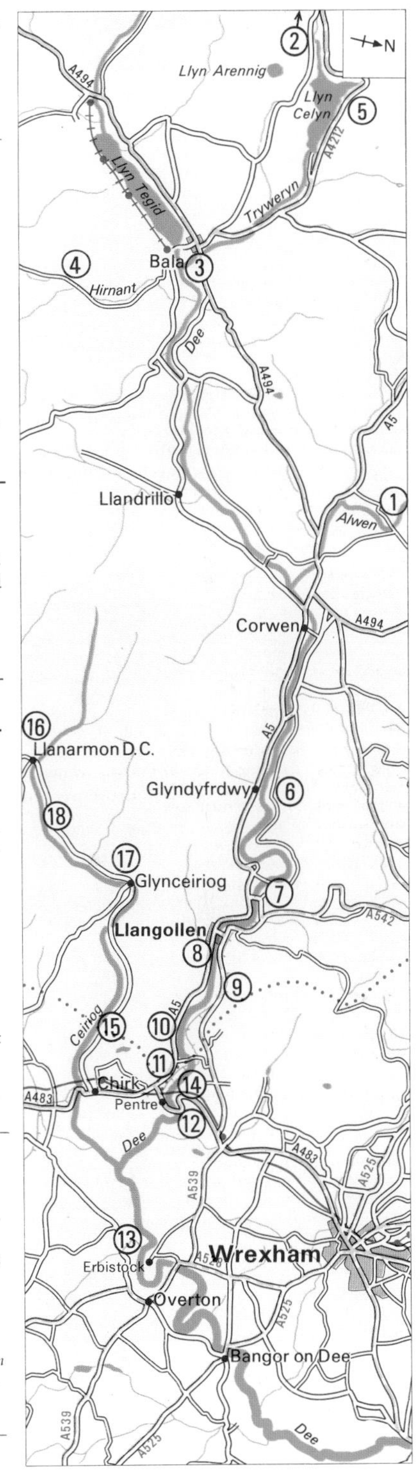

continued from previous page

Welsh Water Authority, Dee and Clwyd River Division, 2 Vicars Lane, Chester. Tel. (0244) 45004.

5. Llyn Celyn: 900 acres reservoir in mountains beside B4391 Bala to Ffestiniog road. Brown trout to 1½ lbs and rainbow trout to 1¼ lbs, average 10 ozs, fly and spinning only. *Permits from: W. E. Pugh, 74 High Street, Bala. R. E. Evans, Bradford House, Bala. J. A. Jones, Lakeside. Charges: Adults (visitors), season £25.00, day £1.50, evenings after 5 pm – 75p.*

Berwyn Arms Hotel, Glyndyfrwdy, Corwen. Tel. Glyndwr (049 083) 210.

6. Dee: 1¾ miles, mainly on right bank from marker post below Mountpool to Glyndyfrdwy Bridge. Salmon up to 20 lbs, sea trout and rainbow trout. *Day permits from hotel; contact N. J. Croft or G. M. Croft.*

Llangollen Angling Association, Llangollen, Clwyd.

7. Dee: 6 miles. On left bank from Rhewl Mill to Horseshoe Falls and right bank 1½ miles above falls to Pendre. Below falls on right bank to old weir and on left bank on Ty Craig stretch to a point above Abbey Brook. Also both banks by Jenny Jones Hotel and Woodlands Hotel. Right bank from canal recording station to Chain Bridge. Salmon and trout with some coarse fish. *Day permits from Neil Elbourne, Tackle Shop, 12 Chapel Street, Llangollen. Tel.* (0978) 786055.

Hand Hotel, Bridge Street, Llangollen, Clwyd. Tel. (0978) 860303.

8. Dee: Left bank along hotel's garden fronting onto river. Salmon, brown trout and coarse fish. 1977: 2½ lbs grayling, 1¼ lb brown trout. *Free to guests of the hotel.*

Bryn Howel Hotel, Llangollen, Clwyd. Tel. (0978) 860 331.

9. Dee: Approximately 360 yards of river in vicinity of the hotel just east of Llangollen. Salmon and some coarse fish, four rods only allowed. *Permits available free to hotel Residents.*

Liverpool and District Anglers Association.

10. Dee: 3 miles between Llangollen and Lower Hall and Holt. Salmon to 12 lbs, trout and coarse fish. *Day and season permits (reduction for OAP's and juniors) available from J. Johnson, 97 Liverpool Road (North) Maghull, Nr. Liverpool. Tel.* 051–526 4083.

Maelor Angling Association, Wrexham, Clwyd. Hon. Secretary Mr. Noel Wright. Tel. (097881) 2592.

11. Dee: 2 miles on both banks from Pontcysyllte to Newbridge viaduct. Mainly trout and coarse fish. *Day permits from Mr. Colin Roberts, 20 Daywell Crescent, Gobowen, Salop.*

Newbridge Angling Association, Hon. Secretary, Mr. Phillip Davies, 10 Lawton House, Ruabon, Clwyd. Tel. (097 881) 2497.

12. Dee: White Bridge, New-. bridge, to Rain Brook, left bank approx. 3 miles. Trout and coarse. *Day permits from Hon. Sec.*

Boat Inn, Erbistock, Nr. Wrexham, Clwyd. Tel. Overton-on-Dee (097 873) 243.

13. Dee: 200 yards on left bank from Boat Inn gate to the stile at car park entrance. Salmon, sea trout and brown trout. *Day permits from inn.*

Golden Pheasant Hotel, Llwynmawr, Nr. Llangollen, Clwyd, Tel. Glynceiriog (069 172) 281.

14. Dee: Near Trevor. 2 pools, Salmon, sea trout, brown and rainbow trout.

---

15. Ceiriog: 2½ miles on both banks from Herber Corner to Pontfaen Bridge excluding fish hatchery above bridge. Also 3 miles on right bank to viaduct. Trout only. *Permits available to residents at hotel only.*

Hand Hotel, Llanarmon Dyffryn Ceiriog, Nr. Llangollen, Clwyd. Tel. Llanarmon D.C. (069 176) 666.

16. Ceiriog: Both banks from a point 1 mile east of Llanarmon Dyffryn Ceiriog, near Keeper's White Cottage, to the road bridge on B4500 in the village. Trout mainly, to 1 lb. *Permits free to residents at hotel.*

Royal Oak Hotel, Glyn Ceiriog, Nr. Chirk, Clwyd. Tel. Glyn-geiriog (069 172) 243.

17. Ceiriog: Various stretches from source to confluence with the River Dee near Chirk. Salmon and brown trout (to 1½ lbs). *Permits to hotel residents.* Also 1¼ miles, mostly both banks on River Alwen.

West Arms, Llanarmon Dyfrig Ceiriog, near Llangollen, Clwyd. Tel. Llanarmon D.C. (069 176) 665.

18. Ceiriog: From the hotel downstream both banks for 1 mile to Keepers Cottage and upstream from the hotel both banks for 2 miles to Glan Gier. (*By arrangement with Hand Hotel*). Brown trout only, about 10 ozs. *Free to residents at the hotel. Non-residents: day 60p, week £1.80, Season £3.*

Tackle shops

Bala. *W. E. Pugh, 74 High Street. Tel.* (06782) 248.
E. Evans, Bradford House.

Bangor on Dee. *S. & A. Adams, The Stores. Tel.* (097 872) 430.

Llangollen. *Miss Lewis, Tackle Shop, Chapel Street.*

Wrexham. *The Angling Centre, 2 Ruabon Road. Tel.* (0978) 51815.

Snowdonia and Anglesey

The choice is wide, varying from mountain tarns, where the trout are small but plentiful, to the stocked reservoirs such as Anglesey's Llyn Alaw. In 1976, for the first time, spinning and bait fishing was allowed over two-thirds of this reservoir in addition to fly fishing, so catches should be excellent and the fish are big.

Welsh Water Authority, Cambrian Way, Brecon, Powys. Tel. (0874) 3181.

1. Llyn Alaw: 777 acres, 3 miles south-west of Amlwch on the Isle of Anglesey. Rainbow and brown trout up to 4 lbs 13 ozs, average 1 lb 14 ozs. *Permit prices: Adult visitors to Anglesey: season £25.00, week £6.00, day £2.00, evenings £1.25. OAP's and juniors 50% of above charges. Boat hire (50% of stated rates after 4.00 p.m.), Day: row £3.00, outboard £5.00. Permits, etc., available from Fishing Office, Llyn Alaw. Tel. Llanfaethlu* (040 788) 323.

Seiont, Gwyrfai and Llyfni Anglers' Society, Secretary Mr. A. Roberts, 17 Castle Street. Tel. Anglers' Society, Secretary Mr. A. Roberts, 17 Castle Street, Caernarfon, Gwynedd.

2. Rhythallt: 1 mile on right bank from outlet of Llyn Padarn to Pont Rhythallt. Salmon and sea trout.

3. Seiont: 5 miles. Most stretches on right bank from Grawiau Bridge to confluence at Coed Helen. Most stretches on left bank between Pont Rhythallt and Pontrug and small stretch at confluence. Salmon and sea trout.

4. Gwyrfai: 3 miles. Certain stretches mainly on left bank in the upper reaches. Salmon and sea trout.

5. Llyn Padarn, 6. Llyn Cwellyn, 7. Llyn-y-Gadair: Boating rights and bank fishing rights on lakes of Padarn, Cwellyn and Gadair. Brown trout. *All fishing available on one permit which may be obtained along with any desired information from the Secretary. Permits also available from Huxley Jones, Tackle Shop, Bangor Street, Caernarfon. Tel.* (0286) 3186.

Welsh Water Authority, Cambrian Way, Brecon, Powys. Tel. (0874) 3181.

8. Llyn Padarn and tributaries: Brown trout and char. *Permits from: West Gwynedd Water Division, Bron Castell, High Street, Bangor, Gwynedd. Tel.* (0248) 52881. *Adult: season £7.50, week £2.50, day £0.75. Boats available at Llanberis.*

The Ogwen Valley Angling Association.

9. Ogwen: 3 miles from Half Way Bridge to Pontwr and from Ceunant Bridge (Ty'n-y-Maes) to Ogwen lake, including tributaries. Salmon and sea trout in late season. *Day permits available.* Also lakes **Ogwen, Idwal and Ffynnon Lloer.** Brown trout. *Permits from Buckley Wyn, Outfitters, 40 High Street, Bethesda. Tel.* (0248) 600020.

Castell Cidwm Hotel, Betws Garmon, Nr. Caernarfon, Gwynedd. Tel. Waunfawr (0286) 243.

10. Gwyrfai: 150 yards on right bank from outlet of Llyn Cwellyn to boundary of Plasisaf.

11. Llyn Cwellyn: From hotel to Snowdon Ranger Y.H.A. Salmon, sea trout and brown trout, 1975. *Day permits available from above address. Boats available.*

Pen-y-Gwryd Hotel, Nant Gwynant, Nr. Llanberis, Gwynedd. Tel. Llanberis (028682) 211.

12. Pen-y-Gwryd Lake: Opposite hotel. Also River Gwryd on left bank from lake outlet downstream. Good brown and rainbow trout to 1¼ lb. *Day permits from hotel.*

The Dinas Lake Fishing Club, Proprietor, R. H. Williams, The Beddgelert Gift Shop, Beddgelert, Gwynedd.

13. Llyn Dinas: A lake lying in Nant Gwynant beside A498. Salmon and sea trout to 6 lb and brown trout. *Day and weekly permits and boats for hire. Apply*

Glaslyn Angling Association has rights to extensive stretches of River Glaslyn.

Post Offices at Beddgelert and Bridge House, Aberglaslyn.

Craflwyn Hall Hotel, Beddgelert, Gwynedd. Tel. 076–686 221.

14. Glaslyn: ½ mile, right bank between Ty Canol and Craflwyn Hall. Salmon, sea trout, and brown trout. *Day and weekly permits from the hotel 50p day.*

Glaslyn Angling Association, Porthmadog, Gwynedd.

15. Glaslyn: Most of both banks from tidal sluices at Porthmadog to Beddgelert apart from some small stretches still in private hands. Salmon to 15 lbs, sea trout to 10 lbs and brown trout. Lake Edno. 3-*day (i.e. M.T.W. or Th.F.S.), weekly and season permits available with reductions on seasons for OAP's and juniors. (Monday–Saturday fishing only: no Sunday fishing allowed). Permits from: Pugh's, 94 High Street, Porthmadog. Tel.* (0766) 2392. *Correspondence and permits: Mr. Gauler, Bridge House, Aberglaslyn Bridge, Beddgelert. Tel.* (076 686) 229.

CEGB Ffestiniog Power Station, Blaenau Ffestiniog, Gwynedd. Tel. (076 681) 465.

16. Tan-y-grisiau Reservoir. 95 acres of the lower reservoir of the Ffestiniog Pumped Storage scheme, maintained on a put-and-take basis. Rainbow trout. (Season 6 March to 31 October.) *Licences and permits available from power station reception centre and by post from CEGB, Bron Heulog, Conway Road, Llandudno Junction.*

---

continued on next page

continued from previous page

Welsh Water Authority, Gwynedd Water Division, Eryi Water Unit Dinas, Llanwnda, Gwynedd. Tel. Llanwnda (0286) 830 575.

17. Cwmystradllyn: Lake of 95 acres holding brown trout. *Day and season permits available from Cwmystradllyn Treatment Works, Garndolbenmaen. Tel. (076 675) 255. Adult: season £7.50, day £1.00.*

Tackle shops

Bangor. *Ron Edwards, 6 Dean Street. Tel.* (0248) 2811.

Blaenau Ffestiniog. *J. F. & B. W. Davies, Lord Street. Tel.* (026 681) 414.

Caernarfon. *Howards, Ironmongers. 72 Pool Street. Tel.* (0286) 2671.

Penrhyndeudraeth. *S. Pearce & Sons, Bank Buildings. Tel.* (0286) 236.

Other accommodation offering angling

Aber, Gwynedd. *Aber Hotel, Aber, Nr. Llanfairfechan. Tel. Llanfairfechan* (0248) 680 639.

Llanberis, Gwynedd. *Mount Pleasant Hotel. Tel.* (028 682) 395.

Maentwrog, Gwynedd. *Grapes Hotel, Maentwrog, Nr. Blaenau Ffestiniog. Tel.* (076 685) 208.

Cymdeithas Enweiriawl Cambrian
Cambrian Angling Association

Hon. Secretary:
Emrys Evans, Garth, Twddyn Gwyn, Manod, Ffestiniog, Meirionnydd. Tel. Ffestiniog (076 676) 630.

18. Fishing around Blaenau Ffestiniog:
The Blaenau Ffestiniog area is undoubtedly a good centre for the angler. The Cambrian Angling Association has its headquarters here and offers excellent lake-fishing. Season, week and day permits are sold by tackle dealers in the area, subject to the angler being in possession of a Gwynedd River Division rod licence.

Rivers

Cynfal. ¾ mile left bank from Talybont upstream between Maentwrog and Ffestiniog. Salmon, sea trout and brown trout.
Goedol. ¾ mile right bank at Rhydsarn, between Maentwrog and Blaenau Ffestiniog. Salmon to 16 lbs, sea trout and brown trout.

Lakes

Gamallt Lakes. 1,534 feet above sea-level, produce the finest trout in Wales. Mid-June onwards gives the best results, with evening and night fishing for preference. The Lakes are reached by a track leading north-westwards 600 yards south of Ffynnon Eiddew, on the Ysbyty road from Ffestiniog. White quartz stones mark the route and from the road to the lake is a 25-minute walk - no climbing. Restocked late 1975 with 3,500 brown trout.
Dubach-y-Bont. 200 yards to the north-east, above Morwynion, on the roadside that leads to Ysbyty. Tales of rods being broken and big fish getting away are accepted as facts, 2½ lbs trout being no rarities.
Morwynion. The lake is 1,500 ft above sea-level and is situated about 200 yards off the lay-by on the Bala road off Ffestiniog. Most easily accessible, easily fished and holds a good stock of fish. Average weight 12 ozs.
Manod Lake. Situated between Manod Mawr and Manod Bach mountains above the town to the east. Fishing is rather rough due to rocky shore conditions. Holds plenty of fish, average weight 8 to 9 ozs.
Dubach Lake. 1,500 ft above the centre of the town. Is well-stocked with brown trout. It is not much use for the fly-fisher when the wind is from the north or north-east as it is well-sheltered from that quarter. Very suitable for dry fly fishing.
Barlwyd Lakes. 1,500 ft. Accessible in 25 minutes from bus route to Betws-y-Coed. Visitors are warned against soft peaty shore and floating islands of the smaller lake. Fully stocked with brown trout.
Cwmorthin Lake. 1,330 ft. Lies between Moelwyn and Nyth y Gigfran above the Tanygrisiau Reservoir. 25 minutes walk from Tanygrisiau. Well stocked with brown trout 8 to 9 ozs.
Cwm Foel and Cwm Corsiog. Situated west of the town on the Moelwyn range. Not easy of access, but well worth a visit. Grand scenery, and trout up to 2 lbs, are caught in these small lakes.
Permits for all above mentioned lakes and rivers available from Mrs. Owen, Royal Stores, Blaenau Ffestiniog: Glyn Parry, Newsagents, Ffestiniog: G. Payne, The Tackle Shop, Ffestiniog: Mrs. John Davies, The Tackle Shop, Lord Street, Blaenau Ffestiniog.

Conwy

Sea trout come in force to its glorious waters around Betws-y-Coed. Salmon also run from early spring, both species as far as Conwy Falls between Betws-y-Coed and Penmachno. Above the falls, on the Lledr, there are plump brown trout.

Alwen and Aled

The Alwen is a notable tributary of the Dee that has been dammed on the Denbigh Moors to provide a water supply. The river itself has salmon as well as trout but the reservoir's trout have been joined by hard fighting perch.

Just the other side of the moorland watershed from Alwen is the Aled reservoir and river .

Pengwern Trout Farm, Glan Conwy, Gwynedd. Tel. Glan Conwy (049 268) 751.

1. Afon Garreg Ddu lakes: Small artificial lakes on Afon Garreg Ddu, approx. 2 acres, located 1 mile above Glan Conwy. Rainbow trout 2–3 lbs, well stocked from breeding tanks. *Details from P.O. Box 8, Colwyn Bay or above address.*

Dolgarrog Fishing Club, Dolgarrog, Conwy, Gwynedd.

2. Conwy: 1¾ mile on left bank upstream from Porthlwyd canal and ½ mile on right bank upstream from aluminium works bridge. Also two lakes above Dolgarrog and connecting streams. Salmon up to 28 lbs. *Weekly and day permits from Club Secretary, F. A. Corrie. Tel. Dolgarrog* (049 269) 651.

Lakeside Cafe, Llyn Crafnant, Nr. Trefriw. Tel. Llanrwst (0492) 640818.

3. Llyn Crafnant: All of the 60 acres lake, ¾ mile long. Brown and rainbow trout to 2 lbs. *Day, weekly and season permits from Lakeside Cafe, Llyn Crafnant, Trefriw. Tel. Llanrwst* (640) 818. Facilities available at the lake include rowing boats, self-catering accommodation and refreshments.

Llanrwst Anglers Club.

4. Conwy: 1¼ miles both banks from Llanrwst Bridge to Old Gwydyr golf links. Salmon to

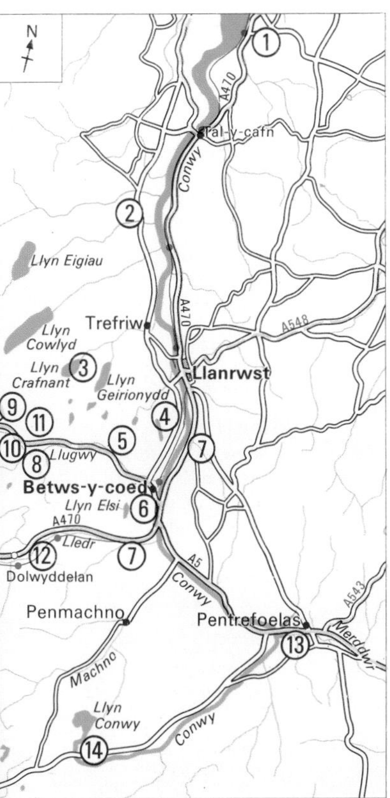

30 lbs, sea trout and brown trout. *Weekly permits available from: The Library Tackle Shop, Llanrwst. Tel. (0492) 640 525. The Radio Shop, Watling Street, Llanrwst.*

Betws-y-Coed Anglers' Club, Secretary Mr. Ernest W. Jones, 25 Bro Gethin, Betws-y-Coed, Gwynedd. Tel. Betws-y-Coed (06902) 498.

5. Llugwy: Both banks from railway viaduct to Swallow Falls and Llyn Goddion Duon. Salmon, sea trout and trout. *Weekly permits only £10.00. Day permits for Llyn Goddion Duon only £2.00. Available from Tan Lan Cafe, Betws-y-Coed. Tel. (06902) 232.*

6. Conwy: 1 mile on left bank from Waterloo Bridge.

Gwydyr Hotel, Betws-y-Coed, Gwynedd. Tel. (06902) 217.

7. Conwy and Lledr: 8 miles on right bank from a point below Trefriw Quay to Gower Bridge at Llanrwst, Monday to Friday only. Advance booking is advisable for this stretch, known as Plas Madog. Also from the Wall Pool above the railway bridge 1 mile south of Llanrwst to the Black Pool on the Lledr, below Gethin Bridge and Llyn Elsi. Salmon, sea trout and trout. *Exclusive to hotel residents. Weekly tickets only. Further weekly tickets are available at lower price for restricted sections of the above waters and the River Llugwy. A limited number of visitors' day tickets are also available for the 2½ mile stretch on right bank from the Wall Pool to the Beaver Pool above the Fairy Glen.*

8. Llugwy: 6 miles on left bank from the outlet of Mymbyr Lakes at Capel Curig to the Swallow Falls. Also Llyn Siabod. Mainly trout. *Day permits available. Trout tickets are also for Llyn Elsi. Season tickets for more extensive waters are available. All permits from the hotel.*

Cobdens Hotel, Capel Curig, Gwynedd. Tel. (069 04) 243.

9. Llugwy and a mountain trout pool. 2 miles, on both banks Afon Llugwy near Capel Curig. Brown trout in pool. *Permits purchased at hotel, available to residents at hotel only.*

Ty'n y Coed Hotel, Capel Curig, Gwynedd. Tel. (069 04) 231.

10. Llugwy: ½ mile, both banks near Capel Curig. Brown trout. *Permits from hotel.*

Bryn Tyrch Hotel, Capel Curig, Gwynedd . Tel. (0569 04) 223.

11. Llugwy: About 1 mile on Betws-y-Coed side of Capel Curig. Brown trout only. *Permits from Mr. Hughes, The Garage, Capel Curig, available to hotel residents.*

Dolwyddelan Fishing Association, Dolwyddelan, Gwynedd.

12. Lledr: 3 miles from a point near Elen's Castle Hotel, Dolwyddelan, to Pont-y-pant road bridge, both banks except for two small private stretches. Salmon, sea trout, brown trout. *Permits available from Siop-y-llan, Dolwyddelan. Tel. (069 06) 137. E. Jones, Secretary, 8 Llwyn Estyn, Deganwy. Tel. (0492) 84669.*

Voelas Arms Hotel, Pentrefoelas, Nr. Betws-y-Coed, Gwynedd. Tel. Pentrefoelas (069 05) 654.

13. Merddwr: 2¼ miles from confluence with River Conwy upstream to confluence of River Nug. Right bank only from upper limit to a point ¼ mile below Rhydlydan Bridge. *Day permits from Voelas Arms Hotel.*

The National Trust, Dinas, Betws-y-Coed. Tel. (069 02) 312.

14. Conwy: 7 miles, west bank between Hendre Isaf and Llyn Conwy and 6 miles east bank between Bryniau Defaid and Llyn Conwy. Brown trout. Day, weekly and season permits from the National Trust, North Wales Regional Office, Dinas, Betws-y-Coed.

Welsh Water Authority, Dee & Clwyd Division, Shire Hall, Mold. Tel. (0352) 2121.

15. Alwen Reservoir: Divided into three sections. Top section limited to four rods on each side of reservoir. Mainly brown trout. *Permits available from the Superintendent's Office, Alwen Reservoir, Cerrig-y-Drudion.* Ground bait and maggot strictly prohibited.

Welsh Water Authority, Brenig Reservoir, Cerrig-y-drudion, near Corwen. Tel. (049082) 435.

16. Brenig Reservoir. 919 acres reservoir offering good brown and rainbow trout fishing, opened in 1978. *Permits: Season £70.00, day £2.50, week £12.50. Boats – motor and rowing – may be booked in advance by telephone.*

Tackle shops

Betws-y-Coed. *Knowles (Betws-y-Coed) Ltd., Carlton Stores. Betws-y-Coed. Tel. (069 02) 229.*

Llandudno. *Westmorlands. 19 Lloyd Street. Tel. (0492) 77126.*

Clwyd

Celebrated is the word the normally reserved local River Division uses for this excellent little sea trout and salmon river. It can be fished more or less along the whole of its meandering way through the Vale of Clwyd, from ancient, castled Ruthin to the sea at sunny Rhyl. Brown trout are found in good numbers, particularly in the less contested upper stretches, because stocking takes place and coarse fish are noticeably absent.

Elwy

The region drained by the Elwy is a quiet backwater remote from the more boisterous coastal resorts strip of North Wales. It rises on the fringes of Hiraethog Moorland to bubble and burst its way through quiet country villages near the small cathedral city of St. Asaph. Rhyl anglers have an arrangement permitting visitors to fish their waters, mainly for brown trout.

Rhyl Angling Association, Secretary Howell Jones, Belmont, 51 Pendyffryn Road, Rhyl, Clwyd. Tel. (0745) 50342.

1. Elwy: Beats of Maes Elwy, Pont-y-Ddol, Upper Pant-y-Ddol and Dolganned.

2. Clwyd: Beats of Bryn, Bryn Clwyd, Wern Ddu and Bodfari. Salmon, sea trout and trout. *Permits from Arthur H. Fogerty, 29 Queen Street, Rhyl. Tel.* (0745) 54765.

St. Asaph Angling Association, Secretary Ian D. Jones, 18 Heol Afon, St. Asaph, Clwyd.

3. Elwy: 200 yards on left bank between St. Asaph Bridge and flyover. Salmon up to 10 lbs and sea trout from ¾ lb to 2 lbs from end of July. *Permits from Mr. Cosnett, Newsagents, High Street, St. Asaph. Foxon's Newsagents, Penrhewl, St. Asaph. Tel.* (0745) 583583. *Plas Elwy Hotel, The Roe, St. Asaph. Tel.* (0745) 582263, *also has four permits available on this Association's waters to persons staying at the hotel.*

Cambrian Fisheries, The Fisheries, Afonwen, Nr. Mold, Clwyd. Tel. Caerwys (035282) 589.

4. 18 acre Ysgeifiog lake near Ddol: Fishing from 8 boats or from bank. Fly only for brown and rainbow trout. Best 1975 rainbow trout of 8 lbs 12 ozs by M. Dixon. *Booking in advance day and season permits available from above address. Boats for hire.*

Cilcain Fly Fishing Association, Cilcain, Clwyd.

5. Cilcain Reservoir: 12 acres of brown trout fishing up to 2½ lbs in the five reservoirs near the village of Cilcain, 4 miles west of Mold. *Permits from the Association at 9 Maes Cilan, Cilcain, Mold.*

Warburton Hotels (Chester) Ltd., c/o Ruthin Castle Hotel, Ruthin, Clwyd. Tel. (08242) 2664.

6. Clwyd: 22 miles. Many stretches on both banks between Eyarth bridge and Llandyrnog Junction Pool.

7. Clywedog: *Both banks near* Bachymbyd Bridge below Rhewl. Brown trout up to 1 lb and occasional salmon and sea trout. *Exclusively for hotel guests.*

Wrexham and East Denbighshire Water Company, 21 Egerton Street, Wrexham, Clwyd. Tel. Wrexham (0978) 2259.

8. Penycae Reservoirs: 11 acres of trout fishing on the upper and lower reservoirs. Restricted to six rods per day. 24 hours notice required by reservoir keeper. *Season permits from the Water Company.*

Tackle shops

Bangor-on-Dee. *S. & A. Adams, The Stores. Tel.* (097 872) 430.

Connah's Quay. *Mrs. I. M. Williams, 216 High Street. Tel.* Deeside (0244) 813373.

Mold. *Blundells Sports Centre, The Cross, Mold. Tel.* (0352) 3695.

Rhyl. *Arthur H. Fogarty, Fishing Tackle Specialist, 29 Queen Street. Tel.* (0745) 54765.
W. M. Roberts (Rhyl) Ltd., 131 High Street. Tel. (0745) 53031.

Ruthin. *Hughes & Roberts, 7 Clwyd Street. Tel.* (08242) 2726. *Trigger & Tackle, St. Peter's Square. Tel.* (08242) 3739.

St. Asaph. *J. A. & M. Foxon & Son, Penrhewl Post Office. Tel.* (0745) 583583.

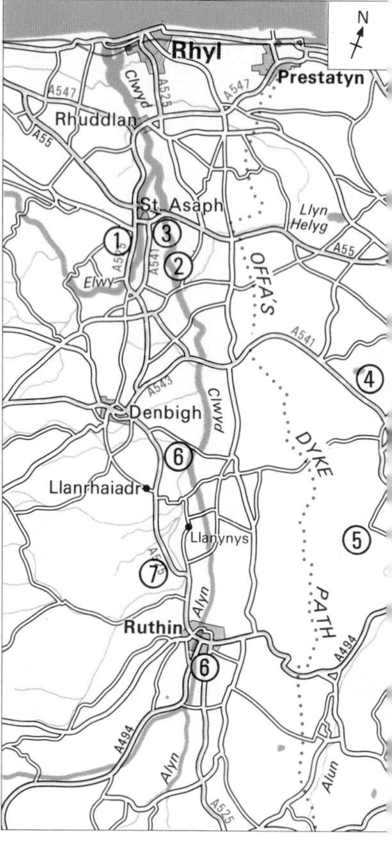

Coarse fishing

F. W. Holiday's advice to the angler visiting Wales is to leave off coarse fishing for a while and enjoy the change of sport its rivers and lakes offer in abundance (*Fishing in Wales, F. W. Holiday, An Angling Times Book*). It's good advice of the kind most anglers are happy to take. But for those who would enjoy the coarse fishing that is available this short section has been compiled. Only the coarse fishing available in recognised rural or coastal holiday areas has been listed here, though this understates this branch of the sport. Short of listing the well-stocked pools, lakes and tranquil stretches of canal and river in south-east Wales where coarse angling is much practised, the references to it here must of necessity be scanty. The best advice still is, contact a local tackle shop in the area and you will be well advised and directed. Their addresses are found on the previous pages in the sea angling and game fishing sections.

Bream form a major part of the catch in the moat waters of Caerphilly Castle.

Welsh record coarse fish list

	lbs	*ozs*	*drm*	*Caught in*
Barbel	8	0	0	Vacant (*qualifying weight*)
Bleak	0	0	0	Vacant (*qualifying weight*)
Bream, Bronze (Common)	4	10	0	R. Severn
Bream, Silver	1	0	0	Vacant (*qualifying weight*)
Carp	25	0	0	Vacant (*qualifying weight*)
Carp, Crucian	2	0	8	Wepre Pool (Connah's Quay)
Catfish	0	0	0	Vacant (*qualifying weight*)
Char	0	6	0	Vacant (*qualifying weight*)
Chub	4	0	0	Vacant (*qualifying weight*)
Dace	1	0	0	Pochin Pond
Eel	6	5	0	Trawsfynydd Lake
Grayling	1	15	0	R. Dee
Gudgeon	0	2	8	Vacant (*qualifying weight*)
Gwyniad (Whitefish)	1	4	0	Mr. J. R. Williams *Llyn Tegid (Bala Lake)*
Perch	3	9	4	*Astra Lake, Anglesey*
Pike	32	0	0	*Kenfig Pool*
Roach	3	1	8	*Bala Lake*
Rudd	2	10	0	*Kenfig Pool*
Ruffe	0	0	0	Vacant (*qualifying weight*)
Tench	6	10	0	*Kenfig Pool*
Zander	0	0	0	Vacant. (*qualifying weight*)

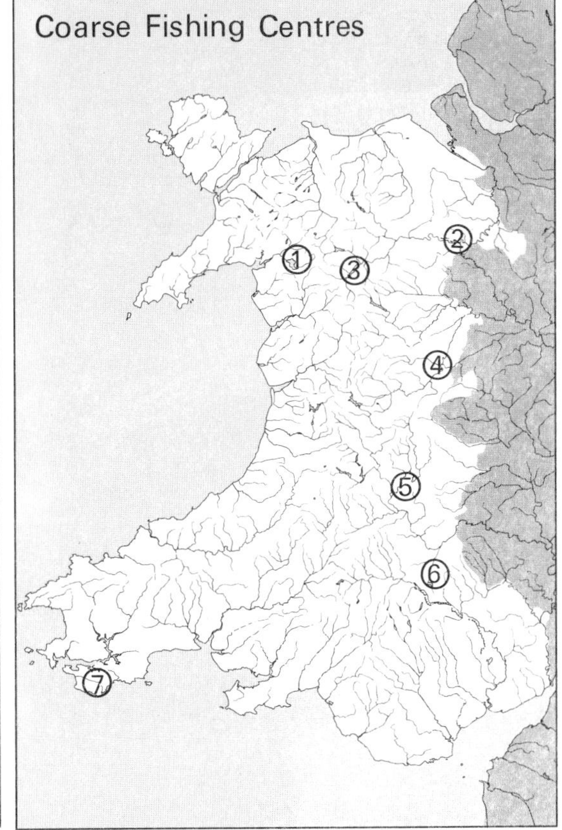

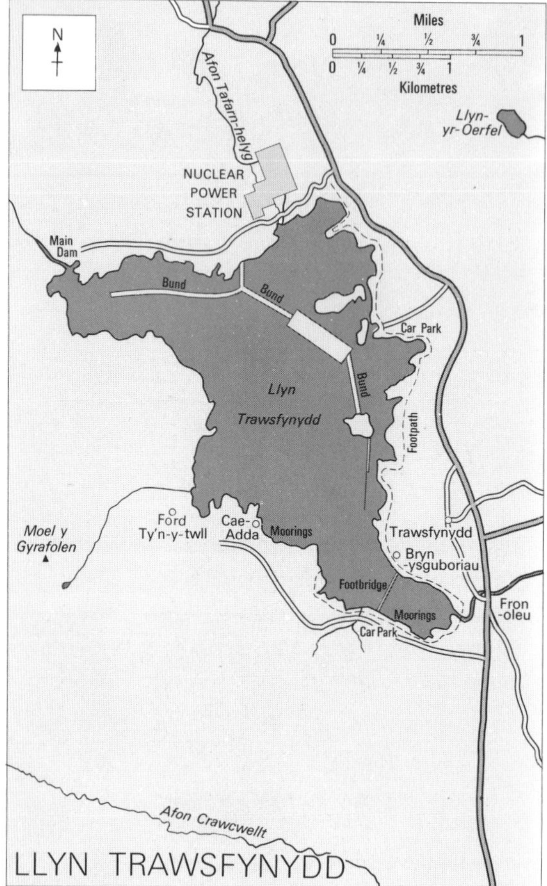

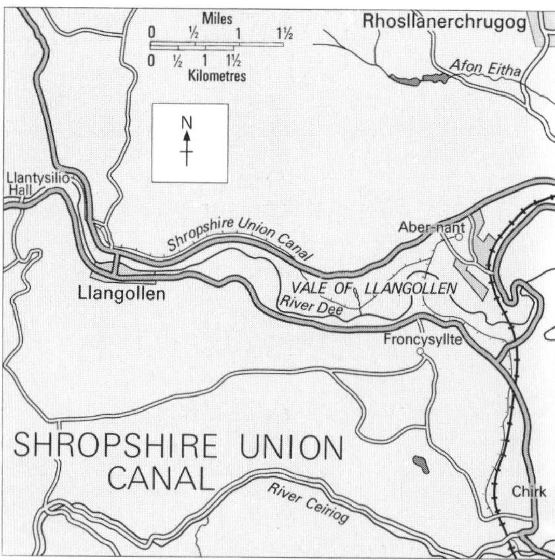

1. Llyn Trawsfynydd

Trawsfynydd's 1,200-acre artificial lake was conceived as long ago as 1928 as part of the Maentwrog Hydro-Electric Scheme, but it was only with the building of the nuclear power station on its banks in the early 1960s that the lake took on its present character. Prysor Angling Association and the CEGB have formed a Lake Management Committee. Fishing times are from dawn until one hour after sunset, and you may fish on Sundays. Perch fishing is available all the year round, but during the winter months it is only allowed in the warm water channel.

You may enjoy fly fishing on all the shores of the lake, and bait fishing and spinning are also allowed on the village side (marked A to B on the map) so long as live bait is not used. Fly fishing only is allowed from boats but fishing from the bridges is not allowed.

Permits

Before you go fishing at Llyn Trawsfynydd you will need a WWA river licence and a Lake Management Committee permit. They should be obtained in advance from Mr. H. K. Lewis, Lake Management Committee Secretary (address below). Permits are not transferable and cover the use of only one rod.

There is also fishing on the nearby rivers, Prysor, Cain and Eden; the first two for brown trout and the last named containing also late season salmon and sea trout, though none abundant. Permits can be bought at the undermentioned Tackle Shop.

Tackle shops

Trawsfynnydd

Mr. H. K. Lewis, Newsagent's Shop, Trawsfynydd. Tel. (076 687) 234. Tackle supply only; flies and lures; advice on where to fish; WWA river licences sold; permits sold for Llyn Trawsfynydd.

2. Shropshire Union Canal

Clearly, one of the most scenic stretches of the extensive Shropshire Union Canal should find a place in this book. It is the length from the canal's bridge over the River Ceiriog at Chirk to the famous Horseshoe Falls at Llantysilio above Llangollen. Fishing, good coarse fish of size and quality, is leased by the waterways authority to Shropshire Union Canal Angling Association.

Secretary: Mr. R. Brown, 10 *Dale Road, Golborne, Lancashire. WA3 3PN. Tel. Ashton-in-Makerfield* 76917. Day permits are issued by bailiffs on the water.

WWA river division licence is needed and these can be obtained from

Niel Elbourne, Tackle Shop, 12 *Chapel Street, Llangollen.*

Mrs. L. M. Davies, Groes Lwyd, Rhewl, Llangollen.

J. Ingham, The Bull Inn, Castle Street, Llangollen.

W. F. Nicholls, Church Street, Chirk.

3. Llyn Tegid (Bala Lake)

When Bala Lake was created in the Ice Age, a species of fish established itself and has remained to this day – it is the gwyniad. This lavaret is very similar to its very close relatives the powan of Lock Lomond and Loch Eck, and the schelly of several Lake District waters. Superficially, it resembles a small herring in appearance; you may see some preserved in jars at the White Lion Hotel, Bala. The British record, from Bala Lake, stands at 1 lb 4 ozs, caught in 1965.

The lake is owned by:
Gwynedd County Council, County Hall, Caernarfon.

Llyn Tegid's 1,200 acres extend 4½ miles and are 1 mile wide. Apart from brown trout, it offers good coarse fishing with 13 species in all, including roach, pike up to 20 lbs, perch, grayling, gudgeon and eels. Best recorded trout 5 lbs 10 ozs caught on a spinner.

Permits

Day permits obtainable from:
The Lake Warden, Lakeside Office, 24 Ffordd Pensarn, Bala. Tel. (067 82) 626.
W. E. Pugh, Tackle Shop, High Street, Bala. Tel. (067 82) 248.
R. E. Evans, Tackle Shop, Bradford House, Bala.
H. T. Jones, High Street, Bala.
Boats are also available for hire. Day and evening rates. Apply to the Lake Warden at the Lakeside Office.

WWA river licences are available at tackle shops.

Tackle shop

Bala
W. E. Pugh, 74 High Street. Tel. (067 82) 248.
Tackle supply; worms and flies, advice on where to fish; WWA river licences sold; permits sold for Llyn Tegid.

White Lion Hotel, Bala, has specimens of the rare Gwyniad, an Ice Age fish surviving in the nearby lake.

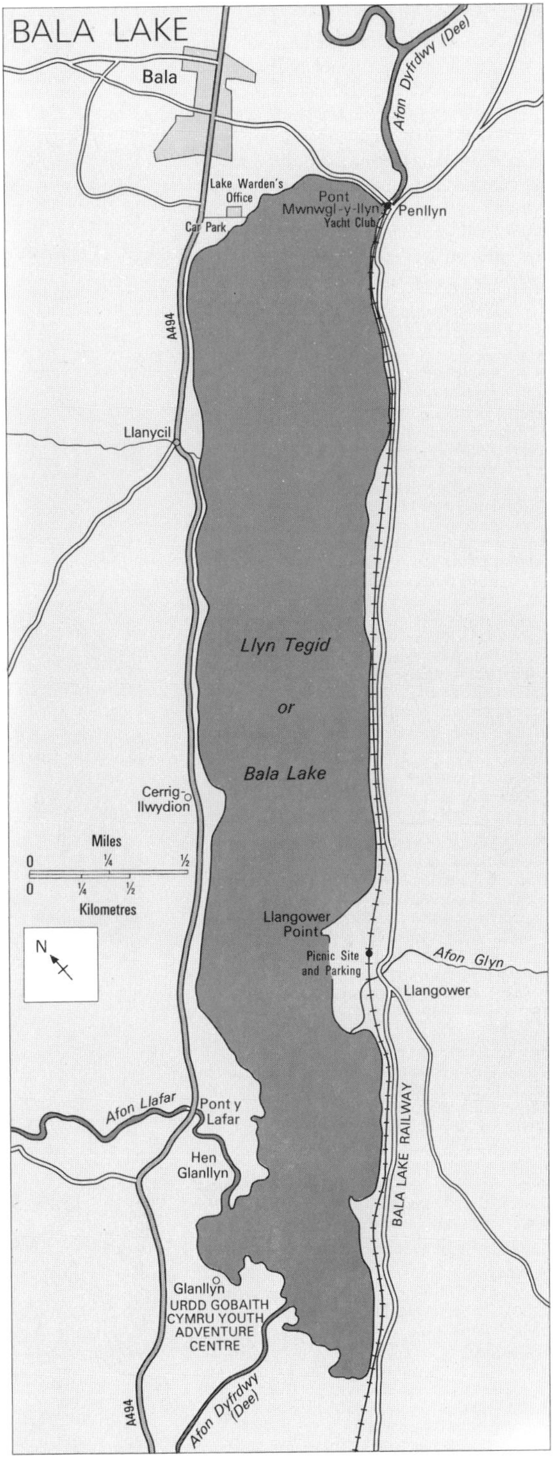

4. River Severn

The Severn's upper reaches beyond Caersws are noted for the excellence of their trout fishing. Caersws to Welshpool has more sluggish waters suitable for chub, dace and roach with perch, pike and eels in both river and canal, part of the old branch of the Shropshire Union Canal which still remains in the vicinity of Welshpool; the latter holds tench as well. Barbel introduced lower down the Severn under an *Angling Times*/River Authority scheme are slowly coming along. The chub can run to a specimen 5 lbs, dace to ¾ lb.

Montgomeryshire Angling Association, Secretary Rev. Robin Fairbrother, Vicarage, Bettws, Newtown. Tel. Tregynon (06867) 345.

This association amalgamates the Newtown and District, Welshpool and District and Llanfair Caereinion and District Angling Club.
The association offers 80 miles of river, stream, brook, canal and lake to the visiting angler.
A detailed list of their waters can be obtained from the association's secretary. These include the coarse fishing stretches of:
(a) Shropshire Union Canal at Welshpool.
(b) Lower Leighton Water, Welshpool.
(c) Woodland Water on River Camlad, Forden.
(d) Abermule Water, restricted to 25 rods.
(e) and (f) Dolerw Water, Newtown. The water east of Newtown has been subjected to a flood alleviation scheme and has been drastically altered.
(g) Penstrowed Water.
(h) Fachwen Pool, Aberhafesp. Trout fishing.

Edderton Hall Hotel, Forden, near Welshpool, Powys. (*Tel. Forden* (093 876) 339.

Two pools in grounds of hotel. Tench, roach and carp. *Free to residents at hotel. Day visitors 60p.*

It is worth recording that Birmingham Anglers' Association have considerable water on the Severn and its tributaries. Membership is open to any angler at the Association's rates. (See game fishing section of this book.)
Secretary, Birmingham Anglers' Association, 40 Thorp Street, Birmingham B5 4AU.

Permits

Permits for the Severn, restricted permits and unrestricted permits for other waters for adults and juniors are issued by the tackle shops listed below and also from:
Westwood Park Hotel, Welshpool.
Red Lion Hotel, Llanfair Caereinion.
Trading Post, Church Street, Welshpool.

Severn River Division licences available at tackle shops listed below.

Tackle shops

Newtown

Mr. L. Bebb, 15 Short Bridge Street. Tel. (0792) 26917. Tackle supply, flies; advice on where to fish; Severn River Divisions licences sold.

Welshpool

Bonds, Hall Street, Welshpool. Tel. (0938) 3327. Tackle supply and minor repairs; worms when available (June–August) and flies; advice on where to fish; Severn–Trent licences sold.
The Trading Post, 3 Church Street. Tel. 2563.

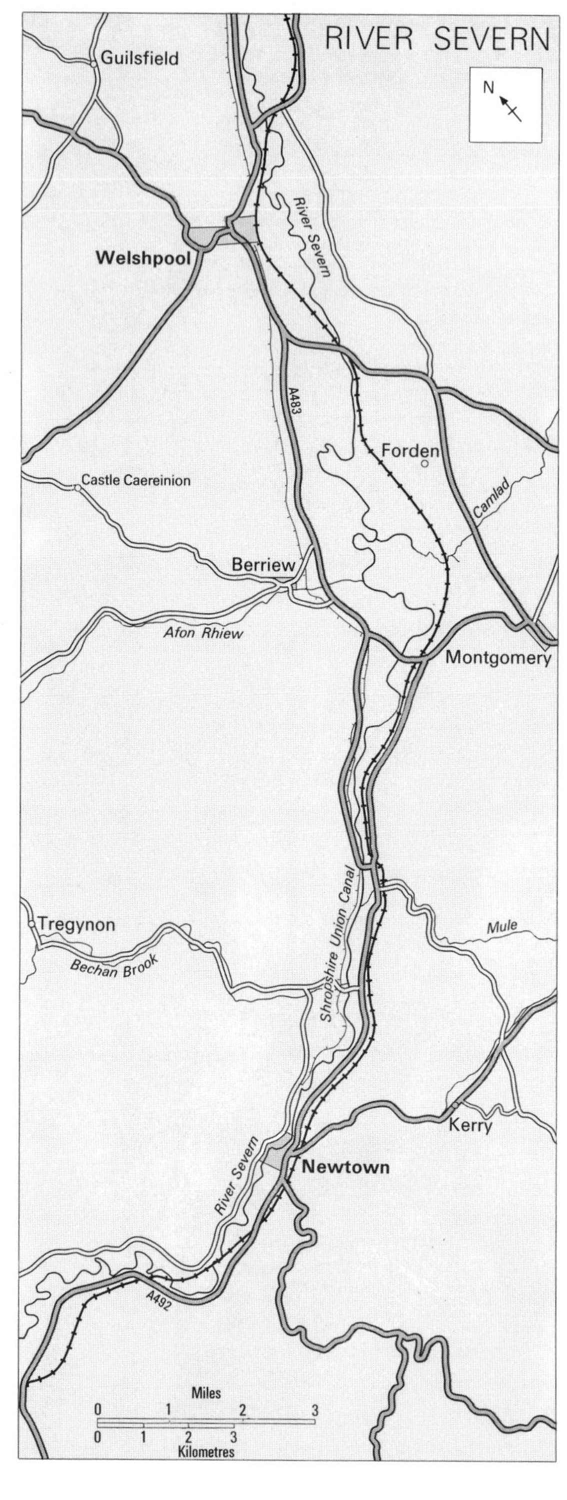

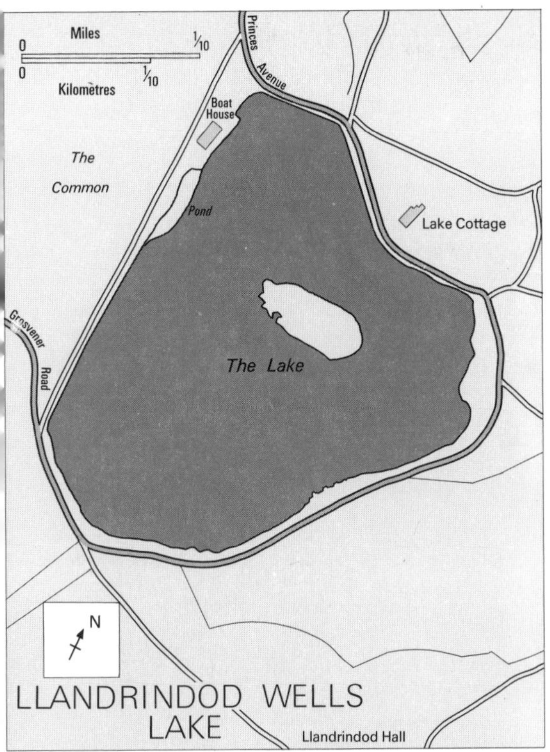

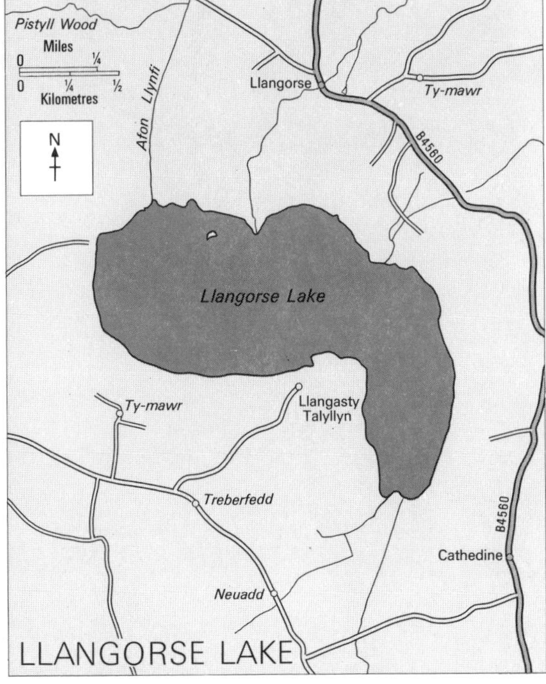

5. Llandrindod Wells

The 14-acre lake at Llandrindod Wells is a popular summer retreat for visitors to this pleasant Mid Wales spa town, which was an important holiday centre when 'taking the waters' was in vogue. Coarse fishermen have a particular interest in Llandrindod for the lake's carp, up to 20 lbs, as well as other species, provide exciting sport. A pleasantly optimistic note is set in the lake's fishing rules, which underlines how good it can be, for it says that competitions of over 4 hours duration can lead to the overloading of keep nets, so carp should be weighed immediately and set free. In fact, all fish except gudgeon – which must be killed – should be returned to the water as quickly as possible.

Tickets to fish are bought at the lake boathouse; fishing is from 8 am to 8 pm. Normally roaming is allowed – as are two rods – but on busy days a spot, either on banks or island, may have to be indicated to fishermen by the lake manager.

Permits

Banks and Island. Seven day weekly ticket. Reservation by clubs on the island. (A ferry service operates to the island which is included in the permit price.)
Youths under 14 (banks only).
WWA river licence for coarse fish can be bought at the tackle shop in the town.

Tackle shops

C. Selwyn & Sons, Tackle Shop, Park Crescent, Llandrindod Wells. Tel. (0597) 2397. Tackle supply and repair; flies; advice on where to fish; WWA river licences sold.

6. Llangorse Lake (Llyn Safaddan)

Only a true prince of this area can successfully command the water birds of Llyn Safaddan to rise as one from the lake, says tradition. Some of the ski boats that skim the lake must be driven by descendants of these same princes, for they manage to do the same thing. It's still an important coarse fishing water, with excellent pike and perch, as well as carp and roach. There are some fairly big eels, too, and these may be fished for, regardless of season. No permit is required for this water, merely the WWA licence. It drains north, to the Wye not south to the Usk. Llangorse is convenient to the A40 London-Fishguard trunk road. Leave the A40 road at Bwlch, 10 miles west of Abergavenny, for the B4560 which takes you to the village of Llangorse where boats may be hired.

continued on next page

continued from previous page

Nearest WWA licence sale points:
Llangorse. *R. P. B. Davies, Lake Side.*
J. M. James, Royal Oak Camp.

Tackle shops

Abergavenny
P. M. Fishing Tackle, 12 Monk Street. Tel. (0873) 3175. Tackle supply; flies; advice on where to fish; WWA river licences sold.

Brecon
R. & C. Denman, Watergate. Tel. (0874) 2071. Tackle supply; worms, flies; advice on where to fish; WWA licences sold.

7. Bosherston Lakes

Five miles south west of the castled town of Pembroke, is a group of lakes called Bosherston. Dating from the Napoleonic Wars, they present an interesting coarse fish habitat. Just over the dam that created them is Broad Haven and Barafundle Bay, some of Wales' best beaches for shore tope. It's an interesting combination that attracts holidaying anglers. Tench and pike predominate in the lakes, both running to useful figures – one pike weighed 32 lbs. In addition there are good perch, roach and eels.

Note: In common with all other coarse fishing waters Bosherston Lakes close season is March 15 to June 15.

How to fish

Averaging 5 ft to 8 ft deep, the lake may be fished with a permit only as no River Division licence is required. The tench, believed to reach 7 lbs, but averaging 3 lbs to 4 lbs, frequent quiet swims and take light floated tackle on a suitably pre-ground baited stretch. Pike take ledgered live or dead bait and are best taken when the summer vegetation has died back. (No live baiting until 1st October). An idyllic spot for a family outing, the lakes hold a vast crop of water lilies. Perch are taken with small spoons, small live bait and, of course, worms and maggots. Fishing rights are leased by Stackpole Estate to Pembroke and District Angling Club who issue permits through local tackle shops and cafes.

Permits

Permits for visiting anglers:
Day, week; Juniors and OAP's obtain permits at a reduced rate.

Mr. Smith, Pembroke and District Angling Club, 2 Belmont Terrace, Pembroke.

Permits can be obtained from:
Ye Olde Worlde Cafe, Bosherston.
H. Bagshaw's, 24 Main Street, Pembroke.
F. J. Donovan, Tackle Shop, 61 Bush Street, Pembroke Dock.
W. T. Humber, 46 Dimond Street, Pembroke Dock.
Morris Bros., St. Julian Street, Tenby.

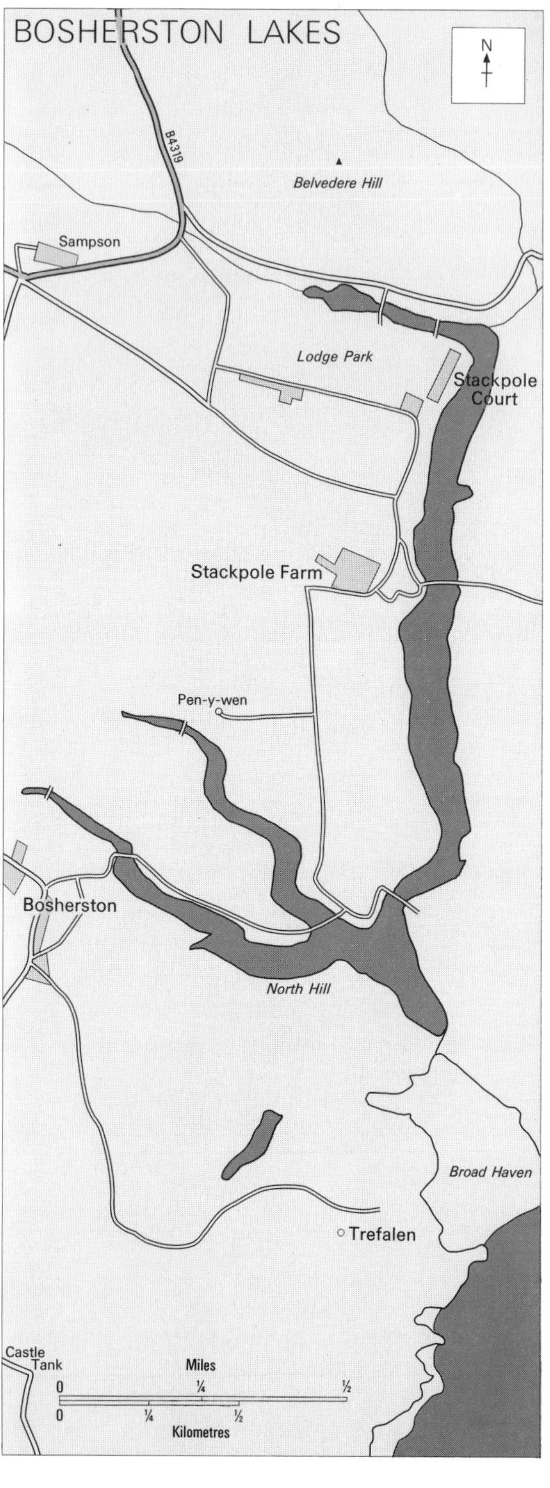

INDEX